GI Jive

An Army Bandsman in World War II

Frank F. Mathias

THE UNIVERSITY PRESS OF KENTUCKY

D0920201

For Florence

Scholarly publisher for the Commonwealth,
serving Bellarmine College, Berea College, Centre
College of Kentucky, Eastern Kentucky University,
The Filson Club Historical Society, Georgetown College,
Kentucky Historical Society, Kentucky State University,
Morehead State University, Transylvania University,
University of Kentucky, University of Louisville,
and Western Kentucky University.
All rights reserved.

Editorial and Sales Offices: The University Press of Kentucky
663 South Limestone Street, Lexington, Kentucky 40508–4008

05 04 03 02 01   5 4 3 2 1

Library of Congress Cataloging-in-Publication Data
Mathias, Frank Furlong. (1925-   )
    GI jive.

    Includes index.
    1. Mathias, Frank Furlong. 2. World War, 1939-1945—Personal nar-
ratives, American. 3. United States. Army. Infantry Division, 37th—Bi-
ography. 4. Bandsmen—United States—Biography. 5. Soldiers—United
States—Biography. I. Title.
D811.M3617   940.54'81'73   82-4792
ISBN 0-8131-1462-4   AACR2
ISBN 0-8131-9009-6   (pbk. : alk. paper)

This book is printed on acid-free recycled paper meeting
the requirements of the American National Standard
for Permanence in Paper for Printed Library Materials.

Manufactured in the United States of America.

Contents

Foreword

A good memoir is a delight but how rare they are. There is a tendency to think of autobiography as the province of the famous who, often with the help of ghostwriters, satisfy the curious with an explanation of their actions and their opinions of peers. If the author is a public figure, the book is apt to be crammed with documents to shore up his case in whatever controversies involved him. If a show business celebrity, one can expect to find little more than an explicit description of varied sexual romps or what Star A or Starlet B was "really like." These are books one picks up from the counter and lays down after a glance at the photos, a search through the index for a person or incident, and perhaps a scan of a paragraph or two. Their superficiality jades even on brief exposure. They have little resemblance to the novel that the Kentucky writer Jesse Stuart said was the story of each individual's life.

A well written memoir illuminates the life, the places, and the time of the author. He may be obscure but if he has the ability he can make his life fascinating. James Herriot is a good example. Who would have thought that the experiences of an unknown veterinary in rural Yorkshire would be of interest? Yet, Herriot's talent and his warm, humane perspective provide the reader with a rich and interesting account of a life that one might assume to be, at best, dull, and, at worst, grim.

Military memoirs have a special appeal, one that is presumably starkly different from that of *All Creatures Great and Small*. Cast against the background of historic events which magnify the significance of the activities of even the lowliest participants, they attract those who seek descriptions and explanations of times when societies most clearly focus their energies in mutual endeavors. The books of generals and statesmen, however, are apt to suffer from the fault noted by the British general, Ian Hamilton, of having fit truth into a uniform. Their concern is to chronicle actions and to justify decisions, not to delve into their deeper thoughts or to develop the mood of a time. Field Marshal Viscount Slim's account of the Burma campaign in World War II, *Defeat Into Victory,* is a rare exception. For too long, the view from headquarters has not just dominated the study of military history but virtually monopolized it. In recent years, there has been an increasing awareness of the rich source available in the memoirs of those who observed war from far down the chain of command, in the ranks, or even at home. While these add a new dimension to military history, if well done, they also have the broader appeal of the novel Jesse Stuart envisioned. What happened to an average person caught up in the cataclysm of war and what he thought of the experience has an inherent fascination. Of course, the average man does not write a book and the average book is not that good anyway, but the possibility is there.

Frank Mathias's *G.I. Jive* fulfills that potential. After three decades, this middle-aged history professor looked back on his share of World War II. Fortunately, his mother saved his informative letters so he had those to help his memory. He took excerpts from the letters and skillfully blended them with his reminiscences in a frame of the historical account to create a book of historical interest and literary merit. Here are aspects of World War II familiar to millions of his generation: the introduction to military life, the journey to battle, and the fear mixed with awe of the horror and the spectacle of war. He remembers the rough humor—complete with dialogue—of the barracks, the Saturday nights in towns crowded with soldiers, the interludes of loveliness made more intense by war, the repulsive face of the jungle and the tropical sun, the grotesque sights of death, and the gritty feel of the dust that shells and bombs leave on their targets. Such memories, as well as his reactions to leaders and to such major events as the dropping of the atomic bomb, and the pride in belonging to the 37th Infantry Division should satisfy the interests of students of World War II. There is also a basic theme, which the author handles with sensitivity and ability—the coming of age of a small-town youth during World War II. Drafted at eighteen, just after high school graduation in 1943, he entered the Army as a sort of game tinged with the excitement of going out into the world. He met strange people for the first time— Jews, Mormons, Mexicans, Melanesians, and Filipinos; saw wondrous sights—the Pacific Ocean and many of its islands; and took part in historic events. At first the report of the deaths of childhood friends, then his own experiences made him realize that he was involved in a serious, deadly business over which he had little control. This element of chance became particularly apparent to him as his talent as a musician time and again rescued him from drudgery and danger. During the fighting, however, he had to lay aside his saxophone and pick up a machine gun. When the war was over, he returned home a twenty-year-old sergeant—a veteran—who had seen a good deal of the world and learned much of life. His story of those two and a half years is as gripping as a good novel. It is a memoir well worth reading.

EDWARD M. COFFMAN
University of Wisconsin, Madison

Acknowledgments

I am grateful for the patience and constructive assistance offered by my colleague Antonio E. Lapitan, who read the manuscript from the critical viewpoint of one who was present as a civilian on Luzon during the events described in this book. James Rigdon, who soldiered on Luzon with the 158th RCT, has my gratitude for his thorough reading and masterly criticism of the material, and my colleague Edwin King, who served throughout the war as Ernie Pyle's orderly, my thanks for many good suggestions. I thank Leroy Eid and the University of Dayton History Department for aid leading to a quicker completion of my task. University librarians share a full measure of my thanks: Ray Nartker, Robert Montavon, Ed Starkey, Marjo Maxwell, Linda Hinrichs, James Rettig, David Buckley, Mary Ann Walker, Joanne Maynard, and George Anna Jackson. I also thank the gracious librarians at the Fort Benning Infantry School. Typist Linda McKinley merits thanks for her excellent work.

Many people read parts of the manuscript, and I especially thank my former comrades in arms, Gil Silvius, Pasquale Marchette, John Moum, Merle Sickmiller, and John Willer for helping me write of the years we shared during World War II. Joseph H. and Joan Conley were of great help in checking my material on Carlisle, whereas the Maysville section was read with equal care by Clarence Moore, Mary H. Campbell, Lewis Kilgus, Walter Hines, and Clair Adair Hendrickson. Heartfelt gratitude goes to Doris Wander and the 37th Division Veterans Association for its gracious support in all things. Finally, I thank my wife, Florence, and Nancy, Frank, Jr., and Susan, for they have lived this book with me.

Preface

The Second World War was the last of the great shooting wars. There will never be another one fought, as it was, with gunpowder and piston engines. It may well be the last great war in which the issues were starkly outlined in black and white. It was a war of ideologies—"gentlemanly" war having ended long before its grim masses of civilians and soldiers fought to an "unconditional surrender." Finally, World War II was by far the most extensive and bloody war fought in the long history of our planet.

The above is hindsight. The war did not seem complicated to me as I left high school in 1943 to enter the army. I left with a thrill of adventure, a feeling fully shared by my classmates. My adolescent mind, formed in a village during the Great Depression, was unprepared for the follies of life in four stateside army posts, or for the grim uncertainties of combat in the Pacific. This book is the story of a teen-aged youth and his friends who were caught up in the burning fabric of global war. We hardly counted for a thread in the cloth of this conflict; the war could have done very nicely without us. If this book has any importance, then, it is precisely because we were utterly unimportant. The view from the bottom of the heap, where we young privates lived and died, was often more revealing than the one from the top. We experienced the war as it was, not as highly placed civilian and military officials believed it to be. They seldom write of the war described in this book.

How can a memoir, purporting to show "the war as it was," be written from a memory eroded by the wear and tear of some forty years? It would have been impossible without some three hundred letters, documents, and photographs saved by my parents. I also saved letters addressed to me, shipping them home in bundles so that I might later "see what I was up to back here in the army." These letters form the backbone of this book. They not only reveal "the war as it was" for me, but do it with all of the pettiness, snap judgments, and occasional insights of a very young soldier. They also refreshed my memory, bringing intellectual and emotional recall of events and people I had not considered for decades. I found myself nostalgically in love again with Libby and Nita, my palms sweating as I wrote of the shells smashing in at Tumauini, and as confused now as then by feelings of love and hate for General Douglas MacArthur.

Most soldiers live in a box constructed of army traditions, regulations, and their own personalities. Unlike many, I lifted the lid of my box, hoping throughout the war to find answers for knotty and sometimes frightful problems I had never before encountered. I have yet to find answers for some of those questions. I might have done as well had I left the lid in place, but a curious and optimistic personality made this impossible.

The lid of my box was loosened considerably by two fortunate circumstances, the first being my assignment as an army musician. Military bands are assigned to unit headquarters, where they encounter streams of rumor and gossip, but also factual information denied most other soldiers. More important, bandsmen lived somewhat different lives, like thrushes nesting in a half-track. The contrast of our lives with those in the war machine on all sides sharpened my perceptions and aided my pen. This is especially noticeable during my year at Fort Benning and Camp Wheeler. The contrast is not so vivid after I entered the 37th Division Band, for we were often a part of the war machine itself.

Entering the 37th "Buckeye" Division was a second fortunate circumstance, for it greatly broadened my literary horizons. This division's story probably reflects the course of the war in the Pacific better than most other divisions, whether Marine or Army. During its 592 days in combat, it fought in every type of terrain the Pacific had to offer—steaming jungles, huge mountains, sandy beaches, table-flat plains and grasslands. It hurled the only blitzkrieg of the Pacific War down Luzon's Cagayan Valley and took the major part in the capture of Manila, the only metropolis involved in the Pacific conflict and the site of its deadliest single battle. The 37th alone was responsible for the fall of Intramuros, a walled city in Manila built by Spain, which had withstood various assaults for 350 years. The 37th also mingled exceptionally well with civilian populations, whether in New Zealand during the war's early months, in the Fiji Islands, or on Luzon, the most populous island taken by Allied forces. Civilians here erected a monument in its name, the only instance of this, I think, in the Pacific war. My story is in some ways the story of this division, but the story of this division is in many ways the story of World War II in the Pacific. I amounted to nothing personally, but I was busily writing my letters in the right places at the right time.

I have presented this story as it happened, letting the letters speak for themselves whenever possible. Gaps were filled in from memory and through correspondence with men who shared many of the experiences in this book. Names are sometimes changed to protect privacy, and conversations are sometimes included, even though not written as such in my letters. I cannot, for example, remember old "Pump's" lecture to me on venereal disease verbatim, but I am sure I have written a close approximation. The same can be said for several conversations with girl friends or with fellow soldiers, such as the one glorying in the news of the Battle of the Bulge while we swam in the tepid waters of a tropical lagoon.

I did not change the wording of the letters, although I often deleted irrelevant or repetitive material by use of ellipses. Phrases of explanation clarifying certain items for the modern reader were inserted within brackets. I use "Japs" and "Nips" throughout, instead of Japanese and Nipponese, hoping the reader will accept this as revealing of the harsh wartime sentiment of a bygone era, rather than any lingering hatred for Japan and its wonderful people.

No enlisted man had access to the tactics, strategies, statistics, and chronology of events I explain in this book. I turned to other sources regarding these things. I made extensive use of Stanley A. Frankel's *The 37th Infantry Division in World War II*, one of the best unit histories to emerge from that conflict. Almost of equal value was the multivolume *United States Army in World War II*, often referred to as "The Green Series." I found the following volumes particularly useful: *Chronology, 1941-1945*, compiled by Mary H. Williams (1960); *Victory in Papua*, by Samuel Milner

(1957); *Triumph in the Philippines,* by Robert Ross Smith (1963); *Strategy and Command: The First Two Years,* by Louis Morton (1962); and *Cartwheel: The Reduction of Rabaul,* by John Miller, Jr. (1959). My memory of Fort Benning and its environs was greatly enhanced by a return to its library in 1979 where I read pertinent issues of *Pine Bur* and *The Bayonet.* I was thrilled to find the buildings of ASTP headquarters company intact, including the band barracks.

I have written this book as the historian I am, and not as an "old veteran" intent on gilding the lily. The things set down here actually happened, and have not been exaggerated. But errors do creep into a manuscript written years after the fact, and I accept sole responsibility for them.

1. The Sax Section

I awakened to the sound of a file rasping a razor's edge on a trench knife blade; a soldier was hunched under a dim circle of light cast by the red lamp on my ship's troop deck. I lay stiffly in my bunk in the pre-dawn darkness, dry of mouth and hollow with fear. How could this have happened to me, I thought, for I had "had it made" for so long back in the States—first in the Army Specialized Training Program (ASTP), then in the bands at Fort Benning and Camp Wheeler—anything but the infantry. Yet, here I was this morning of January 9, 1945, a member in good standing of the 37th "Buckeye" Infantry Division, aboard the troopship U.S.S. *Simon Bolivar*, rocking gently in the swells of the vast Lingayen Gulf, part of the largest invasion fleet in the history of the world except for the one that had hit Normandy seven months earlier, and scheduled to land with the assault wave on Luzon's beaches at 9:30, just five hours from the time I had awakened. Most intelligence reports indicated that General Tomoyuki Yamashita, the "Tiger of Malaya," could muster up to 275,000 Jap troops to give us a hellish welcome to Luzon's beaches. After all, Luzon was the key island in the Philippines. Lord! I thought, what's a nineteen-year-old like me, with everything to live for, doing in a place like this. Since I had already done my praying the night before, my thoughts went back to my home in Kentucky. I had left there just a year and a half ago, yet it seemed as far removed from this place as a single star beckoning from some inaccessible sky. But that is where my thoughts began and ended that morning, for a boy lacks the frame of reference that might have supported deeper thoughts.

My thoughts started with my father as he walked me to the bus that August morning of 1943 when I left for Fort Thomas, Kentucky, and induction into the U.S. Army. "That damned Roosevelt got this war going," my father muttered as we walked the two blocks from my home on Main Street to the Nicholas County Court House. The school bus which would take thirty of us to the Fort Thomas Reception Center was already there. I was surprised at Dad's steady cursing of Roosevelt, for before this he had just as steadily voted for him. But this was different, for Roosevelt was taking his oldest son to war, and his oldest son had barely begun shaving, weighed only 130 pounds, and measured just 5' 8". Moreover, Lucky (as my father was called in reference to his fishing luck) was not noted for mincing words. "They ought to hang that son-of-a-bitch right along with Tojo and Adolph," he said, spitting a rusty, red stream of tobacco juice on Main Street.

In a few minutes we saw the crowd of draftees milling around in front of the court house. Many of them were from the Class of 1943 and had graduated with me from Carlisle High School in May. Today was August 25, and although it was only seven in the morning it was going to be hot and humid in a few hours. Lucky kept up his tirade against Roosevelt, but everyone was on to him and paid little attention. Doc Bradshaw, the local druggist, came out and gave each of us a "Flat Fifty" of Lucky Strike cigarettes. To me this was a puberty rite—the first time anyone had ever openly acknowledged my manhood. Instead of former warnings against cigarettes—"they'll stunt your growth"—everyone now beamed as we took these tin boxes full of "coffin nails." At this moment I began to think I might like the life of a soldier, a life certain to be much different from any I had known over the past eighteen years.

I had long endured conflicting teen-age sentiments concerning my "boring" home town. Carlisle, Kentucky was a town of 1600 people located on the rim of the state's fertile Bluegrass region, some 35 miles northeast of Lexington and 70 miles southeast of Cincinnati. It was the county seat of Nicholas County and was the kind of place and society Thomas Jefferson had in mind when he advocated a nation based on small farmers and mechanics. There was no person or family of real wealth in the vicinity, nor was there any factory or mill to seek economic and political privileges at the expense of the people. Nearly everyone was White, Anglo-Saxon, and Protestant, with only a sprinkling of Negroes in the county, no Jews, and only eighty Catholics, of whom I was one. Agriculture provided the entire economic base, and tobacco farming brought in most of the cash income. The Great Depression caused no real problems of want in this rural setting; moreover, the people stuck together, helping those who needed it, and were firmly optimistic in the belief that better days were coming. But no teen-ager can long stand boredom, and my crowd longed for the bright lights of Cincinnati or Lexington, and each one of us openly hoped the war would not end until he "got into it."

I did not mind leaving Carlisle so much as I minded leaving what I had going for me in nearby Maysville. This little Ohio River city, thirty miles to the north, had been my birthplace in 1925, and nearly all of my mother's side of the family still lived there. I was related in various degrees to hundreds of people there, including Rosemary Clooney, who had been born in Maysville three years after I was. My mother, Nancy Browning Furlong, had been a Maysville schoolteacher who delayed marriage until she was thirty-five, then married a forty-three-year-old salesman named Charles Mathias who, as a typical drummer of his day, had gone through life unmarried, getting by on a shoeshine and a smile. My younger brother Charles was born in 1928 and that rounded out our family of four. But Maysville now entered my life in a way which would stamp a musical theme on my army career and greatly increase my chances for survival. Late in December, 1942, I received a phone call from Clarence Moore, a dance band leader in Maysville. His band, the "Kentucky Kavaliers," played throughout northeastern Kentucky and southern Ohio. I held the phone in stunned delight as he said he had heard that I was a good sax man—"Could you come and audition with us?" I barely managed to utter a hoarse but happy, "Yes Sir!"

Was I a "good sax man," as Moore said? I did not know. I remembered getting my first tenor sax back when I was twelve years old. My mother had cashed in $120 worth of her World War I war bonds to buy it. Its gold laquer shimmered in a "red crushed plush" case, the most exciting thing I had ever seen. My identity was soon tied up with it, and I worked hard to win a spot in the Carlisle High School band. At several state contests I was criticized by the judges for "affecting jazz techniques," showing fine talent, but "going astray." I could not help "going astray," for I imitated every great sax man I heard on the radio—Coleman Hawkins, Ben Webster, Flip Phillips, Jimmy Dorsey. Each night I huddled over the Crosley radio at home, more alert to the music than anything I studied at school. My parents sighed, but I sat there, listening and yearning as radio announcers brought me "the great Benny Goodman band from the Hotel Sherman," or "Tommy Dorsey from Castle Farms," or "Glenn Miller from Frank Dailey's Meadowbrook." This was the Swing Era and I was part of it. My generation was part of it, too, but I yearned to play that music myself, to share the work of a sax section as it swung the lovely ballads and exciting jump tunes of the day.

My pulse pounded wildly as I walked in for my audition. The other musicians were seated behind blue stands with *Kavaliers* stenciled on the front. "God," I prayed, "let me pass; let me belong." Moore seated me behind the second tenor parts, kicked the band off, and after several numbers told me I was hired. He was disturbed that I could not double on clarinet, but I promised fervently that I would learn to do so "or die trying." A wild elation swept through me as I left the audition. I had everything I wanted.

I returned home in triumph. I was no longer "little Frank," the kid trapped in such a slow growth cycle that the fame and fortune of football and basketball had passed him by. "Are you *really* going to play with the Kavaliers?" old girl friends asked, but with a delicious new interest in their voices. "Sure," I replied, relishing the questions and the perfume as the sweatered bobby-soxers clustered about me. Questions were blunt. "How much will you make?" June Stewart asked, though all wanted to know. "I get six dollars a dance—that's for four hours—as much as I make working a whole weekend at Krogers!" This caused a ripple of "Gollees!" to run through the crowd. We were all frugal children of the Great Depression, and six hard dollars for four easy hours of work was cause for amazement. But on the sidelines there lurked the males, puzzled now but greening with envy as the former duck began preening himself like a swan!

Most of us can look back to a time of perfect harmony, an

unforgettable skein of months when formerly discordant parts of our lives suddenly blend together, as if deftly arranged by a master musician. My life during the first eight months of 1943 fits this description. I had more money than I needed, new friends in every town within range of our band, and complete acceptance in front of every juke box in Maysville. And there were the girls—new ones, lovely ones, interesting ones—clustered like butterflies around these drugstore juke boxes. "Frank, what do you think of that new record over at Kilgus's Pharmacy, you know, the one everybody's talking about—Glenn Miller's 'Moonlight Cocktail'?" I had to have an opinion, for I was a musician, and even if I had never heard the song, I fabricated an answer. "Yeah, that's a great one, typical Miller sax voicing. We'll have it in the Kavalier book real soon." My opinion was usually the last word on the subject. I did not fully realize that there were really two subjects, music being only the first one. "Frank, you just know *so* much; why don't we walk over to Kilgus's and listen to it—together." This second subject, romance, was part of the music, at least for the girls. It was all one subject for them. I abandoned all dry analysis of chord structure and embouchures in such pleasant situations, content to sense the soft, sweatered presence beside me in the booth, sip cokes together, or get up and jitterbug in a flash of bobby sox and saddle shoes. Nevertheless, music was a separate subject for musicians, and I was studying and practicing hard to guarantee my spot in the band.

Gradually I learned to double; at least I could play the clarinet parts on most of the printed "stock" arrangements. Tough ones, like the clarinet chorus on "Josephine," I committed to memory. There were thirteen other musicians in the band, and I watched and learned from them. I chuckled when the leader broke up a fight on the dance floor by calling up "The Star Spangled Banner." Everyone, including the fighters, stood at respectful attention; it was war time, and this clever use of social pressure ended the fight. I learned that "Stardust" would get a slow dance started by forcing couples out on the floor—it was "everybody's song." An experienced leader like Moore knew how to keep a dance going once it started. The trick was to call up sets tailored for each type of crowd, ones that did not wear the band out, and that fit the time and place. A typical "set" would have two ballads, a waltz, and a "jump" number: "Heaven

Can Wait," "Mood Indigo," "The Waltz You Saved for Me," and "White Heat." At least once during a dance we would answer pleas to "turn the drummer loose!" After a long drum solo, heads would nod knowingly as the crowd agreed that "he sounds just like Gene Krupa!" We were always pleased at this response, for we tried to sound like the big bands of the day. In our segment of the Ohio Valley the dancers expected to hear things they heard on juke boxes, and they wanted them played exactly as they heard them. We obliged them, seeking out stock arrangements based on the originals. I was learning rapidly and piling up experience I could have gained in no other way. If the time ever came when I had to fall back on this experience, I would be ready. The time was not far off.

As things stood that August morning of 1943, I did not mind leaving Carlisle for an adventurous Army life, but I knew I would miss Maysville. I would miss the music, and the girls—I think I was exuberantly in love with all of them, as only an eighteen-year-old can understand! Yet, given the choice, I would not have hesitated a moment in choosing the Army!

Any youth felt besmirched if he failed to pass induction exams into World War II. Patricia Purdon wrote me in the army that her brother "got his papers to leave the 18th of this month. He has already started celebrating." Another letter came from a friend who had tried desperately to get in anywhere, including Canada: "I'm going to try to get in again and not tell the doctors about my stomach trouble this time." He made it, but later was discharged when his pancake-flat feet attracted attention. A high school buddy wrote wistfully that "I only wish I was in there, but I guess we all can't get what we want. I flunked my physical but I think I can make it now. I have been checking my pulse everyday and they haven't been over 87 per minute." These rejects, known as "4-F's," were treated with great understanding by most people, but "draft dodgers" were not.

My father was still grumbling as we boarded the bus. He pulled me back, holding me in a heartfelt hug. "Good luck, son." I was too young and too excited to understand the tears in his eyes. The bus pulled away for the seventy-mile trip to Fort Thomas. A classmate soon got sick from the tension and puked out the window. All of us behind him caught the spray. "Hey," someone shouted, "Smitty's seasick already—don't he know he ain't in the Navy?" I had been seated behind him wondering how many of us would make it back, wishing some sort of "red mark" would appear above those destined to die, and wondering if such a telltale sign would appear above my head. If such a mark had appeared above the heads on that bus, one would have hovered over Smitty's head, for he was killed in action the next year.

Fort Thomas was a typical nineteenth-century brick army post. Perched solidly on a Kentucky bluff high above the Ohio River, it overlooked hilly eastern Cincinnati. Our bus unloaded in front of the huge drill hall where we would bunk with 416 other nervous draftees for the next twelve days. After claiming my bunk, I met my first supply sergeant. I learned for the first time in my life that I wore 30-31 pants, size 37 jacket, and a 14½-32 shirt. I also got my first whiff of moth balls, but I thought for years that this smell was in some way part of the army. I had never smelled them at home, for my mother was not the type to spend good money on a moth, or anything else she could swat.

The army's two greatest social lessons were painfully hammered into us at Fort Thomas. A group of mountaineers came in drunk after bed check the first night. A sergeant told them to shut up and get to bed. "Boy," one of them slobbered, "you rattle on like a bell clapper up a goose's ass!" The sergeant said nothing, and the drunks clattered around the latrine, finally staggering into their bunks. I thought the army had gone soft. The next night everyone in the drill hall was denied passes out into the city owing to what had happened the night before. We were enraged at the mountaineers, and they were in turn humble and terrified, possibly for the first time in their lives. Order and quiet prevailed everywhere. In any army the most effective force comes from within, or, "We cannot *make* you do something, but we sure as hell can make you sorry you did *not* do it."

The second lesson began when a sergeant asked for "volunteers who know how to run a typewriter." We were lined up on the drill field. Several of us stepped forward, smug in our superior knowledge. With a haughty backward glance at our unenlightened comrades, we followed the noncom down to a railroad siding. "Well, here it is boys," he grinned. "Here what is?" someone asked. "Why boys," he drawled, "this here boxcar is full of typewriters; you typists is going to carry them over to that warehouse and stack them neatly in storage. I'll be back later this afternoon to check on you." The three-striper swaggered away, confident he had fooled some more dumb recruits. We were mad until someone said, "Fool me once, shame on you; fool me twice, shame on me." We would never be fooled again, for we had learned a second important rule of Army life: *"Never volunteer for anything."*

The army at first appealed to my romantic nature. I had been reared on stories told by World War I veterans—voluptuous French women, hilarious pranks, and a little fighting somewhere, but nothing to worry about. I lay thrilled in my bunk as a talented Fort Thomas bugler sent *Taps* drifting out on the warm night air. I wrote home that "you either like the army life or you hate it. I love it. It's a lot like Blackhawk scout camp, only more so. I feel better than I have ever felt in my life." I was euphoric; I had escaped my small home town for what must surely be a life of adventure. I was with the youngest group in the army, kids who believed things and put up with things older men could never accept. We lived in different worlds in the army, just as we had in civilian life.

My army future hinged on the various IQ and aptitude tests. High scores on all of them won me assignment to the Army Specialized Training Program. The ASTP was to provide college training for young men throughout a war of as yet unknown length, thus preventing a shortage of engineers and physicians. Before entering college, however, each trainee had to undergo thirteen weeks of basic training in infantry. When I left Fort Thomas it would be as an ASTP infantry trainee.

"Move 'em out," a buck sergeant shouted, and we boarded trucks for the Covington railroad station. Scores of ASTP boys crowded aboard passenger cars on a typical, packed, wartime civilian train, where we sat impatiently, listening to a stuck record on the station juke box: "Way down south in Columbus, Georgia . . ." repeating itself over and over and finally fading away as the cars swayed down the tracks. We later recalled this as "magical prophecy," for we were rolling south to the great Infantry School at Fort Benning, just a few miles south of Columbus, Georgia.

2. ASTPeewee

We unloaded at Fort Benning, and a noncom (noncommissioned officer) took us to our barracks in the Harmony Church area. "What's it like here?" I asked, adding "Sir" to my question to play safe. "I wouldn't mind living in Georgia," he replied, "if I didn't have long to live." We laughed, then turned thoughtful, Midwestern boys for the first time trying to puzzle out life in the deep South— blood red soil, pungent pine forests, cotton, strange accents, and the labels of racial segregation stuck boldly on doors and fountains. This was not like our Ohio Valley, and a Cincinnati lad complained that it "doesn't even seem to be much like *Gone With The Wind.*"

We were unsure of Georgia, but Fort Benning was an exciting place to all of us. God but it was big! Somewhere out on its hundred-thousand acres were a hundred and fifty thousand men—the Seventh Armored Division over in the Sand Hill area, thousands of paratroopers at the Jump School, other thousands in Officers Candidate School (OCS), the training cadre, and twelve thousand in ASTP. Benning was "Old Army," dating from 1919, with a main post resembling a college campus. There sat the beautiful Infantry School, backed by huge, multistoried brick barracks, giving way to tree-lined streets, theatres, chapels, and many blocks of Spanish-styled officers' dwellings. This place was the infantry's home, the source of anything of importance to that crucial branch of the army. Its symbol was a bayonet in an oval frame, the words "Follow Me" standing boldly across the bottom. I was to like this post far more than any other place I lived during my two and a half years in the army.

The Fort Benning Basic Training Center (BTC) for ASTP had opened in May, 1943. There were three training regiments, the 4th, 5th, and 6th. I was assigned to the 3rd platoon, 16th company, 4th battalion, 5th regiment. My 250-man company was captained by David C. Garvin, a soft-spoken Carolinian who, with the "top kick" or first sergeant—an "elderly" soul of perhaps thirty-five years—represented god-like and never-to-be-tampered-with authority. I liked my platoon sergeant best. Jim Overton spoke my language, for he was from Tennessee, "the next best thing to Kentucky."

The regular army men on the post had a low opinion of us. The best thing we were called was "ASTPeewee." I wrote home that "the regulars call us male WACs. They don't like us and call us 'dodgers.' I don't like it." To men going through basic and then on overseas, it seemed unfair for thousands of boys to be sent to college instead. In the same letter I told my mother to save my letters home, the reason being that "I might want to see what I was doing back here in the army." I would also save letters to me, I said, and ship them home in bundles. These hundreds of letters provide the backbone of this book, but I had no such intentions at the time.

After a few weeks, I wrote the home folks an analysis of army life:

No one can imagine the army and the life in it. It's impossible. In the first place not one single thing in life is private, yet we are called privates! Even trunks and barracks bags are inspected. There are no window shades, chairs, carpets, wall paper, or blinds of any kind. Everybody dresses the same. Every single shoe and hat must be in its place. The lights are strikingly bare with no shades on them as they protrude from their sockets nailed on bare rafters and braces. Everywhere you go you must have a pass or somebody's "permission." Everything is very democratic. Nobody attempts to be better than the next fellow or he soon regrets it. Millionaires and former farm hands work side by side cleaning a urinal or bowl in the latrine. Latrine is a word that was never spoken in civilian life. It seems natural now.

You soon learn that generosity is the cardinal rule. Everything is split up among the other fellows, packages, magazines, soap, hair tonic, anything from home at all. Eating is never a problem except for being on time. The Mess Hall is open 15 minutes every chow call and it closes on the exact "dot." You eat regular and sleep regular unless you are a big operator with a lot of chicks in town. Everybody wants to be a "big operator," but there is usually too much competition.

Basic training was easy at first. I was elated when handed an '03 army rifle, thinking "Gollee!" as I hefted and played with it, then spent hours cleaning the cosmoline out of it. We moved everywhere "on the double," strained to keep up with a rapidly mounting training regimen, and welcomed the relief of sitting through lectures. We listened to historians telling why we were at war. No one doubted why we were at war—Pearl Harbor and Hitler needed no explanation, so we were bored with this. The movies and lectures on VD were much more to our liking. VD meant venereal disease, and judging from the material, the Army feared this stuff more than Japs or Nazis. I knew it was horrible, remembering the long scruffy line that formed every Saturday morning in front of the Nicholas County Health Officer's clinic. "They're all getting their weekly shots for syphilis," I was told. My informer was a very crusty old man nicknamed "Pump," who hung around my father's filling station. Dad had quit his salesman's job and started running a Gulf service station in 1942. "If you think syphilis shots are bad, you don't know nothin'," Pump said. "Get the claps and they stick a metal rod up your pecker, open up scrapers on it, and pull it back out with all sorts of stuff sticking to it. Boy, that smarts!" I nearly fainted thinking about it.

Pump was a storehouse of sex lore for the kids who hung around the station. He liked to shock people, but VD films proved Pump still had a lot to learn. No female was to be trusted. *Good Girls Have VD Too* was the film proving that. Classical music plays as a "real lady" lures a poor soldier to her bedroom. A few days later he feels a stinging as he urinates, but dismisses it as caused by spicy food. Soon something called a chancre appears, turning rapidly from pimple size to a raging, virulent, leprous growth enveloping his organ. The treatment was even worse than Pump had claimed. College boys in the crowd made catcalls throughout the show, but in this pre-penicillin era, no one could walk away from such films untouched.

"The Infantry School will officially go into woolens Oct. 18." This headline in *Pine Bur,* our ASTP newspaper, meant that although Georgia afternoons were still a sweaty 90°, the Army had settled on an "average" date to ease administrative problems. Flexibility in such a matter was never expected, so we winced as we pulled on the woolen OD's or Olive Drabs, and discarded the comfortable cotton chinos or "suntans." By this time I was moving into the fifth week of basic training.

Weaponry and camping appealed to me more than any other part of basic. I had often used a .22-caliber rifle to shoot sycamore balls from the tops of giant trees along Licking River. By autumn they mark a clean hit with a satisfying puff of dust. I scored better than most at Benning's Carmouche Range, and I did as well with the light machine gun, a weapon I would later use on Luzon. Emotionally, however, I was unable to make my adolescent feelings accept the fact that I was learning to kill people. I wrote my anxious parents about the "Night Infiltration Course": "Soon we crawl under live fire from machine guns. I'm not scared of it. It will be fun. Just like a game."

I was in step with my buddies in developing a pride in the infantry. We were in ASTP and unlikely to have to carry this thing any further—so we believed. A letter home held that they "should not think of the infantry as something awful. When I got in the army I thought anything but infantry for me. Now I'm really proud to be a member of it. They are the guys that win. They do the suffering for America while the aviators, signal corpsmen and other branches get the glory and praise."

Living in tents during tactical bivouac was a pleasant repeat of earlier scouting experiences. By this time I had made three good buddies, from Ohio, Texas, and Massachusetts. Reveille and assembly roll call was very casually done, so we decided to sleep through the thing and show up later for breakfast. "They finally caught up with us," I wrote home. "For three mornings now we have slept through reveille and left our beds unmade, tent flaps down and the tent in an uproar. The sgt. and lieut. came around and discovered our ramshackle tent. We will be on KP as soon as we finish our march home." Mother was not impressed; she replied that she had "been on KP for almost twenty years."

My fun-and-games idea of basic training took a severe jolt one black November night. Several of us were along Upatoi Creek, perhaps in a border area between our own Harmony Church area and the Sand Hill area, which was occupied by the Seventh Armored Division—the "Lucky Seventh." This division was soon to be shipped to Europe, and it was finishing up its training. There was no moon, and we were standing in the center of a huge field learning compass coordination with maps, finding grid lines—true, grid, and magnetic north. The phosphorescent dial of our compass shone dimly in the velvet darkness. The silence was suddenly shattered by the rumbling, grinding crash of tanks as they burst through the pine scrub that bordered our field. They would be upon us in seconds, and panic gripped us. They could not know we were in the field and we had no flashlights; we would be squashed like bugs under their whirring tracks. We ran in aimless circles, confused and shouting, until someone pulled paper from his pocket and lit it with a match. Anything we could find was burned, including paper money. We were ripping our shirts off to feed the fire as the tanks roared by to the left and right of us, their sirens screaming. We huddled numbly around the embers of our small fire, deciding not to tell our comrades about this; they might not understand how soldiers out studying maps could wind up so far off center. Nor did the tankers ever file a complaint about the fire bugs trespassing in their pasture that black autumn night.

I did not write home about my narrow escape with the tanks, but I included other information gleaned on bivouac:

Just got back from camping last night. We ate C rations which consisted of instant coffee, hard candy and 4 hardtack biscuits which resemble cow crackers [a hard round cracker of the 1940's] and meat hash. It contains 2600 calories and tastes very good. I cut my finger as usual on the meat can. We warmed our food over the fire by sticking our bayonets in the can before opening.

We learned how to improvise bombs and grenades with

T.N.T., dynamite or nitro starch and nails and other metal. Next Halloween if I'm home I'll go out and blow up the courthouse! We learned how to handle fuses, caps and lay all kinds of charges of our own makings.

One type of fuse burns at 23,000 feet per second, yes, 23,000 feet per second. Daddy has probably heard of this. In the last war we were caught short of grenades. The Germans were well prepared. The Allied soldiers however would improvise a grenade out of metal and 8 ounces of T.N.T. and 1 foot per 40 second fuse. They would cut off 5 seconds of fuse, light it and throw it over. The Germans caught on and got to pulling the fuse out before it went off and lighting it again and throwing it back. Well, the Allied soldiers got hold of some of the "red, rough, and ready," as this 23,000 feet per second fuse was called. They would make a grenade and put this fuse in it after rubbing soot on the end of it to make it look like it had died out before going off. The Germans would run up and happily pick up these grenades. When they lit them to throw them back they got their heads blown off.

The very nature of infantry training gave country kids advantages over "city dudes" and boys from the desert or plains. We lived off the land. I soon had a knapsack full of pecans, picking them up under the trees and swapping them for various things from boys who wondered "where Mathias gets all his nuts." As often as not, these boys would be standing under a pecan tree and walking on the unhusked nuts. Occasionally I was able to add wild grapes and onions to my swapping, as well as honey taken out of an old tree bull-dozed by a tank into Upatoi Creek. I tried to run fish to riffles and grab them, as I had done back home, but Georgia's sandy creek bottoms stymied this. "If I could just get hold of a jeep or truck battery, I could 'telegraph' us a good mess of fish," I told a buddy. "All you have to do," I explained, "is stick wires from the negative and positive battery poles down into the water. This stuns the fish and they float to the top." Such refined equipment proved beyond the meager powers of army privates.

My greatest success, however, came in developing a ready cure for poison ivy. I was immune to it, but most others were not. I found a weed that resembled Kentucky's jewel weed, crushed its pithy stalks and smeared the juice over the blisters. It stopped the itching immediately, just like jewel weed, and soon the blisters dried up. This won me some grudging respect, even from the New York City crowd! But I failed miserably one afternoon to prevent a woodland disaster. Our infantry column had stopped for a ten-minute break along one of Benning's sandy roads. "I wonder what's inside that funny thing?" said a city soldier sitting beside me. I missed grabbing him as he grabbed a stick and shoved it through a low hanging hornet's nest. The enemy's reaction was immediate and decisive. They won, routing an entire cursing and swatting platoon of U.S. infantry!

Religion had been an important part of life in Carlisle. I had grown up a Catholic in a thoroughly Protestant environment, sometimes wondering if there were really any other Catholics in the world after all. In the army I soon found Catholics on all sides, and also the first atheists I had ever encountered. Carlisle's parish priest, a gentle soul appropriately named Edmund Priest, wrote me that "there is really great possibility for our good Catholic boys to influence soldiers who have no religion." I did not know what to make of this advice, but I welcomed his assurance that Catholic servicemen could eat meat on Friday: "I am of the opinion that you may take all you can get of it, on any and all days." From then on I deliberately ate all the meat I could find every Friday.

My mother worried continually about my morals in the army, convinced that all armies were long on rape and pillage and short on prayer. One of the first things she sent to Benning was a letter full of advice and instructions "to carry this little gold miraculous medal with you. Father Bauer gave it to you when you were a baby. So don't lose it." I promptly lost it. Although I attended mass rather regularly at the Benning chapels, I spent little time thinking about religion until I got overseas.

Another turning point in my life came in mid-autumn, 1943, when I flunked out of ASTP. My platoon had just returned from a long hike when we were given a battery of tests. I was crushed to find that I had passed everything but the mathematics, but this subject was crucial to the engineering courses awaiting most ASTPeewees. I had barely passed math in Carlisle High School, but this small school offered nothing beyond algebra and plane geometry. My lack of study along with a lack of opportunity had combined to end my hopes in ASTP.

I had plenty of company in my misery, for perhaps one-third of us had failed this final "weeding-out" exam. We searched frantically for excuses and scapegoats as we talked it over. The facts had to be faced, however, and college was not one of them; instead, we would finish basic with the rest of the guys, then be shipped out to a line company in some embattled infantry division! God, but we were trapped. Most of us had already tried and failed to get into the air cadets or navy; in my case defective color vision had barred the path. ASTP had then rescued us in the nick of time. Now it was gone. Even worse, it had started us through infantry basic training. In flunking out of ASTP we had no place to go but on into the infantry.

Most draftees and volunteers of World War II believed fully in this often repeated axiom—"anything but the infantry!" There was something frightfully personal about the infantry. It was here you saw the enemy face to face, here that the casualties mounted the highest, and here that soldiers labored the hardest and lived in the most primitive conditions. Further, most were generally aware that the War and Navy Departments used intelligence and aptitude test results in assigning recruits to the Army Air Force, the navy, and the technical branches in the army. Men at the lower end of the scoring tables went to the infantry. This latter fact galled many former ASTPeewees in a special way, for in our case very high test scores had paradoxically dumped us into the infantry. We had outsmarted ourselves! This gnawed on us much more than any feeling that the infantry was beneath us, or that it was an insult to our intelligence— our training had belied most such notions—rather, we keenly felt the irony of our entrapment into a laborious and dangerous job we could have avoided with better luck.

I somehow screwed a smile on my face and wrote my mother a sour grapes letter. "Who wants to piddle around in an old college anyway?" I wrote. "Likely as not I'll get corporal stripes before long and be assigned to the training cadre here." I knew there was not even a slim chance of that, and she probably did too. In her return letter she hit the crux of the matter by advising me not to "take

ASTP too seriously, the main thing is getting back home safe and sound after the war."

My tough break did not hold me back long. I had the cocky feeling of omnipotence that usually goes along with superb physical condition and an optimistic bent of mind—to hell with the ASTPeewees, nothing will happen to me anyway! With this settled, I began to enjoy my stay at Benning, and the new friends I had made. The best place to have fun was in nearby Columbus, so I set out to have my share of it every weekend.

Columbus was a city of fifty thousand located along the Chattahoochee River in southwestern Georgia, about 130 miles north of the Gulf. Across the river was Phenix City, Alabama, correctly called "Sin City" by the soldiers. Fort Benning had a hundred and fifty thousand soldiers in late 1943, and a hefty percentage of this mob descended on Columbus every weekend. It was a tremendous experience to be with and watch this crowd as it surged like a khaki tide through Columbus.

The bus ride into town was an adventure in itself. Huge, articulated trailer busses of the Howard Bus Lines followed six routes through the post. Fares were paid through a rear cab window as soldiers crammed into these clattering and steamy steel tubes. It was only a ten-mile trip into the Ninth and Broadway terminal, but strange things could happen, especially on the trip back after a night at the bars. I wrote home that "on the way out to Benning on the bus a drunken soldier started shaking the dew off his lily and about half of it went right into my shoe. No kidding. I couldn't figure out what was happening when it hit my ankle. You have to watch for vomit all the time, but I never expected this!"

Another time I stepped off the bus into a roaring big fight at the station between members of the Seventh Armored Division and a gang of paratroopers. It did not take much to get something like this started, but it took a lot to get it stopped. Before this battle was over several men were seriously cut up, and rumor had it that several had been killed. Droves of military police dropped into the affray. By that time, my buddies and I had retreated to safer streets.

Walking downtown Columbus's two major streets was like lifting a rock without knowing what would run out from under it! Here, for example, were the first tattoo parlors I had ever seen. They were clustered together, and proud soldiers stepped out (or staggered out) showing off garish skin pictures in reds, oranges, and blues. We would stand in the windows or doors and watch the artist at work over hearts, wreaths, arrows, girls' names and the "Follow Me" motto of the Infantry school. A great favorite was a woman's head floating in a wine glass, captioned "Man's Ruin." Couples often came in, getting tattoos pledging eternal love, or perhaps just a butterfly on each wrist.

The United Service Organization ran five or six popular USOs in Columbus. I liked the Eleventh Street USO best, but I have the fondest memories of a small, church-run USO on a side street— perhaps it was Episcopalian. In any event, I showed up at the door with Edgar Nash. We had already scouted the larger clubs, and found all the girls occupied by guys either bigger or wealthier than we were. We decided to try our luck at this small club with the flag in the window. I knocked and a little old lady opened the door. She was in an ankle-length dark dress, with silver hair and a tasteful small array of jewelry on her person. Nash and I started to enter, but she halted us.

"Just a minute," she said, looking us over as only an old lady can. "And where are you from?" she asked, looking straight into my blue eyes.

"Kentucky, mam," I replied, "Carlisle, Kentucky."

"I see," she said, and turned on Nash with the same question. "And you, sir, where are you from?"

"I'm from Texas," Nash drawled, "Seagraves, Texas, mam."

Suddenly a warm glow came over her formerly suspicious face. "Why boys," she beamed, "come right on in—you're one of us!" For her the Civil War was far from over.

Strolling through downtown Columbus on a Saturday pass combined two freedoms—freedom from the army and also freedom from the earlier restrictions of civilian life. Few of us analyzed it, but we relished this temporary sense of well earned irresponsibility as much as children delight in a circus or carnival midway. These precious hours of freedom were seldom wasted in movie houses, although we checked the marquees of the Bradley, Springer, Royal and Rialto from force of habit. I wrote home that *Stage Door Canteen* and *In Old Chicago* were playing in the Columbus theatres, but "we have later movies out in our Benning theatres." Civilian restaurants, however, attracted soldiers in droves, for ASTP food supplies at Benning were rather limited that autumn of 1943. My gang tried out Smitty's, Hartins, Hayes, and the Goo Goo, but we eventually settled on a downtown cafeteria where mountains of good food could be bought cheaply. We sneered at the R & R, which advertised that it was "for officers and their guests." But Phenix City across the river had no such restrictions; in "Sin City" no holds were barred. The lurid reputation of the place snared the attention of every red-blooded soldier—either "put up or shut up!"

Phenix City's night spots, such as the Bama, Matag, or Southern Manor, held little attraction for my crowd of poverty-stricken privates. Gambling halls were ignored for the same reason. We were long on talk about the whorehouses, but extremely short on action, for all of us admitted our virginity as well as other fears entailed in facing off with a "real, live whore." Instead we liked Idle Hour Park, an amusement park with some unforgettable attractions. Anyone entering the park had only to look to see a naked woman lying seductively on a red plush pad above the "Electric Eye Rifle Range." Twenty or so hits on a moving target below the pad would ring a gong and drop her bouncingly into a huge bed below. This gave an exciting view of her well structured anatomy, and was not to be sneezed at in an era long before *Playboy*, a day in which nude pictures appeared in no magazine—yet here was the real thing. Many of the riflemen in line here shot the best scores of their lives. She was the first nude woman I had ever seen.

Phenix City came by its reputation honestly, but Columbus had one attraction that rivaled anything available in its cross-river neighbor. An excursion steamboat was based just off Ninth Street, near the Phenix City bridge, advertising rides for a dollar per passenger. A Saturday night trip on this small, crowded steamer was a voyage none would ever forget, and most would not want to repeat. I went aboard one Saturday night with John Molleran, a pal from Cincinnati. A capacity crowd of 700 milled around in anticipation. Numerous whores plied their trade as a seven-piece Negro jazz band thumped away on such numbers as "South," "Basin Street," and "Perdido." The captain blew a fanfare on the boat's wheezing, hornlike whistle, then eased his sternwheeler out to the center of the placid Chattahoochee. John and I were used to the great steamers on the Ohio River, and we belittled all of this, but we were soon proven wrong, for this little boat and its captain had real action built into them.

We paddled south down the river toward the distant red lights on the high paratroop jump towers at Fort Benning. The river was only a hundred or so yards wide, and its banks reflected back the boat's lights as well as the music and squeals of feminine laughter. Clumps of soldiers hung along the rails, perhaps wondering why they had not joined the navy. Suddenly the boat lurched, slowing almost immediately to drifting speed. John looked at me quizzically—"What's wrong now?" At that moment the captain appeared with a large megaphone. He leaned over the top rail as a searchlight picked up a figure swimming toward the nearby bank. "Sink or swim, baby!" he shouted in the megaphone. Since the woman was swimming well, and almost to shore, the captain poured more steam into the boilers and the paddlewheel hissed and splashed in new-found power. Meanwhile, I joined the other passengers in applauding and cheering for the whore who had fallen overboard, all of us with about the same feeling we would have had while cheering at a ball game. A bit later a drunken soldier splashed in, and made it to shore under similar waves of cheers and applause. Almost every Saturday night the warm Chattahoochee caught several such revelers. I suppose all of them made it to shore.

By this time all of us were using army slang, speech that entered American English and which now seems old fashioned or trite. I was no longer angry, but "pissed off," said "tough shit" instead of bad luck, used "snafu" to describe the army's foolish ways, and called all members of the Women's Army Corps not WACs, but "barracks bags." We reveled in using these and other new expressions as if the mere saying of the words magically moved us out of our adolescence and into an all-knowing adult world. Letters from high school classmates now in the service were heavily larded with the new expressions. One, from a friend at an air force training center, is an uninhibited example of this new language in its purest form: "When we went into that first spin I coulda shit a brass rod. See you've got your self a stripe. I'm a P.F.C. too (poor frigging cadet). We get slapped in the face with a fist full of chicken shit everytime we turn around. It's a great life though."

The most used slang expression of the war was "GI," meaning "government issue," which was stamped on all equipment along with a number, and, by implication, also stamped on every soldier. It was used so much that it hardly was noticed. Even the Filipinos, kept from news since the Jap occupation, were soon calling us "GI Joe." A case of diarrhea was always a case of the "GIs," and never simply diarrhea. Libby Grierson, a girl friend back home, sent me a poem entitled "Government Issue":

> Sitting on my G.I. bed,
> My G.I hat upon my head,
> My G.I. pants, my G.I. shoes,
> Everything free, nothing to lose,
> G.I. razor, G.I. comb,
> G.I. wish that I was home!
> . . . .
> Everything here is Government issue,
> G.I. wish that I could kiss you!

3. Mail Call

Mail call brought soldiers a chance to compare their lot with that of the home folks or with friends in the service. Letters let the steam out of army life or added to it, but no matter the good or bad news, the effect produced by a platoon sergeant standing with a fistful of letters shouting "Mail Call!" was always the same—a stomping of feet as everyone clustered around the noncom hoping to hear the sweet sound of his name.

Love letters were welcomed above all others. They were easy to identify, for most girls chose pastel blue or green stationery. Even before opening, there was the exciting smell of perfume dabbed heavily on the letter. I wrote more love letters than any other kind, nor did I feel like a hypocrite in promising undying love to a flock of girls back in Kentucky. "They all have my love," I reasoned pragmatically "and I'm just trying to narrow them down to the one I love and want the most." Behind this desire to keep them on the hook lay a feeling that I could get away with it. A letter from Grandma Furlong indicated that supply and demand was in my favor: "Are your girlfriends here in Maysville writing you? I never get to see any of them, but when you come back they will still be waiting for you as there is no boys left around for them to go with." There was nothing like a straightforward love letter to play ripples over the keyboard of a soldier's emotions. Phyllis Perkins, a lovely, blue-eyed blond of sixteen-going-on-seventeen, wrote me:

Gosh I miss you every day—that's what love does to you.
I still remember our last night together. I wish you were here
for I am so lonely for you tonight. I guess love does strange
things.

I'm going to Doc's dance. Gosh do I wish I was going with
you. It would be so wonderful to be in your arms, holding me,
oh so tight. The lights would be very low except in one corner
and we would dance there.

Such letters usually aroused feelings of helpless frustration with
Fort Benning, World War II, and the five hundred miles between my
drab barracks and Phyllis.

The war had turned the world of my generation upside down,
nullifying many old ways of doing things while changing youthful
expectations. Love letters helped iron out this time warp. Patty
Carpenter replied to one of my letters: "I do remember those good
times. I sure wish I could live that summer [of 1943] over again.
Those were the good old days. They won't be like that this summer
with everybody away, but the fun will start again when everybody
gets back home again." Patty had aged a year, as had her old boy-
friends, but they were all in the service and she was left stranded in
an all-female world. The past summer was recalled by her with a
nostalgia not normal for a teen-ager, yet now normal in the light of a
seemingly endless war. Patty undoubtedly knew, although she would
never have written it to me, that not "everybody" was going to "get
back home again."

Another letter reveals how everything, even a love affair, had to
be interpreted in reference to the war—the war was the camel in
everyone's tent. Phyllis wrote me that "Harry James is playing *Now
I Know* on my radio. It makes me want you here oh, so bad, to be in
each others arms—this war—Do you know if it wasn't for this war we
may not be going with each other. Maybe we would still just be good
friends. . . . The Gingham Dance was a lot of fun and I wish I could
have taken you, but this old war wouldn't let you come home. When
will you come home? Oh, in about a couple of years, sure that is
when it will be and not before." She was just three months short of
being correct, but two years to her seemed like an eternity.

A letter from Libby Grierson indicated, however, that although we boys of the Class of '43 might be missed "something awful," the Maysville high school crowd was not going to surrender the wonderful necking spots along Jersey Ridge Road. "There isn't any news to tell," Libby wrote from force of habit; then she proceeded to tell all:

> Don't tell this because I don't know whether Gaylord wants it known yet, but he is going to quit going with Bonnie Jean. Crockett and Miles have split up. Billy P is going with some little blonde in the 9th grade. Gayle C has an awful crush on some boy that works in the Washington theatre. He likes another girl. Joyce McChord likes Jimmy Jones. He lives in Aberdeen. Patty Carpenter said Doc and her brother went to Lexington yesterday to see Claire and Ricky. They had lipstick all over them when they came in. They must have had a good day! Mary Milton has the chicken pox. There really isn't much to tell. This town is so dead you don't even have a shadow to call your own now that the war is on.

I had not been at Benning long before I found that writing letters to servicemen had become a patriotic duty at Maysville High School. Jane Wood wrote: "We've declared a week at school to write boys in the service." I began to receive letters from exciting girls I had hoped to know better. Before long I had developed love-letter love affairs with two of these—this in addition to three regulars I had been writing all along. Although the girls eventually caught on by comparing notes, it was exciting while it lasted—I was getting pastel, scented letters at nearly every mail call and was becoming the envy of the barracks.

Nearly every love letter passed along the newest "little moron" joke. These were widespread throughout the army and the home front. Libby asked me if I had heard about the "little moron bridegroom who wore his suit to bed because someone had told him he would be going to town around midnight." She also told me of the little moron "who was glad his parents had named him Frank Mathias because that's what everybody called him anyway." Phyllis asked if I had heard about "the little moron who swallowed five pennies, then went around asking if anyone could see any change in him."

Every mail call brought letters from classmates in service. I sighed in envy or skepticism at the eye-popping contents, but always answered fire with fire—no darn flyboy, swabby, or gyrine was going to get ahead of me and the infantry! The air force provided the strongest challenge. From Maxwell Field: "I went to Birmingham last weekend. Boy what a town. I felt like I had been turned loose in a cherry orchard. Most of them are pushed up so far they look like tail lights. No kidding, all you have to do is flash a quarter. (I sent home for a quarter and I'm going back this weekend.)" From Creighton University Air Force Cadet School:

There are 15 women to one man here in Omaha. Our air force cadet uniforms really attract women. Believe me when I say that there are so many pretty women out here that you feel guilty to stay with one more than a half hour. You'll walk into a bar with the most beautiful blonde on your arm that you could ever want, and there at a table are 3 beautiful red-heads or brunettes just begging you to sit down with them, but you already have the blonde so you make an excuse to the blonde and forget where you left her. No kidding it's really that pitiful—no stuff."

"I dream in my sleep about the exciting feminine figures that are in Carlisle and are going to waste," chipped in a marine from Camp Lejeune. This worrisome thought was heated considerably by the tantalizing report from a seventeen-year-old still waiting the draft: "All the girls at home really have changed and all are smoking, cursing, drinking etc." Another seventeen-year-old lad—such were labeled "draft-bait"—wrote that he had "found a fair maiden over in Ohio. She thinks I'm going to marry her, but I'm not. So you see I'm in the 4–F Club now: *f*ind them, *f*ool them, *f*rigg them, and *f*orget them. I'll get 20 years for breach of promise!" He wanted to pass on the 4–F joke to me, for in real life he married the girl.

Griping and bitching were embedded in most letters. It was a relief to read of others caught in similar webs. "I am now at Kearney, Nebr.," wrote an air force trainee, "and it's the asshole of the 48. Kearney is about 8000 population and nothing going on but the time. . . . From the shit we eat here it's a wonder I exist." A bitterly critical letter arrived from a sailor in Brooklyn: "I'll be glad to get this frigging war over. If we could get rid of our great white father (namely Roosevelt) maybe we could do some good. I am really glad to see that Alben Barkley got fed up with this petty dictator. He is just selling American boys to Europe and the god dam Jews are getting all the money."

I was part of a generation that ran outdoors to watch any airplane flying over town. We entered World War II with high hopes of jockeying a P-38 high into the "wild blue yonder" and sending down in flames any Zero or Messerschmidt foolish enough to challenge us. Most of us were not destined to update *G-8 and his Battle Aces,* a pulp magazine of the 1930s full of World War I dogfights, but we truly envied the few who won their silver wings. I followed the life of George Judge, my best high school friend, with envy. He wrote from Lowry Field: "I finished my course here but was chosen to go to new CFC (Central Fire Control) school which deals with the new B-29 bomber. I doubt you have ever seen one but believe me it is a beautiful ship. It is a great deal larger than a B-17 and has four 2850 h.p. motors with four-bladed props." He wrote again, a few weeks later, to let me know he had gotten his wish. "I have been studying the B-29 wiring system and I didn't know such a complicated thing existed. Boy this 29 is a really a hunk of a ship and boy things are really going to happen when it gets into combat. By the way, I saw the new 'black widow' the other day and the new P-63 (enlarged P-39)." Since I had never been up in a plane, his next letter lifted my senses in sheer admiration: "I am at Pratt Air Field and am a member of a B-29 crew and head CFC man. I fly about 7 hours per day in the 29 and it is really fun. I was down to Jacksonville, Florida and back Saturday morning. You should see me in my heavy flying suit. We have had a flock of overseas shots and I expect to be sent to Burma or India by September [1944]." Later letters, written after bombing runs over Japan, convinced me that being in the air corps was not as much fun as I had imagined.

Racial and religious prejudices trooped into the army with everything else. The fact that the army was segregated was taken for granted. I never gave it a thought, for that is the way it was back home. Some 200 blacks lived in Nicholas County, but they might as well have been invisible, so little did they occupy the thoughts of the white majority. I had been taught to call them "colored folks," yet I wrote my mom repeating an often heard racial slur that "it has been raining pitch forks and nigger babies here in Georgia." A classmate wrote me from Texas that he had "become black as a nigger in this hot, old Camp Wolters sun." Another noted that his Anti-Aircraft battery had "picked up a little black dog for a mascot. We named him Nigger." From Fort Bliss, Texas, a buddy let me in on the surprising fact that "in El Paso there is the damndest bunch of Mexicans you ever saw. Can't understand a word they are saying." I had entered the army unsure whether Jews were a race or a religion, for there were none in Carlisle, but I had heard the name bantered about while half asleep in the Bible studies at church. I noted in a letter home that "some Jew boys have been pointed out to me, but I have never met any yet. My friends claim that they stick together like glue and act like they own the place. Some go to the PX [Post Exchange], get some candy and comic books and come back and sell it at double the price. The New York boys call them Kikes, Heebs, or Joes."

Mail from my parents and older people in Carlisle was full of the gossip that flows under the surface in every small town. Mother summed it up in a letter concerning a local businessman: "Mr. Pfanstiel is back from his Republican political trip to Oklahoma. That is where he went instead of Chicago. Don't know any particulars yet, but it won't be long until the whole town will know, no doubt."

The "whole town" did know any time a local girl joined the military! Mother wrote that "Mabel Maxon is going to join the WAVES soon. Our priest thought it was about the limit. He told me that she may think she knows a lot now but that she'll know a lot more before she gets out." An elderly spinster informed me that "Fay Rand has joined the WACS. Won't she make a pretty one, though I suspect when she gets in training she will have to do what someone else tells her, don't you? There will be no taking the studs and balking like she has always done with the family at home, and it may be fine for her." Neither my mother nor the spinster friend realized that I had recent letters from the above girls telling me of their plans. Mabel had written that she "would join the WACS but their reputation isn't very good and so I'll join the WAVES or something." Fay simply felt she "had to do something for the war effort."

I shared mixed feelings with many men of my generation concerning the changing behavior of women during the war. I felt it was "old fashioned" to oppose women in the armed services, or, like "Rosie the Riveter," in industry, but I also sensed a loss in the erosion of the femininity I had been reared to expect and respect. I was too young, however, for much comparison of past and present on this matter, nor to understand the vast changes the war was imposing on all segments of American society.

Small-town support for "our boys" was never in doubt. A letter from Miss Jimmie Henry, an elderly neighbor, reveals her feelings as times changed:

> It seems so queer to us to be writing to our little friends and neighbors in so many far away places, and we think of you more as a fine young boy growing up, and one of our good little neighbors in our community rather than as a soldier. But we are sure you are a good one. The boys all have such a fine spirit about what they are doing and of course it goes without saying we are proud of everyone of them.

The town, whose support for service men was rock hard, was also rock hard against anyone suspected of dodging the draft out of cowardice or for personal gain. Mother complained that "that big hulk of a Nall boy is still out. His dad is trying every way under the sun to keep him out, but a friend told me that she thinks he will soon have to go." Even students for the ministry were scrutinized closely. A letter from an older friend in Carlisle reported that "John Dox is still going to Bible School. Mr. Rigdon told me that they threw a party for him. They invited Mr. Rigdon, but he did not attend. They asked Mr. Rigdon later why he was not there, and he told them he didn't believe in stabbing the service boys in the back." One would think that a farming community would go easy on farm boys, who were needed to feed the troops and the nation. This was not always the case. "I've heard," confided a letter-writer, "that the draft is about to get Matt Binford. His father thinks he can keep him out with farm units." But I was in the army with no such worries, for my name was openly inscribed with the "elect": "Daddy says your name is on that big board in the Court House yard so I'll have to take a stool up there and try to find it."

Sometime during World War II the Armistice Day celebrations marking the end of the "War To End All Wars" became redundant. This day had always brought Carlisle's blue-capped Legionnaires marching into the high school auditorium, followed by prayers, then a hush over the student body as taps were played while bells tolled the eleventh hour of the eleventh day of the eleventh month— November 11, 1918. By 1943 the irony of this was apparent. Bob Cunningham, a seventeen-year-old, wrote: "We had the Armistice Day parade in Carlisle today. The home guard had a big part in it. I guess this Armistice Day didn't mean very much considering the present situation."

Many shortages plagued the home front. Mother's response to my plea for cookies shows some of them: "I baked some muffins and a blackberry jam cake this afternoon and they are on the way. I couldn't get any raisins so I put in black walnuts and think they will do. I could make those cookies you spoke of if I could get the ingredients. It takes chocolate, and I don't suppose there is any in town."

Gasoline was a source of continual problems on the home front, and this was especially true for filling station operators. My father owned and rented several commercial buildings in Carlisle, one of which was a Gulf service station. When the operator was drafted, Dad tried to run the station, a decision he soon regretted. An Office of Price Administration (OPA) agent checked the station and thought he saw a violation of rationing law as my brother handled the rationing stamps. My thoroughly enraged father was summoned to an investigation in Lexington where he was proven correct and the OPA man wrong. During this episode Mother wrote that "we don't get around much anymore. We have trouble getting gas so we stay close to home. The first of December [1943] a B & C stamp is good for 5 gals. instead of 4 gals. Every few weeks there is a change of some sort. Daddy sold 4903 gals. of gas this month. . . . Isn't it funny with all this rationing that the sales stay about the same as usual?" Although it was unknown to most citizens at the time, gas rationing was used in great part to cut back on rubber usage. There was plenty of gasoline in the nation, but the main supply of natural rubber was now controlled by the Japanese.

When General George Patton slapped some sick soldiers in Europe, he also hit the home front a solid blow. Mother wrote on November 24, 1943, that she hoped I would "keep in good shape with all that exposure in those pup tents. If you don't, Gen. Patton will come over and box your ears! His picture was in the Lexington *Herald* today and he doesn't look like much. Guess a good many are in high positions in the army that are not deserving."

Mother's letters usually lifted my spirits, transporting me home through information suiting my needs and likes, and offering a humorous perspective on my overconfident claims to manhood: "The fact of the business is that most of you still need nursing bottles instead of Night Infiltration." I was proud of her. She had prepared herself well as a teacher, first at Eastern Kentucky State Normal College and then at Chicago's Gregg School of Business. She set out to see the country, teaching in many regions, but I was most impressed with her stay at Mason City, Iowa, where she taught Meredith Willson, a flutist later to compose *The Music Man,* and at Rocky Mount, North Carolina, where she again had a lad in her class destined for musical fame—Kay Kayser of the "Big Band Era." She often used these "musical connections" to goad me into practicing my saxophone.

Dad's letters came less frequently, and were always headed: "Dear Boy." He was always hopeful that the war would soon be over: "The way they are bombing those German cities, the war simply can't last much longer in Europe as something is bound to crack. My guess is that Germany will offer peace terms by Jan. 15 [1944] ." His formal education ended in 1895 when he finished the eighth grade, but his sharp, analytical mind educated itself in a life-time of reading. A third-generation German immigrant, he had spoken German at home, but "poison pen letters" during the First World War brought a family decision to use only English. This deprived my brother and me of easy access to a second language. He had good historical insights, often arguing that "if Germany had won the first war by Christmas, 1914, as planned, we wouldn't have all the trouble we have today." Few modern historians would disagree, knowing as he did that it was the extension of this dreadful conflict that made possible the rise of Communism, sapping of empires, the entrance of America, and the emergence of Hitler and World War II. His belief that "aircraft carriers will doom battlewagons" was vindicated early in the war when the Japs sank *Repulse* and *Prince of Wales.* He found little belief and even less encouragement for such "unpatriotic" views, so he followed his salesman job with humor, and fishing with a passion, justly earning his nickname, "Lucky," as his talented rod pulled an endless supply of fish from Kentucky's clear streams.

4. Sharps and Flats

Nothing was going right. I was depressed as I entered the last week of basic training. Many of my friends were already guessing which college they would attend. The only "educational experience" I had coming was that of rifleman in a line infantry company. My life seemed used up. I opened a letter from Gayle Clark, a girl friend and the lead alto sax player in the Kavaliers. I studied it wistfully, as if it had come from some foreign land. It seemed impossible that only four months had passed since I had last played in the Kavaliers. It seemed equally impossible that I would ever do so again. She wrote: "We sure do miss you in the K.K.'s. The new guy can't play the tenor rides. We play the Carnation Company Dance tomorrow night at the Legion Hall. I hope it isn't as tough as the one the Cotton Mill had up there when the beer keg blew up!" I laughed briefly as I recalled the mill dance. An over-pumped beer keg had erupted, spewing a geyser of beer over the dancers, wetting many of the wartime crepe paper dance skirts and causing them to peel away. The band played on as many of the girls finished the dance in panties or petticoats. All of us had had trouble keeping our eyes on the music. I chuckled as I remembered, but the memory only added to my blue mood.

Laying the letter aside, I took a walk down a company street, dejectedly kicking pine cones along my path. I approached a cardboard sign tacked to a corner barracks: AUDITIONS HELD HERE FOR MEMBERSHIP IN THE 184th ARMY GROUND FORCES

(AGF) BAND: THE OFFICIAL ASTP POST BAND. My God! My heart pounded as I read the date and hours—I was in the right place at the right time. Now was the hour. I hurried in and saw several soldiers trying out for the band. A corporal was seated at a piano. He looked me over as I approached, asking what instrument I played.

"Tenor sax; I was in a dance band back in civilian life."

"Get one of those tenors over there and I'll try you out."

I shook as I wet the reed, then screwed it back on the mouthpiece. It was a good Conn tenor, with a comfortable "lay" for my fingers. I knew I must calm down; the alternative facing me if I goofed this audition had to be forced out of my mind. My mouth was dry, but my optimism was up.

"My name's Klausner, Jerry Klausner. What's yours?" I told him as he pulled out a stock arrangement and set it on my stand. "What's your name again?" he asked, as he rippled a frighteningly competent arpeggio along the keyboard. I groaned to myself: "Hell, I'm far out of my water here."

"I'm Frank Mathias, Corporal Klausner," I said, somewhat startled to hear the sound of my voice.

"O.K. Frank, I'll kick this ballad off and back you while you play the second tenor part—let's see how well you can sight read." He tapped his heel four times and the die was cast. I was soon reading well, and my confidence soared, prompting me to relax and "groove" or "swing" the musical phrases. Klausner tried me out on a variety of written music, from classics to marches. "Enough of this," he said, suddenly leaning back, lifting both hands above the keyboard. "You read well. Can you fake?" I knew he was asking if I could play "ride tenor," creating by ear the usual twelve- or twenty-four-bar solos arrangers demanded by writing *ad lib* into various instrumental parts. I nodded "yes," and played a ride or two as he filled in the background. I was amazed at his talent and facility; I had never played with a piano man like this one. But he was in a hurry—a usual state for this likeable New Yorker, as I later learned— so he accepted my few solos as typical of what he could expect. He assumed I could also play combo work, with a faking knowledge of scores of ballads, rhumbas, waltzes, polkas, novelty numbers and much else. He did not know how little I really knew, but then, neither did I.

"Well, Frank, where's your clarinet?" Klausner asked. I knew what he meant, and panic gripped me again. I had taken out a Pedlar clarinet and wet the reed, but I was praying that I would not have to sight read with it. I had taught myself enough to stumble through the Kavalier arrangements, and I had memorized some difficult parts, but as I looked at Klausner I knew that judgment day was at hand. The infantry was going to get me after all. He was sure to put up some damned screeching part off the top of a Sousa march, or perhaps a finger-busting classical selection. It would not take much to stop me, that was certain. It never occurred to me that he might be eager to get this job over with; just sign up enough musicians to fill out the band, then make it into Columbus in time for a date.

I sat spellbound before my stand as Klausner put up the rollicking lead clarinet part on "Josephine." My eyes had never seen a more welcome sight! Of the thousands of songs he could have chosen, he selected the only one I was certain I could play. I had memorized it for the Kavaliers, and there facing me was the exact same stock arrangement. I played it beautifully, and why not; I could have played it just as accurately in the stygian blackness of Mammoth Cave.

"Fine, fine," Klausner beamed. "You'll do fine; you're in the band." He was in too much of a hurry to try me out on any other number—thank God. Some weeks later as I struggled to read tough clarinet parts, he growled: "How in the hell did *you* ever manage to read "Josephine" during the audition? That song stopped some pretty good reed men that day." I just shrugged my shoulders, leaving him to ponder the strange ways of music and musicians.

I left the audition wildly elated. My world had changed from lead to gold in thirty minutes. I ran all the way to the service club, took pen in hand, and wrote home: "I was auditioned a while ago for a permanent ASTP band here at Fort Benning. . . . I will be stationed at headquarters company ASTP and receive musical instruction. I will probably be here for the duration." After mailing the good news home, I thought I had better thank God for placing "Josephine" on that music stand, a "miracle" if I had ever seen one. So I did thank Him, promising to learn to play clarinet well enough to pass on my own the next time.

I was to join the band in early January, 1944, but I had a post-basic furlough coming my way. I moved my gear into the band barracks, then took a train to Kentucky. Some fifteen hours later I got off in Paris and took a bus the remaining fifteen miles to Carlisle. My welcome home was noisy and happy, for I had walked in unannounced. I was surprised to learn that my next door neighbor, Andrew Metcalfe, had arrived on furlough just thirty minutes earlier. Andy was a grocer's son, a popular lad of good looks and sharp wit who had left pre-dental studies at the University of Cincinnati to volunteer for the infantry. He had been like an older brother to me. Andy and I decided to get dates and take them to Lexington the next night. I cannot remember who we took, but we went to the Canary Cottage, a popular bar and restaurant.

After taking our seats, Andy said he was ordering "drinks for everybody." I knew he meant mixed drinks with their strange names, but I had never tasted one nor did I know what to ask for. Embarrassed at being thought stupid, I mumbled something. Andy helped me out.

"Did you say Tom Collins?"

"Yeah, that's it," I nearly shouted, "good old Tom Collins."

The gin spiked Tom Collinses kept coming, drowning any remaining feelings of stupidity. I was feeling great, and Andy was reeling off one joke after another, all of them uproariously funny. Our dates had demurred from diving deeply into the drinks with us, and probably exchanged worried looks as they thought of the trip home. I was beyond worry, delighted that Andy had introduced me to something as nice as mixed drinks. "Good ole Dandrew," I slobbered, and Andy feigned a poke at my chin. He somehow got all of us home safely in his dad's '39 Chevy. Next day, we both agreed we had loused up what could have been a perfect evening.

I was eager to see my Maysville girl friends, so brushing aside my parents' protests I left, dropping my bag at my favorite cousin's home. Doc Hines (he was a dentist's son) and I were soon out prowling in his dad's car. He agreed to help me avoid the tangle sure to happen if I blundered into a student hangout and encountered two or more of my love-letter lovers. Doc strolled up to the steamy sidewalk windows of Vance's, Kilgus's, and Caproni's, peered intently through the holiday season decorations, then signaled his findings back to me in the car. In this way, I managed dates with

Phyllis and Libby on the two nights I spent in Maysville. Each night we parked for some "smooching" along the bluffs high above the Ohio River, Doc with Claire Adair, his girl friend, and I with my date. The car radio's big band sounds blended softly with the moonlight, while far below the night-blackened river caught and reflected the city lights. These two nights often glimmered in my mind's eye during the years ahead.

Time caught up with me, and I found myself hugging goodbyes into my parents and brother. Andy and I rode the bus to the Paris train station where he went north and I went south. It was the last time I would ever see him. He rose to staff-sergeant in the 88th Division, but one sunny day in the Italian mountains he won the Silver Star attacking two fortified Nazi machine gun nests with grenades and rifle. As he knocked out the nearest nest, the other tore his life away. It was the last week of the European war, and came as a crushing blow to his parents—my "Uncle Ed" and "Aunt Elsie." He was their only son.

I stared vacantly out of the dusty train window as I returned, thinking of the furlough and things left undone. There was a short layover in Atlanta before catching the Central of Georgia train to Columbus. The only vacant chair in the crowded station was a wheelchair in a corner. I flopped in it, glad to rest. A few minutes later two elderly women walked up and looked me over, then one asked in a gentle Georgia accent:

"How are you feeling, soldier boy?" They assumed I was a wounded hero coming home from a battlefield. It was an opportunity for fun; besides I felt bored and a bit mean as my furlough ended.

"I feel tolerably well, Mam, considering everything."

"Would you like us to get you something—anything at all?"

"No Mam, that wouldn't be right or necessary; I have most everything I need anyways," and I pulled my legs up to me a bit, as if there might be something wrong with them.

The one with the bluish white hair now expressed real concern, allowing that she bet I would really "be glad to see the home folks again. Are you from Valdosta, or Macon, or Newnan?" she ventured. By this time I was ready to leave, for the Columbus train was chugging in.

"Mam," I said, springing abruptly from the wheelchair, "I'm from Fort Benning and I've got to catch the train back. See you later!" They were startled, then started laughing as I smiled back at them while trotting to the track turnstile.

The two-hour trip to Columbus was a pleasant ride through endless pine forests, often paralleling red dirt country roads with clusters of woebegone Negro shanties, with a whistle stop near Warm Springs, President Roosevelt's favorite vacation spot. I hoisted my barracks bag aboard the big Howard bus in Columbus, and was soon rolling out the Cusseta Road. I got off at Old Federal Road and walked up the hill to ASTP Headquarters. The 184th Band was in barracks 4025, its noisy bandsmen isolated between a deep forest and Post Office #6. Down in the forest were war dogs of the K-9 Corps, canines trained for combat duties. The band serenaded them all day, and they serenaded us all night, but their presence guaranteed privacy along the south side of the barracks. The musicians practiced there, the clarinets and flutes always accompanied by the howls of the Dobermans.

I walked into the barracks and into a new life. Merle Denny, a staff sergeant, saw me first. I had met him while moving into the barracks after the audition.

"Hey fellows," he shouted, "Junior's back from furlough." The diversion was welcome.

"Did'ja get a lot of ass, Junior?" This came from Rocco Buccini, a trumpet man.

"No, but I sure smooched up a storm," I bragged, feeling I had said something worthy of the occasion.

Instead it brought a roar of good-natured laughter as several repeated my statement for late comers. I was not quite sure why, but I knew I had made a hit, and I also knew my name would be "Junior" from that time on.

I walked upstairs, approaching my bunk at the rear of the barracks. I blinked, then stared at a soldier clad in shorts standing next to my bunk with long shoelaces wrapped around each arm and over his forehead.

"What in the hell are you doing?" I asked with spaced words and an emphasis on hell. He sucked in his breath, squinting his eyes up in anger as if to make sure he had heard me correctly.

"Whadda you mean, what am I doing—who are you anyway?" I could tell he was mad, and I knew I must have interrupted something important, screwy though it was. Two other guys on the floor were staring at me by this time.

"Well, I dunno," I said a bit obsequiously, "I thought you must be playing some kinda game with those shoelaces wrapped all around you."

"Shoelaces! Are you kiddin', don't you know what these are?" His expression had changed from anger to puzzlement.

"Nope," said I. My expression was as puzzled as his.

"Well, these are *Tefilin,* and I use them to pray."

"I don't understand," I said.

"Because I'm a Jew, a Jew—don't you understand that?" His voice grew edgy.

I stammered—ashamed and afraid—"I didn't know; you're the first Jew I've ever met." I felt like crying.

"Are you putting me on?" he asked, with interest rising in his voice. "Where are you from that there aren't any Jews?" His two buddies moved up to hear my reply.

"I'm from Carlisle, Kentucky. There aren't any there. I've been in the army four months and I reckon I've seen some, but I never met any and I know I've never seen anybody wearing *Tefilin.* I'm sure sorry if I've offended you."

He thought it over, then laughed and stuck out his hand. "My name's Jack Block and welcome to the band. I thought maybe you were a smart-ass, then I wasn't sure what you were, but who can complain about a guy that never met a Jew, much less seen one tied up in 'shoelaces'!" Everybody laughed, me most of all, and Jack's buddies introduced themselves as I unpacked my barracks bag.

By this time several bandsmen had come up from downstairs, picked up the "shoelace" story, and passed it around the barracks. Everytime I met a new musician, I had to repeat the story, or comment on it. My Kentucky accent verified the truth of my claims in their eyes, and added to the humor. Goldy, a sax man, pulled me aside: "Junior, you might as well know that this band is made up of 'Jewsiers and Hoosiers.'"

"How's that, Goldy?" I asked, wondering what he meant.

"The 184th was formed, numbered, and detached from the 38th

Infantry Division before it went to Hawaii. The 38th is an Indiana and Kentucky National Guard outfit, and over half the guys in the band are Hoosiers, but six or seven of us, like myself, are Jews— 'Jewsiers.' The rest of you are from other states, but us Jewsiers and Hoosiers outnumber everybody." He spotted my worried look, quickly adding "I don't mean anybody's pulling rank or taking sides; it's all a joke, Junior, this Jewsier-Hoosier business, you'll like this gang. They already like you!"

When I finally got back to my bunk, Jack pulled his *Tefilin* out and handed them to me. They were leather thongs. "I put them on every day when I pray, except Saturdays, to remind me of God's Commandments." I wrote all of this home, noting that "Jack's little book is copied from the *Old Testament* and it says 'Thou shalt bind them for a sign upon thy hand and they shall be for frontlets between thine eyes.' Catholics do something like that with the scapular."

The home folks were delighted that I had settled into the band, and seemed likely to stay awhile. "Every month you stay in the USA is just one more month toward the war's end and a safe return," Dad wrote, adding that "it was about this time last year you started playing with the Kavaliers. Guess that was your lucky day." Both of us knew that without that experience I would be getting ready for overseas shipment instead of playing in a band. Mother added a note in her superbly practiced penmanship: "Sounds like Mr. Block is a God fearing man. You'll probably learn more from your 'Jewsiers' than from the Hoosiers!"

Any military band is always a bit out of place—like a nest of songbirds twittering in the mouth of a cannon. Our table of organization (TO) called for twenty-eight men. Most lived in the barracks although some of the married men commuted from town. Since we were an infantry band, each day began with a long hike. This was followed with rehearsal, ear training, individual practice, marching band drill, dance band rehearsal, and finally, retreat ceremonies. After this, the dance orchestra, combo, and show band often left for jobs at variety shows, athletic events, service clubs of all stripes, USO Clubs in town, and civilian functions like bond rallies and dedications. The entire band trucked into Atlanta on one occasion, leading a large War Bond parade down Peachtree Street. By this time I was able to play the screeching clarinet parts off the top of the stirring Sousa marches, keeping in step as I did so. In short, I was living in a world of music—this in contrast to the war machine grinding away on all sides.

Army bands were led by warrant officers, a rank bridging the commissioned and non-commissioned officers; our was WOJG (warrant officer junior grade) Julian B. Goodstein, a gentle, likeable soul who wore his rank lightly, good-humoredly accepting his musicians' Pattonesque title for him—"Our Fearless Leader." He was an ideal leader for twenty-eight solo personalities: superbly trained in music at Juilliard, tolerant, firm but fair in his musical demands, and reasonably easy to skin out of a three-day pass to Atlanta.

I would have played twenty-fours hours a day in the dance band, if that had been possible. I had heard big, full-blowing bands like this one on the radio, and now I was in one! The screaming brass, swirling saxes, and driving rhythm section would have blown my beloved Kavaliers through the walls of the Maysville Armory. Our arrangements were patterned after those of Sy Oliver, of the Jimmy Lunceford and Tommy Dorsey bands. Experience made all the difference. Jerry Klausner, our piano man and arranger, had played in the big civilian bands of Georgie Auld, Buddy Clarke, and Bob Allen, while Bob Herrin, a trombonist, had come into the 184th from the Ina Ray Hutton band. Our combo leader, Al Jolly, had worked with the Enoc Light and Bud Freeman bands. Although I saved my top adulation for those from the big name bands, my respect deepened quickly for several studio musicians, men who had played every kind of music as background for radio and stage shows in the Chicago area. One clarinetist was held in awe by everyone, though he played no dance music, for he had played with the Boston Symphony. At the bottom of this heap were several former ASTPeewees, like myself, who struggled to keep up, and learned much from our betters.

Military musicians face unusual nuisances. I found this out while playing a headquarters company retreat ceremony shortly after entering the band. Since my third clarinet part called for a rest, I stood idly holding my instrument as most of the band thundered on. A shouting voice and an ominous presence materialized over my left shoulder, and I spun my head into the flushed face and glaring eyes of a major: "I said earn your pay boy—start blowin' that thing!" My mind was numbed by the powerful gold oak leaves on his shoulder, but I jabbed the mouthpiece between my teeth and faked furiously. Hal Wilson, a drummer, smiled and winked at me as the major crept up behind the front line trombones, then burst out in front of them Groucho Marx style, moving his right arm back and forth like a trombonist and bellowing at the same time. They knew from past experience that he was ordering them to "get those slides moving in unison," so with earlier planned precision each trombonist started playing the same part, and the slides moved in unison, like lines of infantry on a drillfield. The major beamed at this uniformity, deaf to the dissonance his order had caused.

"Well, old 'Shank's' at it again," a trombonist muttered as we walked back to our barracks from the flagpole ceremony. "He got Junior this time, and the trombones as usual."

"Is his name 'Shank'?" I asked.

"Naw, that's short for chancroid. Everybody in Headquarters Company calls him 'Major Chancroid' behind his back 'cause he's so damned hard to get rid of. Also 'cause he's a big prick."

Shank was a gung ho officer who always had to inspect something, convinced he was capable of inspecting anything, even music. There were other types as bad or worse. Nearly every dance had its songbird, an officer afflicted with imagined talent who cajoled or threatened the leader into letting him "sing one." (Enlisted men took a more direct approach by grabbing the mike.) Few, however, matched a pompous bird colonel who called Jerry Klausner aside during a dance at the lovely Main Post Officers' Club: "Corporal, your band sounds entirely too much like Glenn Miller. Miller's air force, you know, and no good infantry band should imitate that bunch." He never realized what a compliment he was paying us!

Musicians have a great tolerance for eccentrics—so long as they are fellow musicians. Our guitar man shaved his head bald every week or so to control "runaway dandruff." A reed man continually penciled his tiny, black mustache, spoke lovingly of his girl friends' "tickets"—"He means boobies, Junior"—and had civilian tailors cut his form-fitting shirts and flared pants. Of course Shank had spotted this violation of clothing regulations, and had chewed out Our Fearless Leader for allowing it, but the violator was one of those self-contained types blithely immune to "logical" military arguments. The time and red tape it would cost to discipline him was more than he was worth, so an uneasy truce eventually established itself between our reed man and Major Chancroid. This truce did not extend to the band itself, for after we set a record score on the rifle range, we heard that Shank had complained that "that damned bunch of queers outshot my best platoon."

Few opportunities were ignored by the 184th's musicians to break the boring routines of barracks life. A WAC detachment lived up the road from the band. These girls, uniformed in ugly, mustard-colored dresses, were enlisted under a regulation calling for the acceptance of the more unattractive applicants—this rule presumably seen as an ounce of prevention. They were a suspicious and hard-bitten bunch, and with good reason, for they were seen as "easy prey" by many soldiers. Some were, but of course most were not. Almost every evening WACs and their dates wandered into an old, typically over-grown cemetery some 200 feet north of the band barracks. Out of respect for the Confederate dead, this graveyard was off limits. The bandsmen strung a two-way public address system out to the cemetery late one afternoon, then eagerly awaited the first returns as evening fell. A couple talked directly into a hidden mike, their conversation somewhat like this:

"You're no good to want that; I won't do it."
"Aw, come on baby, you can't say it won't be for love."
"Just because I'm a WAC you think I'm a pushover."
"Why must you bring that up?"
"You know, I'm scared of you. . . ."

The two voices jumbled together as a bandsman blew a police whistle over the PA system while another sounded "charge" on a bugle. Couples stumbled over each other in the dim light as they ran, some laughing, some cursing, to get out of the rusty iron gate. The racket of course aroused the K-9 Corps, and their mournful howls were imitated by soldier storytellers for weeks afterwards as they related what was soon known in the area as the "Ghoulfriend Tale."

I walked into the darkened barracks one afternoon and was puzzled to see big John Willer standing in his shorts in the center of the floor. A spotlight was on him, also illuminating a sergeant seated on a podium in front of him. The noncom was dressed to look like a judge. A Kangaroo Court was in session! Big John, one of the best liked bandsmen, was on trial for the "high thievery" of snitching coal from the barracks furnace shed and taking it into town to keep his family's home fires burning. Several musicians were in the jury box while two others served as defense lawyer and prosecuting attorney. I joined the gang sitting along the sidelines.

The prosecutor's voice shook in officious outrage: "This soldier willingly, and with malice aforethought, violated the highest standards of the Army of the United States by stealing coal continually from federal supplies ensconced in the furnace shed of Barracks No. 4025, just to the south of Post Office Building No. 5026, at Fort Benning, state of Georgia. According to Article of War 69, he is subject to extreme discipline."

"Yeah, yeah, yeah, yeah, yeah, yeah," the judge droned, nodding his head in complete agreement.

"Yeah, yeah, yeah, yeah, yeah, yeah," the jury sang, in three-part harmony with appropriate key changes.

The defense lawyer then stepped into the spotlight, flatly admitting that "the defendant is the type of soldier that would steal the shit from a blind tumblebug and show him the wrong way home. I can't defend anybody who looks as guilty as that big sonza-bitch!" he shouted, and promptly resigned from the case.

"Guilty! Just as guilty as hell!" screamed the judge, smashing his gavel down on the table.

I joined the audience in shouting for the death penalty: "Hang the big fart! Hang the big fart!"

When the clamor died down, the judge passed sentence: "I sentence this thieving criminal to have his crotch painted with mercurochrome."

Two bandsmen with MP bands on their arms carried out the orders. The judge then ordered Big John home to his wife.

Not long after this, Julian Goodstein inspected the barracks, walking slowly down the rows of neat bunks and footlockers. When he entered the bathroom, all six commode seats suddenly rose in unison, springing to "attention" at the pull of a master cord tied to each. Our Fearless Leader pretended shock at such crude humor and unmilitary conduct. This hoary old army trick was never pulled on officers the men did not respect and trust, as Julian knew.

Sometime that winter a small mongrel dog made mascots of the bandsmen. We named him Follow Me, both for his habits and as a jibe at the post motto. He was as much fox terrier as anything else, and he was not housebroken. Before leaving for a dance job, someone watered him, then packed him inside an empty snare drum case. We set up our stands at a service club, the trapped dog's case being deposited in front of the bandstand. A waiter soon tried to move the case away from the dancers, but succeeded only in arousing the mongrel. The case instantly came to life in his hands, emitting barks, snarls, and water. He flung it to the floor in fright, but the round case rolled out among the dancers, snarling and barking all the way. Most of us in the band were as surprised as the soldiers and their dates, who gathered around as the case was opened. Follow Me hulked inside, growling at the hilarious crowd, but his attitude improved as the dancers petted him, fed him, and used him as a conversation piece for the rest of the night.

The best thing about these dances was the women. The Columbus Military Maids and other teen-aged groups volunteered to serve as partners for soldiers. They and their dates continually drifted up to the bandstand, requesting songs or simply watching in admiration. Here was an opportunity to make a late date, for bandsmen had a much later bed check than most soldiers. The front line saxes were in a perfect position for flirting, a meeting of eyes that occasionally struck sparks:

"You sure did play nicely on "Moonlight Mood"; I just love saxophones anyway!"

"Gee, thanks a lot—I love playing for *you*. What would you most like to have next?"

"'The Nearness of You' would suit me fine."

"We've already played that, darn it, but wouldn't 'Taking a Chance on Love' suit you just as well?"

It was easy to read the response in her eyes no matter the replies to such parrying. The soldier dates were either unsuspicious or watching women they would rather have been with. When time came for the intermission, the soldiers always rushed to the latrine to get rid of the beer, and the musicians rushed to the girls to make late dates.

Next to late dates, I most enjoyed broadcasting. Radio shows with a G.I. twist filled the Georgia air in this pre-television era. Every evening a local station, WRBL, carried "Fort Benning on the Air," and often followed this with "Benning Bandwagon." We played for these, but every musician on the post hoped to play the "Army Hour," a War Department show beamed from various army camps each Sunday and broadcast nationwide over NBC. Fort Benning got more than its share of these shows, and the 184th was chosen several times to provide the music. I warned the homefolks by mail, and they tuned in, no less thrilled than I was. I wrote them afterwards: "The show came off fine. I hope you heard it. I played the tenor solo on Basie's "One O'Clock Jump." Mother wrote back: "The whole town was listening."

The band's most frequent airing over the radio came during dances. WRBL would pick us up for half an hour of music from a dance at the Main USO, the Ralston Hotel, or the Army-Navy YMCA. Klausner would get us ready, calling up enough music to see us through, warn us against four-letter words, then beam with the audience as the announcer took the mike: "From the Main USO we bring you Jerry Klausner and the ASTP Dance Band! Here they are now, kicking off with 'GI Jive'!" I played with great empathy for the unseen listeners, remembering the nights I had spent listening to dance bands. My imagination conjured up thousands of couples in parked cars happily smooching as our sax section smoothly unfurled "Song of India," or "Speak Low," or "Let's Get Lost."

By mid-February, 1944, I was due a promotion. Rank, like everything else in life, is relative. Dave Gilkey, a cousin, wrote: "So you are a PFC (private first class) now. You are really getting there. I'll be a PFC when I finish gunnery school here, but by that time you'll be a corporal!" I was proud of that lonesome stripe, for I had been through a lot to get it. I would have "status" with the basic trainees, and I also got a raise, making $42.47 per month after deductions. When this was added to my dance band earnings, I was making over $90 per month. I felt affluent, laughing to think that just a year or so ago I had been proud to make 28¢ per hour at the Carlisle Kroger store!

I had no sooner become a one-striper than I became the butt of many good-natured jokes concerning the Mason County, Kentucky, draft board. Someone had read my clipping from the Maysville

Independent noting that the entire county draft board had been dismissed as a result of a policy squabble. This was such a novel idea, and so appealing to all of us draftees, that humorous speculation came from all sides. "Mathias is not really in the army because of this," was the majority opinion. A barracks lawyer disagreed, going for a narrower interpretation: "His tenure is similar to a bride who has not been bedded—he can go for annulment instead of divorce." Another held that I "should sue for clarification of the laws involved, for by the time the legal hassles run their course the war will be over." There was even talk of calling another Kangaroo Court to decide this weighty issue. I tried to explain that I had been drafted from Nicholas County, but no one was interested in this simple truth. From this time on, whenever our combo faked any simple B flat blues, it was always announced as "Mason County Draft Board Blues."

The army was strictly segregated, but black servants abounded in the officers' clubs. They had a special affinity for musicians, and we for them, knowing that the jazz music we played had black birthrights. We played their requests, and they did us favors in the kitchen, inviting us back for snacks at intermission or after the dance. One night, not long after I had joined the band, we played the stunning Main Post Officers' Club. Officers and their ladies swirled over the glistening hardwood floors from every part of the Allied world, displaying bemedaled uniforms from Russia, China, France, Australia—even Scotsmen in kilts. I was enthralled. After the dance I followed the musicians back to the kitchen. Everybody was soon sitting around with the black cooks and joking about the night's work.

"Take a handful of these," one of the cooks said as he shoved a large silvered bowl across my table. I looked in amazement at the contents, shoving the bowl back at him.

"I ain't gonna eat no damned skinned crawdads," I said in disgust.

"Crawdads! Crawdads! Man, are you crazy!"

"I know crawdads when I see them—I've fished with enough of them, but I ain't gonna eat one."

"This poor fellow thinks shrimp are crawdads," the cook shouted, repeating himself as a laughing crowd gathered around us.

"These are shrimp, friend, shrimp, haven't you ever heard of shrimp?' Here, try one out," and he handed me one dipped in red sauce.

I gamely bit into it, as everyone watched in grinning suspense, and I quickly asked for more! Few of my Hoosier and Jewsier friends were very surprised at my mistake, most of us having grown up during the Great Depression. We were part of an era when live chickens were killed and plucked for Sunday dinners, frozen foods were unheard of, and thick cream rose to the top of milk pails or bottles. A few weeks later, at Columbus's Goo Goo Restaurant, I relished my first taste of "french fries."

The Goo Goo was a gathering spot for our musicians. It had a friendly and relaxed atmosphere, good food, an excellent juke box, and a location convenient to our needs before and after dance jobs in town. We talked music endlessly in this place, just as everywhere else. Klausner wrote some nice arrangements here in spite of spilled coffee, horseplay, and juke box interference. They were "head arrangements," written without the aid of a piano, and I marveled at this show of talent. Music was here, there, and everywhere, and I thought it would never end. "I am a permanent band member," I wrote home, revealing no understanding of how temporary anything connected with a wartime army really is.

Rumors that the ASTP program might be discontinued began circulating in early February, 1944. The rumors were soon verified by official statements that "the army has abolished ASTP except for some advanced courses." Our band suddenly had no future. The ASTP boys, whether in training at Benning or in college, were to be sent into infantry combat units. Victory seemed assured for the Allies, thus infantrymen for the looming invasion of Europe were needed more than a future supply of doctors and engineers. Most of the bandsmen were resigned to a similar fate.

I was soon receiving letters from friends who had gone to college after I had flunked out. From Oregon State University, Franklin Niblock observed sadly that "it looks like we are all headed back to the dear old infantry. I wrote home yesterday for my birth certificate and papers for the air corps, but it is really crowded now." A cousin in the air force observed that "with the closing of ASTP my brother Joe was taken from college and put in the infantry. He had been in college 9 months. He's a private now which shows you how much ASTP amounted to." Betty Sue Scott, a Lexington girl friend, bemoaned the exodus of the ASTP men from the University of Kentucky campus, and then asked the biggest question of all: "Will they send the ASTP guys into the infantry? I don't blame them for not wanting to go to the infantry." Neither did I, but that is where they did go. Most were sent to Europe where their units were over-run by the German Army during the Battle of the Bulge. Thousands of them were either killed or captured.

In early March the band learned, with great relief, that it was to be retained with only a slight change of duties. Several weeks later the Fort Benning *Bayonet* revealed the entire plan in its issue of March 23: "Fort Benning's ASTP Basic Training Center will be retained to give an intensive eight week's training course to pre-officer candidates. . . . About 6,000 pre-officer candidates are . . . to be selected from present R.O.T.C. students." The band would stay where it was, playing for the Officers Candidate Pool (OCP) instead of ASTP. Once again I had survived.

Meanwhile, the 184th band was kept busy playing on the station platform as the ASTP trainees left for combat units. I was well aware of the irony as I, a "flunkee," tooted them off to their unwanted destiny. "We've been busy playing off the ASTP boys formerly here," I wrote Mother on March 21. "We go to Achillee [train] station nearly every day now and play out 4 or 500 boys to Infantry camps. From there they will go overseas. T.S. for them. I would be at Camp Howze now in the 103rd if I hadn't gotten in the band!" I knew I would have gone to Camp Howze, for all of my flunked-out buddies went there, and had written back in envy.

While I smugly considered the fates of old ASTP friends, World War II was building to a shattering climax. The great D-Day invasion force was assembling in England, Russian armies were moving west-ward, and the Allied invasion of Italy was crunching forward. I paid little attention. From the Pacific that March came news of divisions and places I had never heard of, but which, in a few months, I would never forget. Had I bothered to read beyond the headlines, I would have learned that "the 37th division is engaging the Japanese in a savage battle at Hill 700, Bougainville," that the "1st Cavalry Division has landed troops on Manus Island in the Admiralities," or that "Fifth Air Force bombers have continued pounding Hollandia, New Guinea as MacArthur's troops prepare for further moves up that coast." I had been in the army seven months, and I was surviving nicely, with my world of music intact. There was no reason to read or worry about a war I had probably escaped. I did experience a twinge of guilt when a letter from home revealed that a classmate had been killed at Anzio, but by now I felt that my luck would hold out for the duration of the war.

Life was exceptionally easy for the band during April, 1944. Playing for the smaller Officers Candidate Pool did not take half the time required by our previous ASTP assignment. The axe fell in early May when army administrators decided that the 184th AGF band did not have enough to do to justify its presence at Fort Benning. Our warrant officer told us we had been assigned to Camp Wheeler, near Macon, Georgia. This post was an Infantry Replacement Training Center (IRTC), meaning that soldiers here were given Basic Review Training, or advanced training in a specialty, then sent as replacements to shattered line companies overseas. I had just completed my nineteenth year, on May 23, when our truck convoy unloaded the band at its new home in Camp Wheeler. I wrote home on May 29, my letter exuding the usual optimism, fun and games still uppermost in my mind: "I'm at Camp Wheeler now, just seven miles from Macon. It is a beautiful city. . . . There are four big lakes to swim in, and I was swimming at Lakeside Park yesterday. It has bowling alleys, canoes, dancing, restaurants, etc. and big diving towers floating out in the center of the lake. Wheeler had 125,000 men less than Benning so there are lots of girls here. I had a date 6 hours after I got here."

During our move and adjustment to Camp Wheeler two momentous events claimed our undivided attention, the first being Congressional appropriation of $6.5 billion for a "G.I. Bill of Rights." I wrote home uncertainly: "I can't figure out what I want to take after the war in that free college course we vets will get. . . . I'm not sure about journalism. I guess I'll have a whole new set of ideas after I get out probably two years from now."

D-Day was the second event. The June 6th invasion of Europe brought a letter describing the reaction in Carlisle and concern for my cousin, Bob Mathias: "We were all awakened by the ringing of bells and screech of the town siren about 3 o'clock this morning (June 6) warning us that the Invasion was in progress. . . . About 1500 assembled at the Christian Church. . . . I wonder if your cousin Bob Mathias was among the 30,000 paratroopers." A few weeks later Mother wrote that "the saddest news of the war came yesterday. Bob Mathias was killed in action in France, six days after the invasion. . . . I thought Bob was in danger when I heard the accounts of the Paratroopers being slaughtered." This very personal tragedy stunned me, giving way to sadness, and finally to rage. For the first time I took the war on a personal basis, writing in an earnest letter home that "I wish I could get overseas somewhere." My wish would be fulfilled before summer's end.

Camp Wheeler showed us what a working army band was all about. The privileges and frills so usual at Benning were stripped away. We faced six-day weeks, retreat parades every afternoon, renewed infantry training, and played dance jobs for free. "The band," I sighed in a letter home, "got up at 5:30 and played several battalions in off a 20 mile night march." There was something unpleasant every day. Rumors abounded as to why this might be. It was held that Wheeler's commanding general was trying to prove his efficiency in order to make amends for a deadly goof he had made earlier in the Aleutian Islands. "Seven days before the Japs were cleared out, he ordered a parade; 7 or 8 Jap machine guns suddenly opened up cutting the men to pieces. He hasn't liked bands since then." We all believed this canard wholeheartedly, for explanatory rumors in the army soon take on a life of their own, becoming ever more embellished and exact in detail.

Along with its other duties, the 184th played the usual number of radio shows out of Camp Wheeler. I picked up a discarded script written for one of these shows. Its attempted humor, full of puns and slams at the home post, are typical:

At the sound of the chimes it will be exactly 6:60 Ingersoll watch time—[*chimes*]. Good evening, this brings you your world reporter and interviewer from the far corners of the earth. And now to Africa—[*background of flute and clarinet playing snake-charming music*]. This is your interviewer in Egypt. Gad, but it's hot here. I don't see any pine trees so it can't be—Whee!—Hey, what have we here. Yes, a special treat, a captured German prisoner, taken at Gobblers Knob, out on the Ubangi Turnpike. When our men found him he was in bed sick with dirty shieks wrapped all around him. He hadn't shaved in days and had harem all over his face. He's fine now and wants to say a few words. What's your name, my good man?

Awoll von Pflellhauzen.

You sure that's your name?

Reich.

Did you have any little friends back at prison, Awoll?

Ach! Messers Schmidt (who vas der oldest at von oh nine), und Bare Berger, whose cuzzin Hamm vas killed sefferal veeks before by der ravenous boys from your stadt of Georgia who said it was the first food they had had since cotton vent up.

Ah, yes they'd probably trained at Camp Wheeler.

Gott Himmell No No No Noo Noo. I've got a brudder dere named P. W. (Prisoner of War) von Pfellhauzen.

Don't worry about him Awoll, at least they treat the *prisoners* all right at Wheeler! [*out with baritone sax playing Bee Oh—Bee Oh.*]

German prisoners were part of the local Wheeler scene: "We have hundreds of German P.W.'s here now. They are better looking than most of us in training here. They are very cocky and most believe that New York has been bombed to bits and Germany is winning. Before long, Normandy captives will start arriving and change their minds. These P.W.'s do what the C.C.C. did—dig ditches, reforest, and the like. They get the same pay they got in the German army."

The concert band played throughout the Macon area. A typical job was one some fifty miles away at Thomaston, Ga. The program was designed to get the farmers to grow more cotton. Thomaston had one of the largest factories for producing tire cord in the nation. We introduced the show with patriotic music and stirring marches, then the factory fed us fried chicken, and speakers extolled the virtues of growing cotton for defense.

My life of fun and games ended almost one year from the time I had entered the Army. Rumors of impending change came true with the arrival of a third AGF band. Army regulations called for only two bands on a post the size of Wheeler, but we now had three—the 167th, 184th, and the newly arrived 271st. Army "politicking" now took place beyond my reach as a young Pfc, but the results were easy to grasp. The 167th was dissolved, and its warrant officer took over the 184th, shoving Our Fearless Leader aside. The best fifty-six musicians—and we all knew who they were—were now absorbed into the two remaining bands. This left the deadwood out in the cold, meaning me and most of the old National Guard Hoosiers and Jewsiers. And "out in the cold" really meant shipment overseas as infantry replacements. The bad news stunned them at home: "The axe fell Thursday (August 3). I'm no longer in the band. Even our leader and first sergeant were cut. . . . The whole thing is full of political angles and conniving. The army is just a big political machine anyway."

One of the most valuable friends I have ever made was a young clerk working on replacement assignments at Camp Wheeler. He was enthralled with music and was happy to list me as his friend in the post band. One afternoon in early August I ran into him at the PX.

"Hey," he said, "you know you're shipping out next week."

"Aw, you're kidding; but I know it's got to be soon."

"No kidding, I handled your file today; in fact I corrected it in one spot. They had you down with an M.O.S. (Military Occupational Specialty) for Rifleman, but I knew you were a tenor sax man so I changed it to M.O.S. 439, which is, 'Musician: Saxophone'."

"So what."

"Well, who knows, maybe somebody will pick you up and put you back in a band—at least they'll know what you can do best."

"Fat chance, but thanks heaps anyway." We had a coke, then walked out of each other's lives, his good deed not remembered until much later.

A roaring farewell party was thrown for the men leaving the 184th. We were no longer Hoosiers, Jewsiers, kids, or characters, but men united in friendship and fearful of an uncertain future. Many toasts were drunk to Columbus and Fort Benning—"They Loved Us There"—a toast becoming the theme of the party. Bob Stein, a fellow saxophonist, read a poem ribbing the special weaknesses of each man in the band, shortcomings we all knew and laughed at as we recalled them. He concluded with a tribute to Julian Goodstein: "There was our fearless leader, W.O.J.G., J.G., He did his best both night and day to keep peace in the family!"

A grim future awaited some members of Julian's musical "family." One lost an eye to Nazi shrapnel several months later. Another drove a truck over a cliff in Italy, dying in the wreckage. A German shell extinguished the life of another. Several more were seriously wounded or, like myself, picked up life-threatening diseases. The fun and games were finally over, but all of us took happy memories with us. Young Stein's poem echoed this sentiment in its opening stanza:

If when I am old and grey and know my days are few,
I'll take time off to reminisce, as old folks often do,
One thing that I will dote on will be World War Number Two
And that time I spent while in the band . . . with you.

5. Halfway around the World

Thursday afternoon, August 18, 1944, Pfc. Walter Clark and I were handed our shipping orders and train tickets. We were to board a civilian train at the Macon station at midnight. Our desination was Fort Ord, California. Most of our friends had orders for East Coast replacement centers; we alone were headed for the South Pacific.

Clark and I excitedly packed our barracks bags, then stopped short—neither of us had any shirts or pants; all of our uniforms were in the Wheeler laundry! It was too late to get them out, and also too late to get new issues at the supply shed. We were going to travel four grimy days and five sweaty August nights in the cotton suntans we had on our backs.

A three-striper from the motor pool skidded his jeep to a halt in the gravel in front of our barracks, the little horn peeping like a ruptured alto sax. As we loaded, the usual taunts reserved for unlucky GIs headed for the Pacific jungles were shouted at us: "Have fun with the fuzzy wuzzies!" "We won't see *you* in gay Paree!" "Commit hara-kiri *now!*" "Tokyo Rose eats shit!" "Say hello to a 'yellow-belly'!" Clark and I laughed, giving them the finger, but inwardly we agreed with the taunts. The Pacific was still the great unknown, a fearful region infested with cannibals and stealthy Japs, sans women, sans wine, sans anything else worth having—just the opposite of familiar Europe. We sat gloomily with our thoughts until our driver turned down Cherry Street and stopped, as did the street itself, at the Macon Railway Terminal. We slung our bags over our shoulders and walked the first steps of a journey that would take us half way around the world.

Clark and I boarded the crowded train, found seats, and handed our tickets to a conductor as the coaches bucked at their couplings leaving the station. The conductor returned in a few minutes, shaking his head:

"I'm sorry boys, there just aren't any pullman berths available."

"But we have pullman tickets—don't they reserve the berths?"

"Nope. Can't do that; there's a war on, you know. First come, first served."

We did not realize until too late that the conductor had sized us up, naive pfcs that we were, and sold our berths to civilian travelers, once he had disposed of us. This forced us to sleep on floors or propped up anywhere we could stretch out during the trip.

We arrived in Kansas City Saturday afternoon, changing to the Santa Fe railroad for the trip to Los Angeles. I wrote home later that "we didn't get a streamliner, but a long train that was poky and stopped everywhere." Grime and cinders were embedded in the plush seats of our ancient coach, and light bulbs glimmered inside electrically wired ceiling lamps originally designed for kerosene. Stained glass topped the worn wooden windows. I quickly found that several modern air conditioned pullmans were spaced among the collection of antique coaches. No servicemen sat in these cars. I was enraged, thinking of the great theme continually sent out on placards and radio: "Nothing's too good for our boys in service!" I wrote from Fort Ord: "I went on dirty coaches all the way as big fat, society bridge playing hens took up all the pullmans from soldiers and sailors. Guess they had been to Miami or were going to sunny California."

Not long after leaving Kansas City I picked up a nice-looking girl seated a few aisles from me. She was going to a Kansas town an hour or so down the track. We chatted briefly, then walked to the door at the end of the coach. I swung the hinged top half of the door inward, and we stood there watching shadows engulf the Kansas plains as night fell. We were all alone here, yet aboard a crowded train rushing into the night. I kissed her and she responded eagerly, knowing she wanted to be kissed and also knowing she had nothing to fear or lose. She was just fifteen minutes from her destination, and she would never see me again. It was a "wartime romance," one she would never have allowed a few years earlier. We kissed and petted until the train stopped at her town, then lied as we swore we would meet again in the future. She got off, threw a kiss back at me, and walked into the darkness.

Walter Clark was a good companion to travel with, wait with, or be with. He was a slender six-foot Hoosier from Evansville, handsome and soft spoken, with a gentle sense of humor he would need to see him through combat coming his way on Luzon. I knew he often watched my antics, overblown curiosity, and adolescent traits with patient amusement. He was in his late twenties, but neither of us let this edge into our fast-growing friendship. All we had left of Fort Benning and the 184th was each other.

The train rolled through miles of vineyards and orange groves as we neared Los Angeles. It stopped for some reason in a vineyard, and we got off to pick bunches of the largest grapes I had ever seen. We compared the scenery to what we had seen for years in the movies, and were impressed. "It would be a nice place to live," I thought, not realizing that similar GI thoughts would fill California with people after the war.

Clark and I did not realize how filthy we were until we went to a washroom in Los Angeles' new, Spanish-style station. We wiped white streaks across our grimy gray faces, then stood laughing at each other and into the mirrors above the washstands. We were tattered and worn as we boarded a Southern Pacific train for the 300-mile night ride to Salinas and Fort Ord. Early Thursday morning, August 24, we got off at Salinas and boarded an army bus for Fort Ord. We gaped from the windows at thousands of acres of head lettuce. Suddenly both of us sucked in our breath, staring in silent amazement. The bus had just topped a hill, and spread before us, stretching a straight blue line from northern to southern horizons, lay the Pacific Ocean. We had never seen anything larger than the Ohio River.

Fort Ord was a beautifully situated army post, with its feet in the sea and its body resting on a gentle inland slope. We were puzzled when the supply sergeant issued us woolen uniforms, then delighted when told of the cool weather along this coast. We were assigned to Company B, 2nd Regiment, and reveled sleepily at the sight of our bunks, but first we headed into a shower room full of laughing soldiers. A naked GI stood there with a shaved crotch painted with blue ointment—the classic treatment for "crabs." He had just come from the medics: "I caught the sonza-bitches on that dirty train out here from Camp Howze," he pleaded. Finally he made it out to his bunk and Clark and I got our first bath since leaving Georgia.

Fort Ord filled two assignments for the army, the first as headquarters for special troops, and the second as Army Ground Forces Replacement Depot #2, or, as we soon learned to call it, the "2nd Repple Depple." From here replacements were sent to other "repple depples" in the battle zones, and from these into front line divisions. I did not think of myself, and the troops here, as cannon fodder, but that is exactly what we were. I was overseas before I realized my true position, and the insight changed many of my views of the world. Indeed, my views were already changing in some ways. As long as I was in the band in Georgia, I paid little attention to the real war out in the Pacific. But now I was dropped into it like a frog into a pond. On August 28, I wrote home from Ord that it looked like Hitler may soon be licked,

> but that doesn't mean the war's over. All the soldiers out here are worried that we will be forgotten. . . . The Japs said many times they are willing to sacrifice 5,000,000 men in defense of their island. We haven't even set foot on the Phillapines [sic] yet, and people go about hollowing [sic] that the war is as good as over. I never thought of these things untill I was faced with the fact that I was going to the South Pacific probably.

A few days later another letter reveals that I had finally started thinking about the problem of war itself: "Every kid that is 18 should serve one year in the army. After going through a year of army life there would be no more wars. People would have enough idea of war to want to keep out. The whole thing adds up to months and years of your one and only life being wasted doing the same job as a ditch digger. . . . Oh well, it's got to be done and it was just my luck to be in this generation."

I drew KP at Ord on August 25 and 26. In mid-morning we lowly KPs were startled to see the commanding general of the Army

Ground Forces stride into our mess hall accompanied by other big brass. It was Ben "Yoo Hoo" Lear, who had been the butt of national criticism and cartoons for making some soldiers hike a hundred or so miles for shouting "yoo hoo" at some girls on a golf course. He was determined to inspect a mess hall during his day-long inspection of the post, and soon was peering into garbage pails and chasing roaches out of cracks and crevices. He found us lacking, and we were denied passes off the post that weekend.

Yoo Hoo had hardly moved on to greater things before I drew a detail to load bread at the bakery. I wrote home about this: "While working at the bakery, 3 German prisoners of war came in. They had only been at Ord a few days and they came down today on the P.W. truck to get their bread ration. Boy, when they saw those long lines of sweet rolls, pies, cakes, doughnuts, and loaves they really got excited. They couldn't believe it. Just like kids in a candy shop."

The Germans in the bakery may have pondered the promises of Hitler's Reich, but there was one Nazi at Ord who was still true to the fuhrer. I was walking near the sand dunes one day when several soldiers shouted to "come over and look at this." At the bottom of a twenty-foot-deep sand pit stood a young Nazi officer. He was digging a pit of specified size for punishment. He was mean. He spit up at us in contempt. Every time he spit, we pushed several bushels of sand down on him. Finally, he stopped spitting and stood muttering to himself. Even a Nazi could learn if he had the right teachers!

I had seen plenty of Nazis at Wheeler and Ord, but I had never seen a Jap. Then I saw my first ones: "A shipment of Jap boys came in to go over and fight their relatives. They were in the clinic this morning. They don't look like 'monkeys.' Some were over six feet tall."

Several musicians were among the replacements, so we borrowed instruments from special services and landed a combo job at the Hollister Naval Air Base Officers Club. We played well, and talked with many of the officers. "A lot of the officers there," I proudly wrote, "had flown in the Battle of Midway."

My mail from home finally caught up with me, and I found that Mother was taking no chances. She had been unable to find a St. Christopher medal for travelers, so she advised me to "attach the enclosed Miraculous Medal to your clothes somewhere for your voyage. You must go to confession and communion before you take that ocean voyage. I am enclosing a prayer which is a plenary indulgence." I did as she advised, feeling I needed all the help I could get.

Not long before shipping out, I devised a code for the homefolks while sitting before a wall map of the Pacific Ocean in the beautiful seaside Soldiers Club. They would know which island I was on if they checked the dates heading my letters. Thirty islands were listed and given numbers, one for each day of the month. "Notice the *rd, nd, st,* or *th* after the numeral," I advised, "such as October 3*rd,* 2*nd,* 21*st,* 10*th.* Anytime the date carries one of these I am telling you where I am. A date without these letters is just a date." Since I was not sent to any islands not on the list, the code worked.

The men in my 2nd Regiment were left ominously idle the morning of Wednesday, September 20. Our mounting tension was given direction about noon when a noncom shouted through the barracks door: "Prepare for immediate shipment!" The confusion of packing did not end until we were aboard a troop train to the San Francisco docks. It was night as long lines of soldiers filed up garishly lighted passageways to loading ports in the high, gray, slablike sides of a large ship. I followed along, finally stopping in a huge, humid room where bunks were stacked in tiers five deep. I was lucky to find a bottom bunk. It would be my home for the next twenty-four days.

Everyone said we were aboard "some old tub." They were wrong; we had boarded the S.S. *Monterey,* a 30,000-ton flagship of the Matson Lines. It was a "South Seas" luxury liner, now converted to use as a troopship; there were five thousand aboard, including a thousand WACs destined for duty in Australia. The presence of these women, though isolated on a guarded deck, was to spice the trip considerably. In any event, I went to sleep awakening at dawn to find seasick soldiers everywhere. The decks were slippery with their vomit, but I was sympathetic for I had read of the horrors of seasickness. Heading topside to see the sea, I saw instead the towers of Nob Hill and San Francisco! The ship had not moved all night. "So this is what psychology is all about," I thought, reasoning that if the mind could create "seasickness," it could also prevent it. After we sailed I beat it back by directing my whole attention elsewhere—

watching seagulls, flying fish, seals, counting whitecaps, anything to outlast the initial sick feeling.

Seasickness never got me, but I lost out to two other perils—an overpowering desire for sweets and constipation as tight as a pine knot. The craving for sweets may have come from leaving the home-land—everything good. I fed it by loading my canteen with sugar, then pouring it full of the watery hot chocolate always served at our two daily meals. I sipped it for hours afterwards. Constipation, however, was tightened by more than mere tension. Shipboard latrines (we soon called them "heads") were always wet and always occupied, the users raising their feet like a chorus line as the rolling ship sent miniature tides of water caroming around the row of johns. The deck latrines were worse, being long metal sheds with one end landing over the side. Ten occupants sat on holes above a trough continually flushed seaward by a heavy hose. Jokers dropped burning paper upstream, shouted "Ten-SHUT!" then laughed as the singed users leaped to attention. It was one of the unpleasant reali-ties of troopship life.

By the time we sailed past Hawaii—it was "Blue Hawaii" in the distant sunset—I had decided to sleep topside. Ventilation pipes had been cut full of holes by soldiers on decks above us, turning our hold into a steam bath. My favorite spot was in the angle between a bulk-head and the rail's end. The ship was "blacked out" against sub-marine attack, so clouds of stars filled the clear skies, new Southern constellations coming into view as northern ones disappeared. I studied a Red Cross star chart by day, using the information each night. This, and watching the eerie bright phosphorescent wake of our ship, lulled me to sleep on my windswept blanket. I was at peace until dawn brought sailors with brooms and hoses in answer to a roaring command over the public address system: "Sweepers man your brooms—clean sweepdown fore and aft!"

Clark and I had made several new friends at Ord, and they were sailing with us. One of these, Jack Ehlinger, would be with me for the rest of the war. Another was a New England boy of French Canadian background named Marcel. We could pronounce his last name—"Vell-you"—but we never learned to spell it. In any event, Marcel, Walter, Jack, and I bunked together, sharing shipboard events as they came, whether it was the continual topside crap game, the savagely contested Monopoly games, movies, or an unexpectedly interesting series of lectures given by a missionary. Dean Bodger was returning to his Anglican mission post at Milne Bay, New Guinea. By this time we had been told our destination, so he lectured on what to expect from life in New Guinea. He was soon known as "Bean Dodger" by the GIs, but we listened eagerly to his advice concerning the jungle, the natives, the climate, and the terrain. A twilight movie always followed, preceded by a request over the PA system: "Woodrow Wilson, please come to the projection booth." We relished the irony inherent in the projectionist's name.

Every man aboard ship was aware that a thousand women were sailing with us, and that they were shepherded by WAC officers and military police on an inner deck of the ship. Delightful rumors held that sailors were lowering themselves by ropes into friendly portholes, a risky game, if true, for the unescorted ship was under orders to stop for nothing, even a man overboard. When a call went out for musicians to form a ship's orchestra, rumors of dances soon became fact. I auditioned and won a spot in the sax section.

Afternoon dances were held on a long enclosed promenade deck, its one open side overlooking the sea. Many soldiers and WACs had great fun, jitterbugging wildly to the jump tunes and hugging each other very tightly during the ballads; most, however, either ignored the dances entirely, or stood glumly to the side, lost in their thoughts. Although we enjoyed playing again, the musicians and I commented on a certain aura of unreality that pervaded the scene, almost as if we were watching shadows dancing to the echoes of joy departed. There was too much forced gaiety instead of the uninhibited good times typical of such affairs. Few could forget that the ship was carrying its worried passengers—and the dance floor—closer to an uncertain future with every beat of the drum and whisper of the cymbals. I sat there blowing my saxophone, wondering what it must have been like to have played for the swanky tourists on this great Matson Liner during its expensive cruises into the South Seas before the war.

The Equator was crossed on September 28, 1944, at zero latitude and 160°W longitude. An initiation ceremony followed: "Some fellows had half of their hair cut off and were painted a rainbow of colors with molasses and eggs poured on for good measure. King

Neptune wore a mop cloth for hair. All of us pollywogs got diplomas making us Trusty Shellbacks."

We were now in the south seas explored by Cook, Tasman and Bligh, and storied by Melville, Stevenson, and many others. Strings of islets began appearing to port or starboard, often with only a few graceful coconut palms taking life from land so low that any heavy sea would set it aflood. Lovely atolls slipped by, their coral barrier reefs misty with spray as the ocean thundered against them. We hung on the rail, watching for hours as island mountains rose and fell beyond the horizon, great jagged peaks turned blue by distance and mysterious in isolation.

One evening at twilight I was hanging on the rail, reading some of the thousands of initials and home town names carved into its broad back. A soldier sidled up and started a conversation. He asked where I was from.

"A little Kentucky town nobody's ever heard of," I replied.

"Which town is that?" he asked.

"Carlisle," I said.

"How's old 'Prissy Pants;' is she still taking them on at two bucks a throw?"

"My God," I stammered, "how did you ever hear of her; you know she's one of the biggest whores in town!"

He smiled a knowing smile. "I spent two years at the C.C.C. camp on the west end of town. Remember that place?" By this time we were laughing and slapping each other on the back as we recalled places and names we had in common. The odds against such meetings must be astronomical, but they happened to me so often from this time on that I finally concluded that it was a mystery beyond my solving.

By early October we were threading our way into the Coral Sea. This vast arm of the Pacific is enclosed by land or islands on all but its south side. It is to the Pacific as the Caribbean is to the Atlantic. We watched in the bright morning light as a long, lofty, green island drew nearer. We marveled at the beauty and serenity of its mountain slopes while the *Monterey* cruised a parallel course three miles off shore. After over two weeks at sea, we yearned for solid land, and this island looked inviting. An announcement over the ship's PA system brought disbelief: "Off to our starboard is the island of

Guadalcanal." All of us were victims of our grim expectations, forgetting that its war was over and it had therefore gone back to the business of being an island—and a pretty one at that. I chuckled to myself as I recalled seeing this island's strange name in Maysville newspaper headlines, dismissing it as a "canal" somewhere in Holland, or who cared where. I cared now, for my voyage was nearing its end. Our cocoon, the ship, could not be far from releasing its five thousand GI butterflies to fend for themselves. As I watched Guadalcanal sink into the watery distance, unpleasant thoughts tightened my throat.

Two days and 850 miles later, New Guinea was announced off our port side. We were sailing through Vitiaz Strait, its sixty-mile width separating New Guinea's steep Huon Peninsula from New Britain island to the north. Although Dean Bodger had given us some idea of New Guinea, no soldier was ever prepared for the reality. It is immense, the second largest island in the world. Maps shape it as a pregnant lizard swimming the warm seas between the Equator and Australia's northern coast. Its gaping mouth snaps into the islands of Indonesia, while its stumpy tail, some 1500 miles eastward, crumbles into a myriad of reefs and islands in the Coral Sea. Jumbled mountains range its entire length. Five snow-capped peaks rise above 15,000 feet on this one island. All of Europe has only two, Africa four, and the contiguous United States, none! Mount Carstensz Toppen is the highest, at 16,500 feet. Much of it lay unexplored, for the world's densest jungles cover much of its 312,000 square miles, an area nearly eight times the size of Kentucky. The Dutch had governed the island's western half since 1828, while Australia administered its two eastern sections, one of which had been wrested from Germany in World War I. The other, Papua—"the lizard's tail"—was my destination and the locale of terrible campaigns during the first two years of the Pacific war. Perhaps two million people— no one knew for sure—lived in this inhospitable, disease-ridden land. They were Melanesians, with black skins and extremely fuzzy hair.

The *Monterey* moved northwesterly along the coast, presenting us with an awe-inspiring view. The sinuous arms of great dark mountains plunged from the clouds down into the sea, grasping the white surf in fingers blackened by the lava sands that form the island's beaches. Huge vines laced this green and umber edge of the island world together. We watched our new home in silence as the swift tropic night enveloped us.

The next day our ship docked at Hollandia, a small port in Netherlands, New Guinea, taken from the Japs five months earlier. The *Monterey* had a valuable cargo to unload here, but the troops stayed aboard ship. Hollandia was of keen interest to us for reasons other than its beautiful backdrop of mountains, its cluster of quonset huts, or the evidence of a recent building boom. We could not see the object of our interest, but we knew that this was where General MacArthur lived in a very controversial home. My following letter home should prove that MacArthur never had a chance at popularity with this kind of low-level publicity undercutting him, most of it untrue:

> The picture I'm sending you is of Hollandia. The Monterey was anchored down at the bottom of that road you see. Off to the left (out of sight) overlooking the sea, MacArthur had a $50,000 home built for he [sic] and his wife and brat. He lived there six days. You have some idea of where the tax-payers money goes. The house had all the modern fixtures and appeared as one you'd see in San Francisco. [Adm. Chester] Nimitz or [Adm. William] Halsey, or [Gen. Walter] Krueger or anybody else never took their wife with them but old Mac did.

I was repeating what I had been told. Most of the furor over this house was belied by the facts. The general's subordinates had ordered it built in his absence, leaving him with the accomplished fact. Neither Mrs. MacArthur nor young Arthur ever stayed in Hollandia, and the general spent only four nights in a house made famous mostly by the imaginative pens of war correspondents. I had yet to realize that this thing against MacArthur flourished like jungle mold on leather boots—invisible until first noticed. I never knew anything about MacArthur until I boarded the *Monterey,* then I became an "authority," along with five thousand others.

The presence of a thousand WACs on the *Monterey* rode the shorebound wind! The brightly lighted harbor area filled with everything that could float: aircraft wing tanks with outrigger attachments, innertubes with wooden platforms, simple rafts, rowboats, native log boats, crates tarred to keep the water out long enough to pick up a "broad," and one fellow even had cloth painted to a wooden frame that seemed to work fairly well. All the while the ship's sailors were shinnying down ropes into open portholes, and, I assumed, into the arms of a waiting WAC. Other WACs were lowering bottles on strings to the waiting throng below, notes of assignation were inserted, and the bottles pulled up and into the porthole. Schemes were under way to get off the ship and into the hungry arms of swabby or dogface.

While this fleet of lovers was milling around, I was detailed to guard duty, given a Thompson sub-machine gun, and led down to the waterline. The ship's elevator reached bottom here, opening on a passageway that crossed the ship. A door-sized port was on each side, about six feet above the waterline; another soldier guarded the port facing the sea. The officer that stationed us told us that in about an hour, some $40,000,000 in Philippine invasion currency would be unloaded. We were not to let anyone—repeat, anyone—in through our ports, no matter the reason. We understood, and settled down to watch the festivities outside as the lovers congregated.

The mess hall was only a step or two from my station, and baskets of apples were in there. I took ten or eleven, lining them up on a bulkhead support next to my port. I munched and watched the gleaming eyes of the contestants below, each hoping to be a WAC winner. The sailors were still descending the rigging, "like their daddies used to do," and popping into the portholes. I knew that the perpetuation of the human race was in no danger.

A pall now descended upon the happy scene. A large power launch loaded with naval brass cruised into the picture like a swan into a pack of water striders. The launch paused to pass notes back and forth from a porthole up the ship, and the uninhibited sailors and soldiers of a few minutes ago now retreated to the sidelines. As the launch slowly moved toward my port, I heard the elevator running for the first time that night. It stopped and two WACs ran out, immediately pleading with me: "You're going to let us out aren't you honey?" They had their hands in my hair, and I could feel breasts against my arm, as they planned I should.

"I can't let anyone off the ship—you know that." But I was weakening.

"Come on, baby, can't hurt a thing—maybe we'll come back and get you—you're real cute."

I looked out the port, thinking I would see a GI or a sailor waiting for them—maybe I might wander back into the mess hall and let nature take its course. But when I looked out the launch had arrived, with seven or eight naval officers in full dress. A big rusty-headed one said in imperious tones, "Let them out soldier, right now, that's an order, do you hear."

That did it. I knew I would never let these gals out to those brassy bastards, and that was all there was to it. I also remembered my orders; if they tried to get in I would hold them at gun point.

The launch nudged my port. Suddenly, the rusty-headed loudmouth leaped toward the port. He should have looked before he leaped, for he rammed his face into the muzzle of my machine gun, just in time to hear the hollow clicking sound as I cocked it. He quickly threw himself in reverse, releasing his grip on the sides of the port, and jumped from his squatting position back into the launch. As he landed, a flood of water splashed into the launch from topside. WAC officers had tipped over a large canvas tub of deckwater, drenching the dress uniforms. I picked up my apples and threw them at the officers, bouncing several off of heads and splitting mushy ones on backs as the launch moved away with threats and curses from the men in it. My fellow guard from across the ship joined in the fun. At this moment the elevator opened, and a fat and fortyish WAC officer and two military policemen stepped out. They headed for the two WACs beside me, chasing them into the mess hall. The fat officer followed them as they darted under the chest-high eating tables, leaving a white trail of knocked over sugar pitchers. Finally the officer caught the culprits and the MPs took them up on the elevator. The fat officer sat down for a breath and a smoke before heading back to the WAC quarters. She kept shaking her head back and forth, implying thoughts of "What's the use, what's the use." Finally, she looked up at the two youthful faces in front of her, saying: "Boys, you know it's pretty tough to have to deal with a bunch of whores, and that's what they are." We cleared our throats apologetically. "Yes m'am," we said.

6. The Lizard's Tail

The *Monterey* left Hollandia around October 12, cruising south-easterly for eight hundred miles down the coast to Papua. We unloaded two days later on a long wooden pier at Oro Bay. Spaniards had named the place for the gold in the mountains behind it. Plenty of gold was still there, waiting for war's end and the return of its Australian miners. When I went ashore, I was stepping on foreign soil for the first time.

Trucks took us inland several miles to the 5th Replacement Depot. The 5th Repple Depple made thousands of believers in the Army adage that "no matter where you've been, where you're going is worse!" Everything in the sprawling tent city was impersonal and unsettled, with bad food and a staff fed up with the continual stream of nervous and disgruntled men arriving from the states. A reeking clutch of pit privies was located within thirty feet of pumps providing the depot's drinking water. Military police guarded a beautiful beach for "officers and gentlemen," and the Red Cross girls and nurses they alone dated. Enlisted men swam on a beach featuring rip tides, rocks, and encroaching jungle. The mess halls seldom offered anything but canned asparagus and Australian C-rations. A snafu in logistics may have caused the overabundance of asparagus, and as a steady diet it became hard to choke down, but the first taste of the wooly, stringy mass of unsalted mutton in an Aussie C-ration can was enough to fasten lifelong memories on the taster! We called it "sheepy shagnasty." These cans had to be opened with trench knives, for the opening keys never worked. Perhaps all of this was planned, including the tough training, for the cannon fodder passing through here could hardly help but welcome a friendly well ordered life in the divisions awaiting them. In any event, for the next several weeks my mail came to Army Post Office (APO) 711, Training Group 4, 43rd Battalion.

The 5th Repple Depple was part of the site of one of the most desperate campaigns waged in any war. Our training problems crossed and followed paths bloodied earlier along the northern slopes of the Kokoda Trail, Wairopi bridge, and the deadly fortified triangle of Buna-Gona-Sanananda villages. Our training cadre's reply was the same to all complaints: "You can be damned glad you weren't here in 1942–43!" We were of course glad to have missed any battle, but our relief at having missed this one knew no bounds as our knowledge of the affair increased. It might be well to pause briefly and look at the Papuan Campaign, for it, along with the concurrent battle at Guadalcanal, ended the Jap drive on Australia. Again, it influenced MacArthur's strategy throughout the remaining war years, thereby affecting the lives of most GIs in the Pacific, including my own. Finally, although it equaled Guadalcanal in importance, it has unjustifiably been relegated to a footnote on history's pages.

No other campaign of World War II was fought in a place as bad as the Papuan tail of the New Guinea lizard. Mountain ridges of the Owen Stanley Range reared thirteen thousand feet above the miasmal coastal plains, heavily jungled slopes barely a thousand feet lower than the highest in the American Rockies. Over two hundred inches of rain deluged this cloud-covered area annually, fostering molds capable of destroying leather boots in ten days and promoting death-dealing diseases. The deadliest creature on this planet has been the tiny mosquito, and they whined here in their trillions, infecting Jap and Yank alike with malaria, blackwater fever, dengue, and elephantiasis. Scrub typhus and amoebic dystentery were endemic, further thinning the ranks of both armies. Of lesser danger, but perhaps more repulsive to the individual soldier, were the savagely biting scorpions and centipedes, lurking snakes, huge spiders and leeches, and in lowland estuaries, the giant salt-water crocodiles. On the bottom layer of this pyramid of pain was "jungle rot," a fuzzy brown fungus infection which cracked human flesh, sending men back to the beaches to recover.

Exaggeration? Hardly. America's 32nd Infantry Division entered this campaign on September 15, 1942, with three combat teams totaling 10,825 men. Six months later it had its "victory," but at a cost of 9,688 casualties, 7,125 of whom were sick. Many of these men were chronically ill; thus the division had to drop 2,334 officers and men from its roster, gone just as surely as if killed by enemy gunfire. The Australian 7th Division suffered equal losses, and the Japs fared even worse. The only blessing to be counted was a negative one—the lack of frigid temperatures found in such places as the much heralded "Russian Front," but Nazi cockiness and resultant oversight contributed as much to this debacle as the weather. One can escape the cold in proper clothing, but the climate and terrain of the lizard's tail were beyond escape.

Seven months after Pearl Harbor, General MacArthur realized that the place to defend Australia was in New Guinea. Both he and the enemy were surprised at the ease of Jap conquests. As Nippon smashed southward down the island chains north and east of Australia, their strategists began entertaining plans to isolate the island continent from American aid. Naval victories in the Coral Sea and at Midway blunted these plans, giving the Allies enough time to launch attacks at Guadalcanal and in New Guinea. Although the Nips occupied the northern coast of New Guinea, the southern coast, just north of Australia, had to be held at all costs. Allied reinforcements were landed at Port Moresby, the largest settlement on the island. They and their leaders felt secure behind the "impassable" terrain separating them from the Japs a hundred air miles away at Buna, on the north coast.

The Japs did not wait for further developments that August. Backed by the great base at Rabaul, New Britain, General Tomitaro Horii flung a small army into the Papuan mountains in high hopes of taking Port Moresby from the rear. The key to this operation was the seventy-four-mile Kokoda Trail, a muddy, cliff-hanging track seldom more than one man wide, drenched by incessant rains and plagued with insects throughout its twisting up and down course over the great Owen Stanley mountain spine. Although Australian

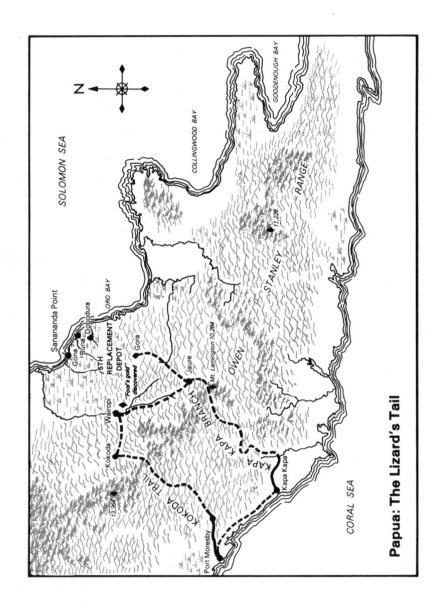

Papua: The Lizard's Tail

snipers and air attack slowed this army, it was New Guinea itself which stopped it. By mid-September, when the tattered Japs were able to see Port Moresby from the trail, it was too late. Supply problems and disease had ground the life out of the attack, forcing a desperate rear guard fight as the remnants retreated back over the trail to the north coast. Australian and American infantry were in hot pursuit--at first--but soon they too fell victims to New Guinea. Dysentery was so bad the men cut the rear from their trousers. Many dropped from malaria, while Jap bullets tumbled others into deep chasms along the trail. In one area, along the Kapa Kapa branch of the trail, the men walked over strangely heated land on Mount Lamington. Their timing was right, for a few years later the entire mountain exploded in volcanic fury, killing over three thousand natives in a sparsely settled region. Finally, the pursued and the pursuers reached the northern coastal plains. It seemed certain to the Allies that nothing remained but a mopping up operation against the bedraggled Japs. They were as wrong in this estimate as in the earlier one concerning the security of Port Moresby, for the worst was yet to come.

When the ragged Japanese mountain army straggled down to the coast at Buna, they were welcomed by reinforcements from Rabaul and incorporated into a new defensive position which can only be described as a masterpiece. Imagine a very shallow triangle, with the beach at its back and an eleven mile front involving swamps and thickets studded with block houses, connecting trenches and interlocking fields of fire. Some 6500 defenders awaited the tired, unsuspecting, and overconfident soldiers of the pursuing Aussie 7th and American 32nd divisions. Allied overconfidence was shot to pieces by January 23, 1943, when the position was finally taken. The two month battle had cost 6,419 dead and wounded, 594 more than the six month Guadalcanal battle which ended on February 9. The entire Papuan Campaign, which also lasted six months, cost the Allies 8,546 battle casualties, to some 12,000 for the enemy. The Papuan Campaign and Guadalcanal played equal roles in turning the Jap tide for the first time, yet Americans think only of Guadalcanal if they think of the Pacific war at all. Who has heard of the Kokoda Trail, or Buna?

General MacArthur learned some bitter lessons from the frightful casualties at Buna. This was the first time in World War II Allied forces had encountered and reduced an area fortified and defended in depth by the Japanese. Never again would he send troops against such positions without adequate planning, or without overpowering air, artillery, and armored support. Whenever possible, he by-passed such strongholds, leaving them to "wither on the vine." He learned his lesson well, for MacArthur's casualties for the remainder of the war were comparable to those incurred in Europe during the Battle of the Bulge!* Although I was to hear continual complaints concerning Dugout Doug's huge ego, I never heard one soldier complain that he wasted his men in the manner of some European commanders.

Not long after arriving in New Guinea I encountered two fearful snakes. While watching planes land at the Dobodura airstrip, my gaze turned to a truck cruising the edge of a nearby thicket. A leaping, curling shape reared up behind it, striking savagely at its body before sliding into an overgrown creek. It had almost vanished before I realized I had seen a giant snake. The truck had bumped over it, sending it into spasms of pain before it dragged its ten or twelve feet of muscled body into the cooling depths. "My God," I thought sickly, "all of us train out in these thickets with things like that!" I told our sergeant about it when I returned. Several friends sidled up to get his advice.

"Hell, boys, them kind ain't poisonous, no more'n a fishin' worm. What you've got to worry about here in Guinea is the devilish little 'snow snake.'"He paused as we gasped, adding: "Now there's a real *bad* one."

"Did you say 'snow snake?'" I asked. The name fascinated me for this place was melting in the heat. "What makes him so bad?"

"Why private," the sergeant replied, shaking his head in mock seriousness, "the New Guinea snow snake is so bad simply because he crawls up soldiers' assholes and freezes them to death!"

Our sergeant had more than snow snakes on his mind. He led us later on a squad problem through head-high Kunai grass and into the

*MacArthur's losses, according to one source, were 90,437 from Australia to V-J day, whereas the Battle of the Bulge cost 106,502 casualties. William Manchester, *American Caesar* (Boston, 1978), pp. 4, 713. Most sources set Bulge losses at around 81,000. Either way, MacArthur's economy of life is evident.

jungle. Once through the sunlit outer wall, a gloomy but open area of vast proportions stretched before us. Vine clad tree trunks disappeared into the green ceiling as much as 150 feet above us. Aerial roots of banyan trees and strangler figs had to be circled, but otherwise we moved easily behind the three-striper. He stopped in a sunny clearing, probably caused by earthquake. A stream from the high mountains, cold and clear, rippled behind him as he stood there, studying our puzzled expressions. "Men," he finally said, continuing with just the hint of a threat in his voice, "we can spend a nice, easy day here, or hike our problem ten miles toward Wairopi bridge and back. What's your pleasure?" We agreed in unison that it would be a shame to let such a beauty spot go to waste.

Not long after learning the art of New Guinea "goldbricking," Marcel and I returned for a swim downsteam from the sergeant's "Shangri-La." Gas masks were considered excess baggage by everyone, and we had cut and shaped ours into excellent water goggles. The crystalline stream ran cold and deep, permitting us to glide and bank under water—"just like birds," I wrote home. Then I saw the gold! Its yellow message flashed into my astounded brain and leaping emotions, sparking here and there as errant sunbeams flashed across it on the sands below me. Marcel hurried over, intent on rescuing me, for I was gasping and flailing like a drowning man as I dived for it. By this time I had a fistful. He whooped as he saw it, both of us thinking the same thing, that the rumors we had heard about Oro (gold) Bay were true. It was said that Australian and Jap soldiers had forgotten their war in order to work the abandoned gold mines in the mountains above us. Officers sent to drag them back had deserted for the same reason. We understood their motives as we worked, ever more silently, to fill a sock with our treasure. Exhausted, we finally hauled ourselves up on the knobby knees of great tree roots forming one side of the stream. We tried to fit our findings into our frustratingly powerless lives at the 5th Repple Depple:

"Suppose I'm shipped out and you aren't," I asked; "Then what?" Marcel suggested that we mark the spot and return after the "stupid war" was over. We pondered this with doubt as we surveyed the ever changing jungle around us. The answer to our problem dawned on both of us at once: "We can stake a claim, just like in the movies!" Our excitement subsided a bit when we realized this was

Australian territory. Did the Aussies have claim laws? Could foreigners do this? We had to have expert advice, but who could we trust? Suddenly I was overjoyed at being a Catholic:

"The priest, Marcel, the priest! I'll go see the chaplain under the seal of confession. If he tells anybody he'll be kicked out of the church."

We trotted eagerly through the jungle with our gold-filled sock, then hitched a ride back to the Repple Depple. I went into the chaplain's office, impatiently telling his dog-robber (orderly) that I wanted to go to confession. The chaplain appeared, smiling a chaplain-smile. He was perhaps puzzled at this midafternoon request, but gamely put his blue stole of authority around his neck. The dog-robber left, and I faced the priest:

"Chaplain, is what we are saying under the seal of confession?"

"Why yes, if that's what you want." He looked puzzled.

"Sir, my buddy and I struck gold this afternoon up near the mountains. Now what I want you to do is tell me . . ."

"Show me all that gold soldier," he interrupted, chuckling at the same time. I hated to hear him chuckle, thinking I had perhaps fallen into the grasp of a holy con man. Paranoia gripped me tighter, but I obeyed his order, pouring the gold out on the table beside us.

"Don't you know what this is?" He looked at me as he smoothed the glittering pieces over the table. "This is 'fool's gold' or pyrites. Hardly a week goes by here but a soldier brings this stuff in to some officer at the depot. The real stuff doesn't shine like this until it has been worked up. If you don't believe me, ask around."

Marcel was waiting as I left the chaplain's hut. He was still deeply under the influence, and it took some time to deflate his visions of wealth. Once back in the tent, we swore our buddies to secrecy, then showed them what we had in the sock. "Where is the creek?" they asked in hushed voices. We recognized the signs of gold fever, giving them explicit directions. Several friends from neighboring tents were included, and a stampede started for our creek. The next day, familiar reports of fool's gold greeted Marcel and me. We pretended dismay at the news, but at least this had verified the chaplain's report. We had not trusted him completely, seal of confession or no seal of confession!

The spirit of capitalism did not apply only to Yankee soldiers. We purchased bananas regularly from the natives, surprised at the varieties of this fruit, especially the squat little three-inch kind with crunchy seeds like charcoal inside. Regular calls on our tent row were made by fat "Bruno," a very ugly grass-skirted saleslady with raised welt "beautymarks" stippling her topless upper body. These pencil-sized welts were the results of knife cuts carefully packed with dirt to infect them. She had pointed, filed teeth, blackened by chewing betel nut. This narcotic fruit of the Areca palm was chewed with a leaf and a dab of powdered sea shell, giving the chewer a light "high" while reddening the saliva which dripped from numbed lips. She was extremely good natured, smiling her bloody smile from under a mass of frizzly hair bleached by lime to a reddish-amber color. Everyone liked her, giving her a monopoly on our banana purchases. Shouts and laughter always greeted her as she waddled her way down the tent row, mixing business with pleasure. We found how easily she mixed the two one day when someone promised to give her a shilling if she would take her grass skirt off. We stared in fascination as she did so, collecting her shilling. She returned to our tent later, standing around and joking until someone again offered her a shilling for her skirt. She coyly untied it, then pulled it away with a business like smile creasing her face—she had worn another one underneath it!

"Me want shilling belongim me other," she demanded in New Guinea's weird pidgin English (which I can only approximate, but which means "give me a shilling and I'll take this one off, too."). We gamely responded to her challenge, but then found she had caught us in a "triple-play." We got her third skirt for another shilling, a total investment of 48¢. She stood laughing and naked on the pile of grass in our steaming tent, a bit puzzled, perhaps, at these laughing men from some strange but wealthy land beyond the horizon.

Infantrymen live closer to the people than men in any other branch of the service. I was soon acquainted with several black skinned natives, correctly called Melanesians, but whom soldiers called "Fuzzy Wuzzies" for their stacks of frizzly hair. Their pidgin English language puzzled me as to its origins, but I learned a few phrases, writing the homefolks that *"hubba-hubba* means 'hurry up,' *totu people* means Christian, *kissim water belong drink he come* means bring some drinking water, and *callim name belong you* means what's your name?" We often lay in our tents listening to village drums "talk" to one another through the jungle, or pound wildly during a festival. Festivals meant fun for everybody. The men fought mock battles, with their black bodies striped with paint and their heads stunningly arrayed with feathers plucked from the island's gorgeous birds. "Just like 'Trader Horn,'" I wrote home, knowing they would recall this movie of the 1930s set in "darkest Africa." No movie, however, could portray the reality lurking behind the fun, for tiny children watched, their bellies bloated with malaria, men sat on the sidelines with limbs grotesquely enlarged by elephantiasis, and a thirty-year life expectancy hung over every one in the happy crowd. We also knew that their relatives back in the mountains still indulged in a bit of headhunting and cannibalism. This never disturbed us; somehow, in a world in which Europeans had produced the Nazis, and Asians the likes of the Rape of Nanking, the dietary habits of these congenial and thoroughly friendly Fuzzy Wuzzies seemed hardly worthy of mention!

Although the average white GI respected the Fuzzy Wuzzy, he did not have the same respect for the American black. Menial jobs awaited black soldiers in the segregated armed forces. Truckloads of white soldiers passing black work gangs along New Guinea's roads would sometimes shout "*hubba-hubba!*" as if confusing them with the natives. This always brought an explosion of curses, followed by picks and shovels thrown after the retreating truck.

Jungle drums serenaded us occasionally at night, but this was nothing compared to music that came with every dawn. The most glorious birds in the world are in New Guinea, and all of them end their vigil of silence at the beckoning of dawn. "You'll never hear anything more beautiful or startling than the singing and raucous noises the thousands of jungle birds make here at sunrise," I wrote. "They are wonderously feathered, and some have voices just like flutes. Others chatter, chirp, click, whistle, squeak and squawk until it makes a very mixed flood of sound." The serenade always stopped with full daylight, and the jungle in daytime was strangely silent, except for the whine of a mosquito or the sound of something skittering away into hiding. The only creatures in full view were the huge, fruit-eating bats, which hung by the thousands from tree limbs, wrapped in their five-foot wings, with foxlike faces staring blankly at the earth below.

Another denizen of South Pacific jungles bears mentioning. I refer to the AW AW bird, which some held was really a lizard. In any event this creature damaged more nervous systems than any other, saving its human-like shout of "AW AW" until a soldier was either creeping up on the enemy or stealing something from the mess tent.

The playwrights knew what they were doing when they substituted *Rain* for the title of Somerset Maugham's famous story of temptation in the tropics. Rain controls the tempo of tropic life, temptation included! Unlike Maugham's missionary, however, I tell here of a soldier unable to refuse "orders from above." It happened during a powerful rainstorm, one which broke a record New Guinea drought of fifteen days. Depot streets were dusty, and the soldier had orders to sprinkle them with his water truck for two hours each afternoon, laying the dust. While he was doing this the drought broke, unleashing trillions of tons of water in unbelievable torrents, assaulting our senses with its liquid fury. We watched with amazement as the soldier sprinkled the flooded streets throughout the storm and for an hour afterward, when his time was up. He had been ordered to do this, and orders were orders, no matter that the streets were under two feet of water. He was typical of a certain type in any army.

When the drought ended, the rains came in a predictable cycle: "About 4 every afternoon it rains, then stops at 5. It starts again at 7 and rains until the open air movie ends at 9:30." The rain was not the only uninvited guest at the movies, for an airstrip was nearby, and "C-47's continually come in or take off. In spite of the noise, I have seen 'Hairy Ape,' 'Gaslight,' and 'Make Your Own Bed,' most of it while peering out from under a dripping helmet liner through a steady patter of rain." The movie had an added attraction, however, on the night of October 20. A terse announcement came over the public address system; "The invasion of the Philippine Islands is under way. Troops landed on Leyte Island today!" We all jumped up and cheered, throwing helmet liners and everything else into the wind and rain. It was spontaneous, an outpouring of tension revealing the unexamined pressures we lived under.

I skipped the movie the next night, going for a walk. I needed time to think. A grim future faced me, and all escape routes were closed. "Maybe I could prepare," I thought, pulling out my trench knife. By this time I was standing in a sandy depression, with high

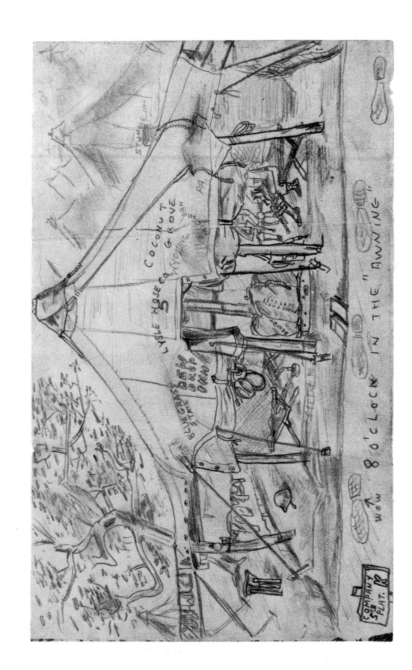

grass on the rims. I practiced swings of my knife in the dim starlight, as if a Jap were there. "This is silly," I muttered, and with that admission my brain began accepting its first insight into my true position. The whole world looked silly—Marcel, Jack, Walter, and I were sane in an insane world. We were here because we had no choice. I hated no Jap; I had never seen one until I went to Fort Ord. We were utterly trapped, with everything to live for and no place left to live it. Cannon fodder. Adolescent theories, fun and games optimism—all gave way to reality as I questioned the war and myself. I slumped to the sand, a sense of hopelessness and futility sweeping me for several endless moments. What could I do about it? Nothing! I would have to accept it, for seven thousand miles of open sea stood between me and home. I did not realize yet that I had taken a long step toward manhood.

I took my new insights to my tentmates, finding that they felt much the same. There was a job to do, we agreed, but no call to glory. Piss on the Armistice Day celebrations of yore and all of their fine speeches. As usual, I tried to spell out my new sentiments in a letter home:

> There will be quite a few of our brave senators and governors that will want to erect gigantic memorials with some hero (minus blood and mud) carved at the top of the $1,000,000 colossus. I saw such a one in Kansas City. We don't want that. It glorifies war and can . . . be compared to putting a gold door on the family privey. . . . It looks fine from the outside and there is no way of knowing what's on the inside unless you enter. It seems that every generation has to learn the hard way. . . . I admit readily that I haven't seen anything yet. . . . Maybe I'm all mixed up.

Questions of war, and of good and evil in the world, had mixed up better thinkers than me, or my buddies. Moreover, we still mixed adolescent actions into our adult questioning of the world. We saw no incongruity in critically discussing abstract issues while pissing on the ground-hugging mimosa vines. This caused an immediate folding of the leaves, revealing barren ground underneath. It was as if summer's foliage had given way to winter's at the command of a soldier's pecker. Acres of the vines grew nearby, giving us something to do while talking our way through larger issues. Youthful zest has never lived easily with the gray hair of philosophy and, in this case, none of us were far removed from pissing up barn doors and wooden fences for distance!

I needed to talk to someone from home after my days of self-examination, and I knew where one was. I had corresponded regularly with Clarence "Junior" Owings, a classmate who had gone to the South Pacific in the 38th Division, the same outfit that had brought together the Hoosiers in the 184th band. One afternoon I learned that this division was located just a few miles up the coast from the Repple Depple! I hitched a ride up the coast, approaching Junior from the rear as he operated a switchboard in the 152nd Regiment communications tent:

"Give me number 82, Junior, the Carlisle Drug."

"My God!" he shouted as he whirled in his seat. "Frank Mathias! This is a dream; to hell with the switchboard!" and he handed the gear to an understanding buddy.

Junior and I exchanged news from home in a rush of conversation, finally deciding to go down to Gona beach for a swim. He got some gas masks and we soon cut them down for underwater viewing. We walked through a mile of dead and shattered trees, torn by shells during the Papuan Campaign. The beach was four miles long and shaped like a half moon. The moon's "nose" was a jetty, and two hundred yards out lay a rusty, fire-blackened Jap ship, bombed to the bottom during the battle. I eagerly prepared for my first swim in an ocean, refusing to count the quick dip I had taken at the uninviting enlisted men's beach at the Repple Depple.

Junior and I raced over the black sand and plunged into the Solomon Sea. The water was transparent in its clarity, as if the air itself had become liquid, and thick enough to swim in. We could see "the length of a football field underwater," I estimated in a letter home. Shoals of wildly colored tropical fish flashed by our masks and out of sight behind castles of coral. We were exhilarated. We had all of New Guinea and its seas to ourselves. Neither of us had the least fear of great white sharks, deadly sea snakes, stone fish, or other dangerous denizens of these waters, for we had never heard of any of them! We swam in blissful ignorance, pausing only to climb around on the sunken Jap hulk. We looked through holes in the deck and sides. Streams of sunlight shot through these holes into the inner gloom, spotlighting debris suspended in the clear, dark water. It had been a troopship, we decided, for bodyless uniforms drifted by in tatters. We imagined the owners, stripped to skeletons, lay in the ever shifting ooze beyond the sunlight—a burial ground better than most. We shuddered, then returned to the warm sea and its live fish.

Junior and I were ending our swim when a huge, batlike thing leaped into the air near us, returning to the water with a horrible smacking sound. We thrashed the hundred yards to the beach in panic; I could feel the teeth of this thing sink into a mental picture of my leg as I flailed along. We staggered breathlessly onto the beach, chattering opinions of our escape. We learned later that we had escaped nothing, that our "great bat" was a harmless Manta Ray stunning a few fish to eat. I did not see Junior again until two years later in Carlisle, where we excitedly talked about our day on Gona beach.

The silken voice of "Tokyo Rose" caught my attention shortly after coming to New Guinea. Hurled out into the ether via 500,000-watt transmitters, her propaganda broadcast reached every corner of the South Pacific. She knew what she was doing, playing the best recordings of the era. When Rose played "Rose of Washington Square" for her GI fans, it was not by some secondary band but by Benny Goodman, one of the best records ever cut by the King of Swing. Her constant reference to the material allurements of home followed the official Japanese doctrine that western civilization had gone soft, needing only a push to topple its defenders. We laughed at her patter, and enjoyed the music. We laughed even more at her accounts of battle losses and victories, for she usually screwed them up as badly as official Jap accounts: "Tokyo Rose said the other night that the U.S. fleet was beaten so badly off Formosa that they fled to the Philliapines [sic] in terror. Funny as hell, since the Japs are in most of the Philliapines [sic]!"

We could hear Japanese and German propaganda broadcasts almost any time we turned on a radio. "The Japs use pretty stupid propaganda," I wrote, "which is just the opposite of the German style which features Aussie soldiers who have been captured. They give their serial numbers etc. to prove their identity. The Aussie captives tell how they feel etc., but between each speaker the Nazi announcer sticks in his propaganda. The Australians back home have to listen to this or else miss maybe hearing from a father, son, or neighbor."

My last three days at Oro Bay were as exhausting as any I spent in the army. We were scooped up and flung into a seventy-five-mile march through jungles, plains of razor sharp Kunai grass, and muddy mountain trails. I could not choke down the "sheepy shagnasty," so I made the entire distance "on one can of U.S. rations, black coffee, and two coconuts. When we got back and got fresh food, our stomachs couldn't take it and we all bloated with gas."

I was serving as the column's flanker as it wound through the old Gona battlefield. As I crashed through thickets, entangled often in the fifty-foot webs spun by colonies of huge spiders, and sucked boot deep into swamps, I cursed the day I was born. I struggled to keep up, my canteen soon hanging empty in the heat. My thirst grew overpowering, for water is never where you want it in a jungle, in spite of the heavy rains. Finally I stumbled up to a tiny stream gurgling its way in gloom through heavy overgrowth. As I impatiently let it trickle into my canteen, I felt I was being watched. I was. Staring at me through lifeless, sunken pits was the raisin-shriveled head of a Jap soldier, its chin dividing the waters into two small rivulets. His punctured steel helmet lay nearby. The sight fastened itself on my memory. I shrugged, dropped several halizone tablets into the canteen, and rushed back to my job as flanker.

The last night out I slept under huge jungle leaves, held above me by sticks across banyan tree roots. I was too tired to worry about the rain or insects. Sometime before dawn, we were shouted out and marched off into the darkness. Everyone was mad and wet. The column finally reached a road brightened by the headlights of scores of parked trucks. We were ordered aboard the trucks and taken back to the Repple Depple. Our ship was in, and we were going to leave New Guinea.

7. The Buckeye Division

When we arrived at the Repple Depple we were told to line up for inspection. Several hundred turned out with packs, duffle bags and rifles. Walter, Jack, Marcel, and I stuck together, choosing the left end of the line. An officer walked up to the middle of the line and divided it. The men on the right side were assigned to the 43rd Division and those on the left to the 37th. That is how I got into the Buckeye Division, not complicated at all. Sometimes the army could do things very deftly!

We boarded the U.S.S. *Oconto* for the seven-hundred-mile trip to Bougainville and our new home with the 37th Infantry Division. Our ship was a new one, drawing ten thousand tons and superior to the *Monterey* as a troopship. The first night out the public address system carried music by Harry Owens and his "Royal Hawaiians," a name derived from the Honolulu hotel in which the Owens band had played for many years. Clark and I knew this as musicians, and we sat on the moonswept deck and listened as steel guitars played "Moon of Manakoora," and many other songs white civilization believed to be typical of the South Seas. We laughed as we compared the Owens band with the jungle drums we had listened to in New Guinea. The reality of the South Seas was on all sides of us and the paradox of the music was evident—it reminded us of the United States instead of the South Seas!

On a sunny November day, 1944, the *Oconto* dropped anchor off the coast of Bougainville. We had watched the island loom ever nearer over the past few hours. Mt. Bagana, a ten-thousand-foot volcano, centered the scene, perpetually breathing out a small cloud tossed back by the winds across its summit. A ridge of mountains, clad in jungle greens and umbers, marched off into the blue distances on both sides of the volcano. Named for French explorer Louis Antoine de Bougainville, this was a big island, over 120 miles long, up to 48 miles wide, and covering 3,900 square miles, an area twice the size of the state of Delaware. We were rolling gently on the swells in Empress Augusta Bay, the heavily jungled "soft underbelly" Adm. William Halsey had chosen to invade in late 1943 precisely because the fifty thousand defenders were expecting him to hit the north coast with its open coconut and copra plantations. The Japs were still there, held at bay by a perimeter around the airstrips. As we rode the ship's rail, someone pointed at the ridges near Mt. Bagana. An artillery barrage was falling with flashes of fire, the lazy white fingers from exploding white phosphorous shells curling through the foliage and falling debris. If our minds could have been read and printed out on paper, just one shaky sentence would have appeared: "My God this is the real thing; this is the real thing; this isn't practice, this is the real thing." We looked at each other and shared our fear through widened eyes and taut lips.

We packed our gear and hefted our duffle bags into Higgins boats alongside the ship. About twenty of us piled into my boat, and the sailor headed for the Division's small docks, perhaps two miles from the *Oconto*. As we plunged along toward the beaches, we sank ever lower in the swells. No one noticed. Finally the water began lapping over the sides, and all of us began shouting. It was too late. We began sinking slowly and sloppily as the water poured in and the boat kept driving forward. Everybody was shouting as the sailor tried to save his "ship." The motor drowned out as the shoebox-shaped boat settled slowly onto Bougainville's offshore coral reef. We were lucky in this, for the water was only a foot or so above the sides and the bottom was securely trapped on the reef.

"Shit! Shit! Shit!" the sailor screamed and wrung his hands. "I forgot to put the bung in."

"The bung? the bung?" we gurgled, "What th' hell is the bung?"

"It plugs up a drain hole; I forgot to put it back in. I'm going to catch holy hell for look who's coming." He wrung his hands some more.

A navy launch with several officers aboard was heading our way and when it arrived the sailor caught the holy hell he was expecting. We now took his side against the brass, laughing and paddling around above the reef. Another Higgins boat soon picked us out of the bay, dragged our sodden barracks bags aboard, and unloaded us on the sands of Bougainville.

Once on dry land and aboard a truck my optimism returned. I liked what I saw. Instead of an impenetrable jungle, there were hundreds of tents and quonset huts in clearings along many miles of smooth coral roads. The division had been here a year, time enough to build a network of roads and improve living conditions. Clark and I and several others were unloaded at the tents of G Company, 145th Infantry Regiment. Marcel and Jack went elsewhere, and we waved them goodbye with regret.

This was it! This was a line infantry company that had seen many savage battles on New Georgia and here on Bougainville. This is what I had thought of with dread from the moment I had entered the army. The reality did not match my expectations. Instead of the grim, hard-bitten, rifle-toting old vets of my imagination, there were friendly faces everywhere. Nobody was in uniform. They ran out to greet us dressed in odds and ends of fatigue suits, Aussie short pants, Marine shirts, sailor hats, and some with nothing on. Hair length suited the owner's tastes, and one fellow had a gold ring in his ear. They reminded me of a gang of exceedingly friendly pirates.

"You're in Ohio now!" one of them shouted. I was puzzled.

"The hell I am," I said. "I wish I were!"

"Well, you are, all right, for this is the 37th and the 37th is an Ohio national guard outfit."

"Suits me," said I; "I've spent more time in Ohio than most of you guys."

"Hey, you guys are dripping wet—did you get torpedoed on the way in?" They laughed at our story of sinking on the reef and brought out a variety of dry clothes. Soon we were as out of uniform as the rest.

I was glad to belong to something again, having lived from pillar to post since leaving Camp Wheeler. Carefully hoarded raisin jack and big green bottles of powerful Aussie beer were pulled out to celebrate our arrival. We were in an expansive mood as we went to supper. After a good meal the regimental commander, Colonel Cecil B. Whitcomb, climbed up on a chair and started off strong:

"You're in the best damned battalion, in the best damned regiment, in the best damned division in the South Pacific—and you damned well better not forget it! We need you and you're welcome." He spoke for a few minutes, then leaped off the chair and shook hands. He was dressed as informally as his men and he made a good impression on the new men. He exuded confidence and toughness, and humor mixed with ability; he obviously had the respect of his regiment. By nightfall, Clark and I agreed that we had done better than we had expected.

We had done even better than we knew, having landed in one of the finest infantry divisions of the Second World War. *Yank* magazine's Sgt. John McLeod wrote of the 37th in an article called "The Heavyweight." "The over-all impression the 37th gives you is one of power and competence," McLeod observed. "Seeing the 37th move toward a new front [is] like seeing Joe Louis step into the ring after the preliminaries. It's a big, tough, skilled division for a big, tough job. It's a heavyweight." McLeod also noted that the division commander, Maj. Gen. Robert S. Beightler, knew what he wanted and got it, whether that might be extra Long Toms and 240mm howitzers, or something as mundane as dump trucks. Also, "you seldom saw a 37th man with the seat of his pants out, and there were few who didn't have combat boots. Up with the lead battalion kitchen, weapons carriers came through with oranges, egg sandwiches and such. The mail goes up every day."

Although *Yank* magazine had high praise for the 37th—and this praise was echoed at war's end by the top enemy commander, General Tomoyuki Yamashita—the Buckeye Division had had to earn it the hard way. Inducted into federal service on October 15, 1940, like other national guard divisions, it had been destined for Europe after completing training at Camp Shelby, Mississippi, but its orders were reversed enroute owing to the rapid Jap advance in the Pacific. Army leaders agreed that "it was too fine a division" to use against the Japs, but they had no choice.

In early June, 1942, elements of the 37th landed at Suva, Fiji Islands, sent there to block what seemed certain to be the next Jap thrust down the island chain in their attempt to isolate Australia. In the process, the 147th RCT (regimental combat team) was permanently lost to the division, for it was detached and hurled into the battle for Guadalcanal with the Marines two months later. This battle, along with the Papuan Campaign and the Midway defeat, stopped the enemy, leaving the 37th idle on Fiji. That September, the 147th was replaced by the 129th, a regiment taken from the 33rd (Illinois) Division. The 129th regiment, with roots dating back to 1810, would carry its full weight alongside the 145th and 148th regiments for the remainder of the war.

The full strength of the division was brought to bear for the first time during the summer of 1943. The 43rd Division had been fighting a grisly campaign on New Georgia to seize Munda airfield. The 37th joined the 43rd, experiencing some of the worst jungle fighting of the war—banzai attacks, knives and bayonets at close quarters, butchery of captives. During the battle a young private from Tiffin, Ohio, found himself and his platoon pinned down by fire from a Nip machine gunner on higher ground seventy-five yards away. The first burst wounded him, but he believed he could save his buddies, so he crawled toward the enemy pillbox, his M-1 spitting lead. The Jap gunner hit him again, but still he came on, killing the enemy with a hand grenade just as the gunner's last blast shot him to death. He had saved his friends, and he won the Congressional Medal of Honor posthumously. Moreover, his actions inspired composer Frank Loesser to write a song that became the best loved theme of American infantrymen throughout the world—"The Ballad of Rodger Young":

> No, they've got no time for glory in the Infantry,
> No, they've got no use for praises loudly sung,
> But in every soldier's heart in all the infantry
> Shines the name, shines the name of Rodger Young.
> . . . .
> On the island of New Georgia in the Solomons,
> Stands a simple wooden cross alone to tell,
> That beneath the silent coral of the Solomons
> Sleeps a man, sleeps a man remembered well.

The last Jap had hardly been kicked off New Georgia before the 37th was shipped two hundred miles north to take over the beachhead established by the Third Marine Division on Bougainville. The

Marines had surprised the Japs by landing at heavily jungled Empress Augusta Bay; nevertheless they had taken heavy casualties before securing the beachhead. It fell to the 37th and Americal Divisions to hold and expand this perimeter with its precious airstrips against the fully aroused enemy. The main body of enemy was on the other side of the island, but an all out attack on the beachhead was expected as they massed to cross Bougainville's mountainous spine. The Nips, as usual, fully lived up to expectations, initiating the "Second Battle of Bougainville" by hurling thousands of screaming infantrymen against the American perimeter in February, 1944. The Buckeye Division sagged, then held against the onslaught, its machine gunners scorching their barrels as streams of bullets stacked writhing Nips ten deep on jungle trails. Still they came, their tin bugles blowing and bayonets slashing as they climbed over their dead or infiltrated through the jungle thickets. The climax was reached on Hill 700, a heavily jungled height whose steep slopes changed hands nightly during deadly hand grenade battles. Before the attack was over, in late March, the 37th had annihilated one of the proudest divisions of the Nipponese army, the infamous 6th, which was involved in the notorious "Rape of Nanking" in China several years before. They would rape no more, but they had inflicted heavy casualties on the Buckeyes, and new men would have to fill the gaps. I was one of the new men.

I was elated at being back in a settled outfit, but this feeling was dampened considerably during my second night with G Company. I was sent out on a patrol, partly as training for the new men but also to sniff around and see what the Japs were up to beyond the perimeter. The entire division had been undergoing intensive training since midsummer in preparation for some as yet unannounced "big invasion." Such combat training was easy to come by on Bougainville, for thousands of Japs had refused to wither on the vine and continued to contest every inch of ground in the upper Laruma River valley. They had screened and blocked most trails into this area beyond the perimeter. Patrols constantly probed the region, some of them unable to avoid fire fights, but most returning with nothing worse than insect bites, chills from the cold night rains, and exhaustion from clambering around the jungled mountains. I had been tabbed for such a patrol.

The patrol I was on did not amount to much—any old hand would have scoffed at it—but my heated imagination pictured it as "the real thing." I checked the mechanism and bullets of my M-1 over and over as we moved out. As the shadows and gloom of the tropic night deepened I started seeing Japs lurking behind every banyan tree. My eyes strained into the flickering misty light as we ambled along an easy trail into the interior. My mind filled with remembered tales of Japs cutting up captives and throwing the pieces back to Yank foxholes. By this time we were moving by the margins of a large lake, its still waters reflecting a myriad of stars. Several of us jumped when these pinpoints of light suddenly jumbled as something disturbed the water. The squad leader chuckled at our reaction, telling us that big crocodiles infested the place. He seemed to be enjoying himself, but I was not. Thoughts were pounding through my mind like hammers: "Why did I complain about that New Guinea march—Wish I was back in Benning— What was that movement off to the right!" The stars disappeared, intensifying the darkness. "If I can't see," I thought, "then neither can the Japs." Clouds suddenly unleashed a heavy steady rain, slicking our ponchos and pattering noisily on our caps. We paused for awhile in a hut, then doubled back over the trail we had covered earlier. I did not know where I had been but I knew I was scared, full of an unreasoning dread, and with no perspective on the true nature of this training patrol. Once back in the dry tent, I prayed at length for deliverance. I dropped off to a few hours of troubled sleep.

As dawn broke over G Company the jungle birds sang their usual happy hymn to the sun, but I was far from happy. Blue notes sounded the depths of my soul as an overactive imagination conjured up endless patrols and who knew what horrors in an unpredictable future. At least I was hungry, so I shaved and ambled off to the mess tent with several of my mates from last night's adventure. We joked about it cautiously before finding that we shared similar worries. "If a bullet's got your name on it there's nothing you can do about it," someone suggested, reverting to ancient infantry philosophy. We talked over this statement, none of us knowing the meaning of fatalism, yet all of us feeling it was too negative to accept; besides, no bullets had yet come our way. We had never seen a man die. Our discussion ended worse than it had begun as we sat with puzzled faces, blank eyes revealing minds lost in long thoughts. I walked back to the tent, still trying to puzzle a way out of my personal enigma.

I fooled around inside the tent for awhile, then the door flap opened, revealing a top kick peering in. Another patrol assignment, I thought, before he spoke.

"Is a fellow named Mathias in here?" he asked as he searched our faces.

"Here I am," I muttered.

"Good, I've been looking for you. I'm Sergeant Bill Rogers. You've been transferred into the Division band. I'm here to pick you up."

"What did you say!" I shouted in stunned disbelief. "You mean I'm in the band!" I was on my feet now.

"Well, it's up to you I guess; if you don't want to . . ."

"I want to! I want to! Don't go away! When do we leave?" I felt like kissing his hand. My emotions were showing.

"My jeep's outside," he smiled. "Get your gear together and we'll leave right now."

Sergeant Rogers joked with his ecstatic new recruit as we drove the mile or so over to Division Headquarters. I thanked God along the way, remembering my fervent prayers the night before. I had no doubt that this was a Heaven-sent miracle and that my lowly saxophone was the tool used to bring it about. Once again, just as back at the 184th audition, my world had changed from lead to gold in the space of a few minutes. I felt I owed my life to my tenor sax and vowed to make it my life's work.

We drove by the Piva fighter strip, with its lines of Marine Corsairs, then turned into Headquarters Company. Rogers introduced me to Chief Warrant Officer Charles B. Hower as we entered the band tent. He was an amiable Tennesseean, perhaps thirty-five years old, and in charge of a fifty-six-piece band which recently had been culled out of the three disbanded regimental bands. We chatted for a few moments, then he noted that he had found me by checking the records of the newly arrived men, spotting my Military Occupational Specialty number, 439—Bandsman, Saxophone. I gushed out the story of the clerk at Wheeler who had thoughtfully put it on my record, and of my experience with the 184th. "Sir," I asked hopefully, "another 184th bandsman arrived with me, Walter Clark, an excellent brass man; can you use him too?"

"I'm sorry," he replied, "we have all the brass we need, but if he was a reed man I would take him." I was in no position to argue the matter, but I knew Clark would be crushed when I told him. Clark later shrugged at the bad news, happy at my break. Both of us would have otherwise have been wed to G Company until death, perhaps, did us part.

I was soon at home with the 37th's musicians, comparing them favorably with the Hoosiers and Jewsiers of yore. One was a Mormon, the first I had ever met. He handled my naive questions concerning multiple wives as good-naturedly as Jack Block had earlier accepted my confusion over his *Tefilin*. I had never known any people of Mexican ancestry, but two were in my tent. Socorro "Chick" Cervantes and Felix "Rudy" Panol were California lads the same age as I, and both were reed men. They were completely bilingual, dubbing me "Paco" (Frank) as I struggled to learn Spanish from them. They became two of my closest friends, as did a stubby, well muscled man from Toledo. Glenn Crosby was a Charles Atlas enthusiast, practicing "dynamic tension," the Atlas art of pitting one muscle against the other. Glenn, for example, lifted himself slowly from chairs with his arms instead of simply standing up. He could do forty pushups with each arm. He had been a hero to the superbly built Fiji Island men, for he knew the secret of pressing heavy weights. Although much smaller, he beat them every time, for they simply bent over and tried unsuccessfully to hoist his huge home-made weights. Glenn's muscles did not extend to his brain, for he was widely read and somewhat philosophical by nature. I viewed him as a man of the world, seeking his advice on numerous things.

After a week of the usual rehearsals and parades I had become acquainted with everyone. They had all been in combat, noticeably edging their conversations and humor with a caution never evidenced by the happy-go-lucky men of the 184th. Instead of wrangling over three-day passes to Atlanta, they were seriously concerned about where the division would strike next. Most were friendly lads from towns and cities in Ohio and Illinois, and I tried hard to pronounce correctly the tongue-twisting Polish names carried by several. Their show and dance band, I thought, was even better than Jerry

Klausner's, playing with the driving power of Count Basie, yet with the taste and accuracy of Glenn Miller. Mitch Zaremba, a Cleveland studio trombonist with a tone rivaling Tommy Dorsey's, led the aggregation, while Hubert Peck, a composer of great ability from Pocatello, Idaho, wrote most of the arrangements. We played often at a large open air theatre called "Lowe's Bougainville" as USO shows toured through from the states or from Australia. I remember only two, the Randolph Scott show and an Australian group, the "Tasmaniacs." The band's comedian, Paul Benzaquin, always got laughs as he smoked a plasma bottle rigged like a Turkish water pipe.

It was exciting to be in division headquarters. Things were different here, for it was the nerve center for twenty thousand men, which now included several thousand soldiers in supporting roles for wherever the 37th was next scheduled to attack. The idea of division units dated from the five-hundred-thousand-man citizen armies of the French Revolution. No one general could command such a mass of men, so divisions were created, each with leaders the overall commander could control. A division contains all kinds of weaponry and supporting units, and is capable of operating alone or with other divisions. Divisions therefore replaced the specialized regiments formerly used. I became familiar with the G-Sections at Headquarters, making friends among the enlisted help in these units. "They are the brains of the division," I wrote my father, "and are directed by staff officers who handle administration, Intelligence, finance and training, and supply."

The division commander, Major General Robert S. Beightler, was a talented leader respected by everyone, including Douglas MacArthur. His ability was such that he alone of all World War II national guard division commanders served throughout the entire war without being removed from office for reasons of age, qualifications, or incompetence. We called him "Uncle Bob," blending pride and affection in this, for he won his battles with one of the lowest casualty rates of any division in the Second World War. He would have agreed with Patton's statement that it is "not the duty of a soldier to die for his country, but to make the other poor bastard die for *his* country!" Beightler did this through careful planning and by massing overwhelming artillery preparations, often in combination with heavy naval guns cruising just off the beachheads. The result of this on Bougainville, for example, was a "kill ratio" of thirty-three Japs to every Yank. MacArthur, another worrier over casualty lists, perhaps admired Beightler more for this than for his skilled tactics and keen strategy. Finally, Uncle Bob and his men had the full support of the homefolks back in Ohio, for he had been the state's highway commissioner before the war. I doubt that regular army men, usually critical of national guard outfits, have ever fully understood the importance of this when a democracy wages war.

I explored the area around division headquarters, finding a small creek nearby, which drained into the Piva River. I stood in a clearing, observing a battered washboard, soap stains, cans, and discarded socks; the place was used as a do-it-yourself laundry for odds and ends. Since I had some socks and underwear that could not wait the laundry pickup, I brought them to the clearing from my tent, picking up soap scraps on the way from around the shower stall duckboards. As I put my stuff in the creek I was startled by a voice: "Hello now, how are yuh?" Stepping through the thicket on the other side of the tiny creek came an Australian soldier, the brim of his campaign hat typically pinned up on the side. "Yank," he said, "hand me that stuff and I'll wash it with mine. I've got a nice hot tub of water going over here." When I objected, he simply took it out of my hands, recrossed the creek, and plopped it into his steaming tub. I followed along, amazed that a man would volunteer to do another man's washing. I liked this guy.

"We came to Bougainville just a few days ago," he said, stirring the hot laundry with a stick. "My division, the Third, is going to take over your perimeter. The 37th is going somewhere for sure—we all guess it's the Philippines, don't you?"

I agreed with him, and we chatted as we washed the clothes. When he heard I was in the band we began talking music. He soon taught me the melody and words of "Waltzing Matilda," the favorite song of Aussie and New Zealand soldiers. I responded by teaching him "Der Fuhrer's Face," a comic number the 184th quartet had sung with success back at Benning. The song requires the singers to make a great farting sound after each "Heil!" and my Aussie friend roared with delight at the idea. Both of us sang it with gusto as the boiling laundry gurgled an adequate background:

> When der Fuhrer sez we iss der master race,
> We Heil! (P-f-f-f-t-t-t-t) Heil! (P-f-f-f-t-t-t-t)
> Right in der fuhrer's face;
> Not to love der fuhrer iss a great disgrace,
> So we Heil! (P-f-f-f-t-t-t-t) Heil! (P-f-f-f-t-t-t-)
> Right in der fuhrer's face!

The song's bridge labels the Nazis as "super-dooper-pooper-men," and we were singing this and laughing loudly when several Aussies and some boys from the band showed up and joined in. This had the makings of a real party, so the Aussies sent back for beer. Aussie beer is powerful stuff, running at close to fifteen percent alcohol, and coming in pint or quart size green bottles. We drank it as fast as it came, and close harmony vanished with equal speed. Before the party was over, the glee club was sitting in the creek. But we sure boiled hell out of those clothes!

I was not feeling too well the next day, and winced as the entire band started shouting and running toward the fighter strip. Chick stopped long enough to say, "Come on Paco, a beer plane has landed!" I stumbled along with the pack, arriving at the edge of the strip to see a huge circle of men forming around a Marine plane, each with a canteen cup. The Corsair had flown in hundreds of gallons of beer in its wing tanks, icing it at high altitudes as it cruised in from Espiritu Santo or New Caledonia. I told Bruce Thomson, a trumpet player, that I was passing it up, but he raised so much hell at my attitude that I promised to get him a cupful if he would get me a Coca-Cola. The deal was immediately made, and I stood in line.

By this time the line was a giant, closed loop, with new guys admitted only in segments with full cups. As I waited my turn, a soldier walked up:

"Aren't you Frank Mathias, from Carlisle, Kentucky?"

I squinted into his sunlit face, knowing that I recognized his features, yet I was unable to recall his name. He laughed as I shouted it at last—"Marion Sims!" He had rented my father's service station before entering the army in 1941, but the South Pacific sun had bleached his hair and sweated some pounds off. "I didn't recognize you at first, Simmy; are you in the 37th?"

"I will be for awhile," he said. "My outfit came in to support you

Buckeyes in the next big push, wherever that is. Have you seen Soda Shrout yet? He's in your 140th Field Artillery."

"Good Lord, Charles Shrout's here too! Carlisle's about to run this show. I'll look him up as soon as I can." We talked over the news from home. I saw Soda soon after, but Sims and I did not meet again. These two, along with the CCC boy aboard the *Monterey* and Clarence Owings with the 38th, made four men from a town of sixteen hundred thrown in my path in a two-month period.

The band was not exempt from the rugged training schedule. We joined in practice landings on the beaches of Empress Augusta Bay. The place was alive with Higgins boats, signal corpsmen with wigwag flags, and hard working soldiers from the motor pools, learning the tricks of waterproofing trucks and caterpiller tractors so they could drive through the surf. While doing this, many of us collected sea-shells scattered in their thousands on the beach. We intended to sell them for big money, for rumor had it that Chaplain Ferdinand Evans had recently sold his fine collection for over $1000. The bandsmen called him "Ferdinand the Papal Bull," a pun including his name, a legendary bull that sniffed flowers rather than bullfighters, and a papal document. I stuffed my pockets full of small "cat's eye" shells, perhaps in the belief that quantity was as good as quality. In a few minutes I started scratching as I worked, then shuddered in horror to see my fatigue suit crawling with spiders. I swatted them wildly as I ran and then rolled into the surf. Everyone nearby stopped working, pointing at me in puzzlement, laughing only when they found out what had happened. Spiders used the hollow cat's eyes for protection, like hermit crabs. I laughed with the rest as I dripped dry, glad to leave sea shell collecting to Ferdinand the Papal Bull.

Between training problems, several of us swam along the great coral reef off Cape Torokina. We hitched rides with sailors in small craft, took the usual gas mask goggles, and leaped in on top of our inflated mattress covers. These things floated like fat white bladders when swished full of air and tied off with their end strings. We rested on them between dives down into the mysteriously beautiful nether-world of the reef. We addicts of the reef never tired of this venture into what we correctly talked of as a "new world." One GI—and we saw him often—did not share our love of the ocean. He came to the division beach with a different purpose in mind. As the great breakers rolled in, he would rush them, cursing loudly as he struck at them furiously with clenched fists. "That guy's fighting the ocean again," someone would say as we watched. "I guess it gets a lot of shit out of his soul," another would venture. The ocean stood between him and home.

It can be doubted that Eleanor Roosevelt ever saw a naked man, other than Franklin and Chalkeye. Chalkeye worked in division headquarters, saw everything worth seeing in spite of a white spot on his left eye, and bragged about his encounter with the president's wife to anyone who would listen. "I was down on Espiritu Santo," he would begin, "and decided to take a swim off the one-lane Bailey Bridge. Now Mrs. Roosevelt, you know how she is always traveling everywhere, stopped off to see Espiritu. While she's coming down my road in a jeep, I'm stripped naked, getting set to dive off the bridge for a swim. Her jeep stopped to wait its turn on the bridge, and I'm just standing there not expecting anything exciting. Then I saw her and she saw me, just as her jeep pulls up. She waved and shouted 'yoo hoo' as I leaped for the water." This always brought laughs, but Chalkeye then shushed his audiences, holding up a hand: "That's not all of it boys," he would say, "Eleanor has sent me complimentary letters ever since!"

Eleanor Roosevelt's toothy but cheery smile was welcome on all battle fronts, and "everyone admires her a lot," I wrote home. Her world-girdling travel attracted the fire of political enemies in the states, for travel was seen as an expensive luxury prior to the war—a rich man's game. Servicemen sensed exaggeration here, for many of them had traveled further than famous explorers of the past. "When I think I'm only 19 and have been 10,000 miles from home, been in 15 states, jungles, Pacific Ocean, Coral Sea, Bismarck Sea, New Guinea, where I am now, and God knows where else, seen 2 volcanoes, fresh battlefields, all kinds of planes, ships and men—guess I'm just bragging but I could still be clerking at Krogers. I'm traveling instead of that and getting $64 a month to do it!"

Few things are more important to a saxophonist than his teeth. While listening one day to the "Man in a Banyan" radio show, I developed a pounding toothache. I lingered long enough to hear the hilarious "interviews," which were a takeoff on stateside "Man in the Street" shows and broadcast over the Solomon Islands' Mosquito Network; then I set out to find a dentist. I wished later I had stayed up a tree with the "Man in the Banyan," for I entered a torture chamber I would never forget.

The dentist's "office" was a small clearing in the jungle. There stood a young lieutenant by a spidery looking drill apparatus, a wooden lay-back chair for his patients, and a GI detailed to spin the drill by pumping a sewing-machine-like treadle. The GI was reading a comic book, continuing this as he pumped the treadle throughout the drilling and filling. I agonized an hour away as the slow moving drill ground its heated way through old fillings and new enamel. I watched and envied jungle birds flying above me as I theorized that the dentist was one of the first ASTP trainees to make it overseas. It felt as if he were using rock candy for fillings. When he finished, my fatigues were wet with sweat and my emotions tattered. I staggered away swearing under my breath that I would never go to another dentist in this son-of-a-bitching division. Ohio may have turned out some good musicians, I thought, but their dentists were not worth a damn!

It was on a hot afternoon in early December that the band was assembled to hear a lecture. An officer stood before us with a large folder propped on an easel. When he announced that what he had to say would be "top secret," we correctly guessed that the division's long awaited next assignment was at hand. Interest and tension gripped the audience as he opened the easel, playing his pointer over a long curving bay and beach area: "The 37th is going to participate in the invasion of Luzon, the largest and most important island in the Philippines. Luzon is the same size as the state of Ohio. We are to spearhead the drive south to Manila. This will be the climax of years of moving from island to island. The Nip general, Yamashita, can probably count on some 275,000 troops to defend Luzon, so this will be a hard campaign." Nervous coughs and sighs greeted this information.

"The map I have here," he continued, "is of the Lingayen Gulf in northern Luzon. We will land here on January 9, 1945, a month from now. The 148th Infantry will land on Yellow Beach, the 129th on Crimson, and the 145th will stay aboard ship in reserve. The 40th Division will land on our right, to the west; the 6th and 43rd divisions will land several miles to our left or east. You will encounter swampy land, riddled with rice paddies and fishponds, and it is land rather easy to defend."

Where did the band fit into this invasion, we wondered? The answer rumbled into our souls like thunder: "The band will land with the Assault Wave." Everyone stared at everyone else, then at nothing in particular as the officer continued. "The Assault Wave will hit the beaches at 9:30 a.m., between Crimson and Yellow beaches. You will be part of division headquarters defense platoon, with heavy weapons. Your job will be to defend the beach and unload supplies in the face of enemy fire. The two regiments will be attacking enemy positions in order to enlarge the beachhead. Any questions?" An oboe player asked if it would not be possible for us to "stay on good old Bougainville." Everyone laughed, but it was the kind of nervous laughter heard at a funeral.

I left the lecture with the rest, but I had no real understanding, as they did, of what it would mean to attack an exposed and easily defended beach in the face of a powerful and well led Japanese army. My thoughts during the lecture had turned to G Company, from which I had escaped with the "miraculous help of the Lord." I fought off a growing suspicion that the Lord may have been playing games with me. The lousy band would hit the beaches first while G Company and the 145th would float invasion day away in a reserve role aboard their ships. I wished I had never left G Company. Then I remembered what my father invariably advised anytime I made a senseless wish: "Wish in one hand and shit in the other and see what you've got the most of!" I finally knew what he meant.

The division began getting ready for its next fight like the "heavy-weight" it was. Night lights burned at headquarters as diagrams were prepared for loading the thousands of things needed by the twenty-eight thousand men of the 37th and its supporting units. The band was reformed as a heavy weapons platoon, a part of the defense of division headquarters. Rudy Panol and I were teamed behind a .30-caliber light machine gun, with carbines as side arms. Strict censorship prevented my writing anything home beyond the fact that I had "finally turned in my M-1 Garand 'elephant gun,' and now have a carbine for which I am thankful because they weigh 4 lbs. less." I also dated the letter "December 30*th*" in keeping with my pre-arranged code, so they knew I was or would soon be aboard ship going somewhere.

Well guarded secrets now came to light. A gambling table, with a highly prized small roulette wheel, had operated for many months in a den cut back into the giant aerial roots of a banyan tree. The owners sold it to some enterprising Aussies. Long saved quarts of "jungle juice," made from raisins and sugar buried in coconuts under the steaming turf, showed up for last blasts. Jungle hammocks were slung, as pyramidal tents were folded and loaded. When properly slung, these things were snug, dry, and bug-proof, protecting the soldier sandwiched between two slices of rainproof material connected with heavy mosquito netting. They were discarded as "sitting ducks" in combat, but nothing better was ever devised for getting a good night's sleep in the dripping depths of a jungle.

Big brass began passing through headquarters to check out things with our general. One of these, Aussie commander Sir Thomas Blamey, paused for a laugh at the humorous signs and cartoons the bandsmen had tacked up around our area. I had drawn one of an Aussie soldier hoisting a big bottle of beer while standing in a can of mutton rations, the can shaped like an outdoor latrine. "By God," Blamey roared, "our rations do take some getting used to, don't they!"

Scuttlebutt concerning the outlook for us on Luzon was everywhere, most of it rather accurate. Bandsmen had secondhand information from buddies working under the brass in headquarters. Jap units identified so far were the 8th, 19th, 23rd, 103rd, and 105th Infantry Divisions. There was much worry about the famed 2nd Armored Division, recently arrived from Manchuria. Our G-section informants painted a dismal picture of the landing area. We would hit a near-sea-level delta region between the Agno and Dagupan rivers. Three miles inland the unfordable Calmay River lay like a sliver of moon around the entire beachhead. Rice paddies, and scores of small ponds shored up to grow fish, completed a scary picture for infantry hoping to have mechanized support. We were to plow smack into the center of this swampy morass. Yamashita would undoubtedly be awaiting our arrival with a cunningly prepared defensive network capable of hurling us reeling and bloody back into the sea. We thought of these things as we boarded our ships, knowing that when we debarked three weeks later we would be entirely unwelcome.

8. A Thousand Ships

The Buckeye Division boarded its ships during the second week of December, 1944. I went with the band aboard the U.S.S. *Simon Bolivar,* an attack transport of some ten thousand tons. We lay off Bougainville several days before the ship slowly swung toward the open sea, its final destination a stretch of beach three thousand miles away. But we sailed one passenger short. Several hours before leaving an officer shot himself, tumbling over the side where he bobbed like a cork until sailors fished him out of the bay. I had never seen a violent death before, much less a suicide. "You can think too much about a thing like this," I told myself, hoping to settle my stomach.

I watched from the deck as the smoky summit of Bougainville's great volcano faded from view, as innocent as the other enlisted men of the scope and complexity of the invasion now beginning. During the next three weeks nearly a thousand ships would assemble from throughout the South Pacific, like the pieces of a giant, watery puzzle, finally fitting themselves together at a rendezvous point off the Leyte coast in early January. This fleet, a double line of ships stretching for forty miles, would then brazenly sail into the heart of the Philippine Archipelago, challenging attack from each Jap-held island along its six-hundred-mile path to the invasion beaches at Luzon's Lingayen Gulf.

General MacArthur was not illogical in choosing the smooth seas of this well defended but shorter inner route. His only other choice was to move the invasion convoy all the way around the northern tip

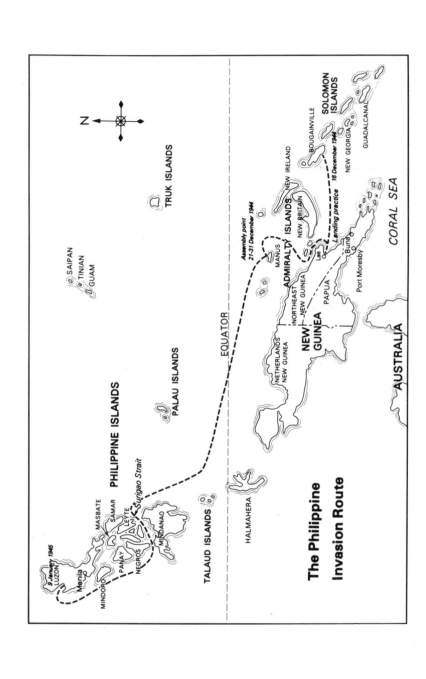

The Philippine
Invasion Route

of Luzon. Although this would have been over open seas, there was the possibility of rough weather and the certainty of attack by Japanese bombers based on nearby Formosa. He made the choice, backing it with land-based fighters from new fields on Leyte and Mindoro. Weakly defended Mindoro lay just south of Luzon and was within range of Clark Field and Manila. The Western Visayan Task Force soon secured the necessary air strips, landing on December 15, the day the 37th sailed out of Bougainville.

Naval operations throughout this vast invasion were directed by Vice Admiral Thomas C. Kinkaid, commander of Allied Naval Forces in the Southwest Pacific. Task Force 77 (Seventh Fleet) transported and guarded the five divisions and support units of Lt. Gen. Walter Krueger's Sixth Army. Within the body of this great mass of fighting ships rode two amphibious attack forces. The San Fabian Attack Force carried the 6th and 43rd Divisions of Maj. Gen. Innis P. Swift's I Corps to Luzon from Sansapor, Aitape and other points. It would land the 6th and 43rd on Blue and White beaches respectively, with the small coastal cities of San Fabian and Mangaldan as their immediate objectives. The Lingayen Attack Force carried the 37th and 40th Divisions, picked up at Bougainville and New Britain, and forming Lt. Gen. Oscar W. Griswold's XIV Corps. It would land the 37th on Crimson and Yellow beaches and the 40th on Green and Orange. The coastal towns of Lingayen and Dagupan were among our immediate objectives. Floating in Sixth Army Reserve was the 25th Division, brought in from New Caledonia.*

The Luzon landing date seemed far away as the *Bolivar* plunged through blue tropical seas. Three days out of Bougainville we raised land again, this time along New Guinea's Huon Gulf, near the town of Lae. The 40th Division was already there, and we joined them in a full dress rehearsal of the landing to come at Lingayen. Thousands of soldiers climbed down the rope nets slung over the sides of the *Bolivar, Harris, Manoora, Sarasota, Westralia,* and *Doyen*—some of the troop ships of the Lingayen Attack Force. We dropped into landing craft and headed for shore as destroyers reeled out eye-stinging rolls of smoke to screen the operation.

*Robert Ross Smith, *Triumph in the Philippines* (Washington, 1963), pp. 659ff.

We had hardly left New Guinea before stopping again, this time dropping anchor in Seeadler Harbor, a vast expanse of water protected equally by a coral atoll and rugged Manus Island. We would remain at this major rendezvous point in the Admiralty Islands from December 20 until we left for the invasion on December 31, 1944. I was astonished at the scores of ships already present—battlewagons, carriers, troop ships, cruisers—all of them talking back and forth across the miles of harbor with flickering signal lights. Other ships arrived almost hourly, adding strength to what would become the second largest amphibious operation of the Second World War and of all time.

Christmas was on our minds as we settled down in the great harbor. Slippery looking little tropical pines had been cut on Manus and set up as Christmas trees aboard ship. Our mail caught up with us, bringing a hunger for home as we looked at the snow scenes on dozens of Christmas cards. The navy cooks pulled out all the stops, treating us to "turkey, peas, slaw, fruitcake, mincemeat pie, dressing, rolls, mashed potatoes, cranberry sauce, and coffee for Christmas dinner." The menu was about the only thing I could write home now without fear of censorship. A greater fear entered our conversations as we wondered where we would be next time Christmas rolled around.

I would never see a prettier lagoon than one I found on Pityelu Islet. We had been given shore leave there to relax and get cold drinks from the Seabees' cold-storage warehouse. The usual crowd of beer drinkers followed me, offering to give me two cokes or more for each of my beers. I left my horde of cokes with Chick Cervantes, then set out to find some privacy. Little Pityelu's pink sands ended in a large grove of coconut palms and shrubs, but within this lay a tiny but perfect lagoon. It covered no more than two acres, with a small opening to the sea and the thundering barrier reef beyond. Shadows from overhanging palm trees penetrated the sun-dappled water, interspersing with seashells, brightly colored fish, and sand to make pleasant designs across the bottom. I sat down with a sigh, glad to be alone with myself and the South Pacific. After an hour, reluctant but refreshed, I rejoined the roisterous beer drinkers.

A day or so later Chick and I went swimming in this lagoon during shore leave. While we were paddling around, our friend Rudy

Panol discovered us, shouting as he waved a copy of *Reveille,* the division news sheet. "Boy oh Boy," he said, "the guys in Europe are taking a helluva beating from the Germans. Says here that a big attack called the 'Bulge' is running them out, and the snow is so deep they're freezing all over the place!"

This fell under the heading of good news to Chick and me. "Freezing, are they," I chortled, "they're the ones who laughed like hell when I got ramrodded out here to the Pacific. To hell with 'em, let 'em freeze awhile. They got all the wine, women, and song—ain't going to hurt 'em to freeze awhile, is it Chick?"

"Hell no," Chick replied, "They'd give up a lot of that good old stuff to be where we are right now." He was floating on his back spitting a stream of water between his teeth.

"Yeah," Rudy agreed as he dropped the paper and stripped for a swim; "we may have a lot of damned bugs over here, but ain't nobody froze to death in the South Pacific yet—I hope they freeze down to their bung holes!" We swam with much increased happiness, taking proprietary interest in the clear warm waters of our lovely coral pool and the sunny blue skies above us.

Our powerful convoy steamed out of the Admiralties on December 31, crossing north of the equator that night. It was New Year's Eve. As 1945 dawned, we came upon deck to see a double line of ships reaching out of sight beyond both horizons. The *Bolivar* was on the eastern or starboard side of the line as we headed north, while running with us a thousand yards to the west was HMAS *Westralia,* an Aussie ship carrying Yanks. We would be watching each other during the next eight days as we shared the dangers of the voyage.

Easy sailing in perfect weather lulled us as our convoy steamed toward "Pen," a navigational control point established between the Palau Islands and the nearby Philippines. Every element of the invasion fleet had to pass this point on a rigid time schedule to ensure its arrival and participation in the landings at Lingayen on S-Day, January 9, 1945. We in the band, of course, knew nothing of this, nor that a powerful group of seven battleships, along with cruisers, destroyers, mine sweepers, and underwater demolition teams were preceding the convoy to clear the way to the objective. If someone had asked us the size of the operation, we might have guessed a hundred ships, some nine hundred short of the reality.

The *Bolivar* was well armed; the rattle of her antiaircraft guns and the THUMP, THUMP, THUMP of her heavy cannons began the day after we left the Admiralties. A B-26 bomber towed a sleeve target down the line of troopships each day, unleashing the world's biggest skeet shoot as gun crews on each vessel awaited their turn to lace the sky with tracers from their pom-poms and other automatic weapons. Surely, I thought, no Jap will ever get near enough to us to do any damage. I was wrong.

Conversation and books from the ship's library occupied our time during the early days of our voyage. I shuddered as I read Bram Stoker's *Dracula,* becoming more frightened of imaginary vampires than of the real wooden stake of war perhaps poised to enter my heart on Lingayen's beaches. Conversation on the breezy decks always turned to women, music, war, and mechanics. "The boys are in a big argument over mechanical brakes versus hydraulics," I wrote as I listened to them. "If it isn't that it's either wimmin or war. We all have our opinions on both. One guy insists you gotta beat em up to handle them (wimmin) and another says he can't handle em no matter what he trys and he's been trying all his life for 30 years." Later, this fellow received a "Dear John" letter from his wife. She had taken his car and moved in with another man. I thought this was "unpatriotic."

We were four mornings out of the Admiralties when we raised land. The greenery of the Philippines slipped by as we entered Surigao Strait, several miles off the coast of Leyte. Buildings and other signs of civilization brought happy sighs from division veterans who had not seen such things since leaving the States in early 1942. Destroyers sniffed among the Filipino craft along shore for signs of Jap trickery. By nightfall we were passing Bohol to the north, with the great bulk of Mindanao looming all along our view southward. During the night we cleared the Strait, turning north up the west coast of Negros. Our route would continue northward, past Panay, Mindoro, Manila, and half of Luzon's west coast before turning eastward into the Lingayen Gulf.

The sixth of January was a beautiful day for sailing. I watched Negros off to our right as the ship plunged along, turning my attention now and then to the Leyte-based Lightnings and Thunderbolts circling in pairs high above the convoy. After a good lunch, several of us decided to play cards, sharing the ominous rumor that Tokyo Rose was predicting the landing at Lingayen. I leaned my back against a spare anchor strapped solidly to a bulkhead. It was a pleasant game of hearts, the queen of spades holding our attention until we idly commented on three planes approaching us at water level from Negros. They were perhaps two miles away. We slowly laid our cards down in apprehension as they approached. By this time they were a thousand yards away and closing on us at four hundred miles per hour. "Japs!" we shouted. I kicked myself backwards from a sitting position, falling on my back behind the anchor, my face to the sky. A plane flashed by at mast level, directly above me; my eyes were full of the big red circles under its wings. Two navy Corsairs were with him, one on each side, forming a tight triangle. I leaped to my feet as they passed, watching in stunned apprehension as they swept toward the *Westralia,* our sister ship to the west. I expected the Jap to hurl his plane into the ship, but again he chose to miss at mast level. Now clear of the convoy, the Yank pilots flew in a rocking pendulum-like motion behind, black dots of smoke punctuating the sky as the multiple guns of the gull-winged Corsairs chewed debris out of the Jap *Jill.* The Jap tried to climb and return, perhaps ashamed of his failure as a kamikaze, but at the top of his turn the plane blossomed into a fireball, careening crazily as it splashed with its pilot into the South China Sea. This was my introduction to combat and also the first attack on the great convoy.

Knots of excited soldiers formed on the decks. The question on every one's lips was why the Jap did not rake us with machine-gun fire as he approached? Again, why did he fail to plunge his plane into the *Bolivar* or the *Westralia*? He had had a perfect opportunity to hit either. We decided that he was a kamikaze pilot who had "chickened out." Perhaps, but I was glad he had, for I had been in his line of fire. Several of the old veterans made light of the attack: "You should have been on New Georgia when they came at us by the hundreds out of Rabaul. This wasn't nothin' compared to that, and it may be nothin' compared to what's comin'." Maybe they were right, but it was plenty for me. I had survived the first attempt to kill me.

The rest of the day we expected other attacks from the islands to the east. None came. The Japs were waiting for night. General

Quarters sounded with a wild gonging as sailors rushed to their guns. We sweat out the attack, fists clenched in fear. Going down at night off Jap-held islands was a fearsome thing to ponder. My respect for sailors rose accordingly, stuck as they were like targets aboard their ships. Life in the ground-hugging infantry had certain charms I had overlooked.

No one had to tell us the next morning that we were just two mornings away from S-Day. The pressure of this date was mounting rapidly, some even counting the number of hours remaining aboard the *Bolivar.* The enemy was not going to let us sail through without a fight. Tiny white streaks forming in the blue skies high above puzzled me; they were the first aircraft vapor trails I had ever seen. Jap Zeros and navy Corsairs were closing rapidly in a challenge for air superiority above the convoy. The trails turned into a spider web of streaks as Yank and Jap pilots engaged in dogfights over a large part of our sky. Some swooped to lower altitudes, their planes losing the appearance of toys. Soon came the smoky black trails of the losers, fiery planes falling with screaming voices into an impartial sea.

Cheers and mumbled prayers were lifted to the deadly contests above us. Cheers from thousands of throats on ships down the line mingled with ours whenever a Yank sent a Jap flaming to his doom. We cried out, throats choked with emotion, when we thought a defending Corsair headed one of those fiery trails into the ocean. We were now off Panay; the great convoy sailed steadily on.

Although the Japs lost their challenge to gain air superiority above the convoy, they had not surrendered plans to rake us with kamikaze "divine wind" suicide planes. Many of the four hundred or so operational Jap aircraft on Luzon were equipped with 550-pound bombs and hurled against the fleet; before the invasion ended they sank twenty-four ships and damaged sixty-seven more.

After the dogfights ended I watched as several kamikaze pilots tried to get through the convoy's defenses. Soldiers were supposed to stay below to avoid falling shrapnel, but I feared getting trapped below decks in a sinking ship much more than I did flak. I stood half in and half out of a bulkhead port as cones of tracers formed around the incoming enemy planes. Shell bursts from heavy guns pockmarked the evening sky, interrupting the fiery fabric knit by the tracers as they skidded on into the clouds. The enemy pilots were brave, flying on until their tiny planes were caught and crumpled in this net of exploding steel. The thumping roar of the ship's guns slackened as the attack failed, giving a navy petty officer time to curse me down below decks, where I belonged.

The next day we were off the coast of Luzon, Manila lying somewhere over our eastern horizon. It was S minus one, and a sense of urgency gripped everyone. Guns were polished and cleaned once, twice, and even three times to settle nerves. A priest, probably Ferdinand the Papal Bull, gave us general absolution, something I had never heard of. Everyone at the open-air mass was freed of sins instead of resorting to personal confessions. Protestant chaplains did an equally brisk business.

Jap kamikazes attacked all up and down the line that afternoon. Solid sheets of flak filled the sky as I crept up to my deckside port, determined to stay there no matter what. "They're going to sink this tub," I thought, "before we get to land tomorrow." As I lurked in the port I watched a low-hanging cloud strung along in front of the *Bolivar*. An aircraft carrier, later identified as the *Kitkun Bay,* was moving directly under it. A kamikaze darted out of the cloud, plummeting as if on a string into the deck of the carrier. Nothing happened when he hit, but a second later there was a flash, followed by the rumble of a great explosion. The smoking carrier was listing as we sailed by, having suffered numerous casualties with much of her insides shattered.

As I watched from deck, I was unaware that two bandsmen were trapped in a coffin-like hold on the *Bolivar*'s bottom. They had been working there but had failed to leave before the watertight compartment doors were slammed in preparation for the incoming attack. They could hear the ship's guns as well as its public address system. The announcer had given a running account of the attack on the carrier, then he screamed: "Here comes another one—he's after the *Bolivar*!" This was accompanied by the din of every gun on the ship. "He missed us!" gasped the announcer, but then shouted again: "He's hit the *Westralia*! He's hit the *Westralia*!" I rushed from my hideaway for a look, but the show was over. The kamikaze had skidded across the fantail of the Aussie ship, knocking the rudder loose. She was able to continue with the convoy. Meanwhile, as the two trapped musicians listened, every phobia possible was given birth or rebirth in their emotions. They were found later by surprised sailors after the attack ended. Trumpeter Chu Curtis allowed that he had sucked his stomach in so far he had developed piles on his navel.

As night fell the great convoy turned west toward China in an attempt to fool the enemy. Later it swung around to the east and entered Lingayen Gulf, an arm of the sea deeply penetrating Luzon's west coast. The waters of this gulf covered several hundred square miles, with a twenty-three-mile width along its southern beach area. The 14th Japanese Army had struck here through choppy seas during a rainy night in December, 1941. MacArthur rejected a night landing, his plans calling for the assault wave to hit the beaches precisely at 9:30 on the morning of January 9, 1945.

When I awoke the ship's eerie silence told me we had arrived. I was too nervous to eat so I joined other soldiers on deck. We were anchored four or five miles north of the beaches. An impressive armada was sprawled across the great gulf, a peaceful scene out of keeping with its purpose. I noticed the Southern Cross, glad to see something that had not changed. It hung alone in dawn's light to the southwest, over the long flat coastline where we would land. Wooded hills formed the western flank of the gulf, but to the east were large mountains, rising from grassy foothills along the coast. This was where the 6th and 43rd Divisions would land. I now wished I had wound up in the 43rd, for it seemed obvious to me that these beaches were not as important as those to the south. The 37th, in striking toward Manila, was sure to hit the enemy's main defensive line. We railside strategists agreed that another Anzio was in the making, fortunately unaware that our commanders saw things the same way!

Our reveries were shattered at 7:00 a.m. by the thunder of heavy guns. Plumes of debris and smoke jumped crazily out of the coastline as the fleet barrage gathered momentum. Broadsides from battlewagons and cruisers were soon joined by multiple rockets launched from LCIs, leaving blazing trails as they whooshed loudly to their targets. Road junctions and other likely targets twenty miles inland were being bracketed with heavy shells. Although it was reassuring to watch, I knew that it was going to take more than this to knock out many defenders dug in behind landing beaches stretching for fifteen miles.

"Now hear this: first wave man your boats!" I went to my assigned debarkation point, slung my carbine over my shoulder, and climbed down the rope netting to the waiting landing craft. It chugged away with some thirty men, joining other boats in our group. We circled until the many small groups assigned to the assault wave were in position, then headed south to the beaches.

A remarkable and inexplicable sense of well being settled over me as my boat bucked forward, kicking up salt spray. I knew—perhaps felt is a better word—that this would be an easy landing. I never doubted this feeling, and was irritated at the silent tenseness of older men as they stared blankly at the sides of the boat.

We passed directly by the squat rear of the *West Virginia*, a battleship sunk at Pearl Harbor but resurrected to deadly new life. Her gold-lettered nameplate inspired me with a sense of revenge, for a Carlisle boy had survived the attack, telling the town about it while on leave. She squatted back on her haunches as broadsides flamed from her sixteen-inch guns. The sea reflected her fiery breath, and I was amazed that I could see the four big shells in flight! They appeared as swiftly receding black dots in the sky, sounding like the jets of a later day as we moved on under them.

Somewhere between the *West Virginia* and the beach I had a strong urge to urinate, an urge I answered by climbing up beside our sailor chauffeur and pissing into the sea as we plunged along. I doubt that this has been done on many invasions, and I claim it as a probable first. As I surveyed the exciting drama unfolding on all sides, it almost seemed as if it had been staged expressly for me—at least, I was the only one enjoying it. "Piss on the Japs" may have been in the back of my mind, but our sergeant took a more realistic view when he noticed me: "Get your ass down here right now you damned fool—you'll attract enemy fire!" Everyone was glaring at me as I dropped to the deck, and I saw nothing more until we ground to a halt on a sand bar some thirty yards off shore. It was around 9:35 when our boat's flat front splashed down. We waded waist-deep and dripping out onto the wide, beautiful beaches of Luzon.

9. Down the Central Plains

Thousands of infantrymen from the 129th and 148th regiments were pouring over the beaches and into the terrain beyond. Where were the Japs? Was it a trick to get us committed and then open up? Bandsmen stood around trying to puzzle out this strange situation. Since nothing had arrived for us to unload, I went swimming in the surf. Tiring of this, I strolled over to the dunes, spotting my first souvenir, an attractive and shiny metal tube almost buried in the sand. As I pulled on it the sergeant gave me a violent pull backward, landing me on my butt. "What are you trying to do, get us all killed!" I winced at his next words: "That's a dud naval shell." I backed up, my anger vanishing in a series of profuse apologies for my stupidity.

Jap planes had been coming in out of the sun over the eastern mountains since early morning, but fighters from the Navy and the air force had so far shot them down. I wandered back to the two-acre fishponds beyond the dunes. As I stood there my gaze darted to a high-flying enemy plane directly above me. The sky blackened with flak as the entire fleet gunned at it. The doomed pilot made it through the flak, but hungry P-38 Lightnings pounced on him, sending him in flames to the ground. A frond from a palm tree dropped at my feet, and the fishpond suddenly dappled with splashes—the flak was falling! Choked with fear, I dived into the pond, digging furiously into its muddy sides. I had left my helmet on the beach. I cringed, halfway into the mud bank, until the heavy jagged pieces of shrapnel, any one of which could have killed me, stopped falling. First the dud shell and now this. I decided to get back to the beach before my beginner's luck ran out.

All of us worked hard unloading supply craft over long roller platforms to ever-growing stacks on the beach. During the day a rumor circulated that a work gang down the beach had struggled to unload a large wooden box. Thinking it a big weapon of some sort, they wrestled it across the rollers. The box split open when dropped, revealing a big piano inside. No one was ever able to account for this wild error in loading the ship, but another rumor soon held that it belonged to MacArthur. I never learned the truth of either rumor, but no extra rhythm was needed that day, for we worked our hearts out to supply our infantry as they rapidly advanced inland.

By nightfall the 37th and 40th Divisions had taken every objective, finding only a few scattered Japs. Trouble came only to the navy, for a kamikaze had ripped into a battleship in the gulf, and another had crashed into the top of an Aussie cruiser. The sun set on a perimeter averaging four miles deep and twenty miles wide. "Where are the Japs?"—that was the big question on every mind.

No one but General Tomoyuki Yamashita could have provided a complete answer to that question. As he revealed at war's end, after Japanese defeats on Leyte he had given up plans to defend the entire island of Luzon. Why not let the Yanks land, he reasoned? He lacked air superiority, sufficient fuel for his tanks, and faced a hostile native population. The best he could do, he decided, was to entangle as many enemy divisions as possible, prevent the use of airfields already on the island, and inflict heavy casualties—in short, he sought to delay the invasion of Japan.

With this in mind, Yamashita divided Luzon into three defense zones, each with a code name and each based on mountainous terrain. The Shobu Group area embraced all of northern Luzon, with Yamashita personally commanding its 152,000 men from mile-high Baguio, the cool "summer capital" of the Philippines. The second defensive group was located in west central Luzon, based in mountains overlooking Clark Field and the Central Plains, the latter being wide flatlands stretching from the Lingayen Gulf southward 110 miles to Manila. He assigned thirty thousand men to this, the Kembu Group. The Shimbu Group was responsible for the defense of all of southern Luzon, but most of its eighty thousand men were concentrated in the mountains east and northeast of Manila. The group included twenty thousand naval troops stationed near and in Manila, commanded by Admiral Sanji Iwabuchi. Yamashita's order to evacuate Manila as indefensible was carried out by the army during the landings at Lingayen, but the navy rejected this order, choosing instead to fortify and defend the city against whatever might come. What was coming was the American XIV Corps and the deadliest battle of the entire Pacific War in combined military and civilian deaths.

We were innocent of Yamashita's plans as we ate our rations at the end of a long day. Rudy and I dug roomy foxholes in the soft sand, emplacing our light machine gun. I lay there listening to the pulse of the surf, content with the balmy night and smug in having sensed an easy landing. I had never lived through a day as full of action as the one I was now losing to sleep.

Rudy and I shook ourselves out of our sandy foxholes the next morning. It was a beautiful day. We commented on this as we ate our K-rations, comparing Luzon's weather favorably with that of rainy Bougainville. The weather for the three-week campaign down the Central Plains was to be so perfect soldiers started claiming with conviction that "Old Dugout Doug even makes the weather bow to him!"

After eating I walked along a dike separating the rice paddies, emerging in the tiny town of Binmaley. I stood in a grove of trees behind a huge church. It had been built by the Spaniards some two hundred years before, but a battleship shell had ripped open its rear end. Climbing over the debris, I peered cautiously into the gloomy interior. A single bright shaft of sunlight streamed in from a shell hole high in a wall, lighting a Hammond organ sitting unscathed and unscratched atop a pile of debris. I chuckled to myself, writing later that "if this had been a statue of a saint, a miracle would have been proclaimed and a shrine started. But what can you do with something like a Hammond organ!"

By the time I got back to the beach the band was ready to move inland. Engineers had taken over the beach job, so we shouldered our weapons and slogged southward with division headquarters. Advertising signs seldom noticed in the States were pointed at with happy shouts—Texaco, Philco Radios, Black Draught-666. Veterans of the Solomons slapped each other on the back at this certain evidence of civilization. Some four miles down the road we entered a small town. Throngs of Filipino well wishers lined the street as we marched under bamboo arches covered with flowers and streamers. Shouts of "Welcome Joe!" came from happy faces on all sides. A beautiful Filipina suddenly blocked my path, putting a hand on my shoulder as her moist dark eyes met mine: "Welcome to the Philippines, blue eyes," her voice soft and very personal. I was pushed on by my laughing buddies, but I knew now that I was going to like this place. My first opinion of these lovely islands and friendly people never changed in the months ahead.

For the next two weeks the 37th Division, as if in payment for past hardships, probably enjoyed soldiering more than any other outfit in World War II. The Nips had failed to show up and we were hailed as conquering heroes by the Filipinos. Three days after landing we were twenty-nine miles down the broad Central Plains. As we hiked along, a murmur swept the column, causing us to look back. "My God, it's the Old Man himself!" we whispered as his jeep inched along the line of soldiers. No one could miss MacArthur's slouchy hat, with the egg salad on its brim, his open shirt collar, and his arms waving as he talked. He was in a jolly mood, chatting with his boys as he moved along. He neared us, his jeep pausing as he smiled and asked: "How are things going, boys?"

"Fine, General, fine!" His jeep moved on by as we shouted and waved at him. We were elated to see him in person, happy to know he was with us. Following his jeep was one bearing a general who had everyone's undivided respect, the Sixth Army's commander, Walter Krueger. Then came our own Uncle Bob, and this time we waved our weapons and cheered. We marched on with a lighter step, sure we had the best leaders anywhere.

By this time I had talked with a number of Filipinos, concluding with unquestioning faith that the Japs had been a hundred percent bad and the Filipinos a hundred percent good. I wrote home that "a priest told me that a 25 lb. sack of rice cost 5000 pesos in Jap currency; an undershirt 700 pesos. People in the cities starve as they can't grow their own food. The people had to bow to Jap soldiers, feed them, and work free. The Japs tortured and killed quite a few for holding out on them. The Quislings [traitors] always have painted houses, but the Filipino guerrillas took care of them as they have in France." I had yet to learn that no small number of Filipinos had initially welcomed the Japanese, albeit with misgivings.

My sense of values changed as the division advanced. I handed a Filipino barber a pack of cigarettes for a haircut, but Gabby Campbell, an older soldier, griped so much over this that I took back all but three of them: "You want to ruin everything?" he asked. It was already too late, for GIs felt foolish dickering over cigarettes, soap, or mosquito bars. GI soap was a surprisingly hot item, good for a dozen eggs or a big bag of *camotes,* the ubiquitous pale-fleshed sweetpotatoes. A mosquito bar brought fifteen American invasion dollars, or a free ride with one of the whores who began shadowing the division. We did not have to swap for the tasty sugarcane candy. It was pressed on us by admiring farmers along every trail or road. We winced in wonder as our tasteless C-rations were eagerly snapped up for fried chicken, rice dishes, bananas, mangoes, fresh eggs, and much else. Many civilians, however, did not have much to trade. One evening there was a long line of men, women and children at our field kitchen, each hopefully holding a large tropical leaf. "We ain't hungry, Sarge," we said, nodding toward the line. The mess sergeant smiled as he and his cooks filled each trembling leaf with S.O.S.—chipped beef on toast, but known to every soldier as "shit-on-a-shingle."

The Tuesday following our landing, January 16, Rudy Panol and I were split up. I was tagged to help man a 37mm antitank gun. Fears had mounted over the division's exposed left flank for no one knew the whereabouts of the shadowy Jap 2nd Armored Division. We had outrun everything to our east because the 6th and 43rd had run into stiff resistance from the Shobu Group shortly after landing. Yamashita had refused to follow our script, striking where least expected while ignoring the 37th and 40th as they cut a deep salient into the Central Plains.

Corporal Jimmy Mayfield of Headquarters Company welcomed me to his small high-velocity cannon. Jimmy was from Alliance, Ohio, twenty years old, and we liked each other from the start.

Private Mathias
on his nineteenth
birthday, May 23, 1944,
Camp Wheeler, Georgia.

The Kentucky Kavaliers, 1943. Frank Mathias is at left end of the sax section.

A Melanesian fiesta honoring the Buckeye Division. *Ohio Historical Society*

The Buckeye dance band plays at "Lowe's Bougainville," an outdoor theater.

Division mortarmen move up through the jungle. *Ohio Historical Society*

A Buckeye flamethrower in action on Bougainville. *Ohio Historical Society*

The deck of a troopship on its way to Luzon. *37th Veterans Association*

Men of the Lingayen Gulf
assault wave descend rope
netting to their landing
craft on January 9, 1945.
37th Veterans Association

Luzon's Central Plain from the coastal village of Binmaley.
Note shattered roof of the old Spanish church, where Mathias saw the
organ perched "miraculously" atop the rubble. *37th Veterans Association*

Eleanor Roosevelt chats with General Robert S. Beightler as they
stroll through 37th Division headquarters. *Ohio Historical Society*

General Douglas MacArthur pulls his jeep into division headquarters to confer with General Robert S. Beightler during the Luzon campaign. *37th Veterans Association*

The Battle of Manila. Intramuros is south of the Pasig River, under the densest plume of smoke; Old Bilibid prison, its buildings like the spokes of a wheel, is in left foreground; the U-shaped building left of the prison is Far Eastern University. *Ohio Historical Society*

The 148th's 3d battalion starts crossing the Pasig River at Malacanan Palace during the Battle of Manila. *37th Veterans Association*

A Buckeye tank rumbles through a 350-year-old Spanish gate into Intramuros. *37th Veterans Association*

A rare Japanese prisoner is brought to a 37th Division command post by Filipino guerrillas. *37th Veterans Association*

MacArthur's prewar home, the Manila Hotel, offers a shattered face to the world at the end of the Battle of Manila. *37th Veterans Association*

The Buckeye concert band, under Charles Hower, plays for liberated civilian internees at Santo Tomas University. Mathias is seated to the right of clarinet player David Briggs. *Ohio Historical Society*

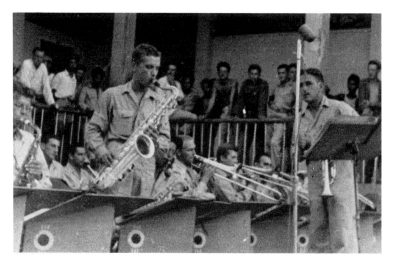

Mathias takes a ride on Charlie Barnet's "Washington Whirligig" as the Buckeye dance band, led by Clete Hennings, serenades GI patients at a Manila hospital in March, 1945.

A Japanese heavy mortar position pounded to rubble by 105mm shells.
37th Veterans Association

General Douglas MacArthur inspects repairs by 37th Division engineers on the
Manila Railroad. *Ohio Historical Society*

One of 100,000 Filipino civilians slaughtered by the Japanese in the Battle of Manila. Note rope-tied hands of corpse. *37th Veterans Association*

In the mountains of northern Luzon, infantrymen lie low until a Japanese roadblock can be knocked out. *37th Veterans Association*

Dead enemy soldiers, probably at Bayombong, where some 200 Japanese committed hara-kiri rather than surrender. *Ohio Historical Society*

A Buckeye unit in action in the Luzon mountains, probably near Baguio. *37th Veterans Association*

Buckeye combo at 129th Infantry's "Mosquito Bar," San Isidro, in May, 1945.
From left, Walter "Bus" Groves, Bruce Thomson, Ralph Freeman, Mathias,
Bill Rogers, George "Gabby" Campbell, and Gil Silvius.

A typical view from the bandstand as GIs dance with Filipina dates.
37th Veterans Association

One of several surrender ceremonies conducted by the 37th Division's staff in August, 1945. *37th Veterans Association*

General Robert Beightler (left) with some of the Japanese soldiers who surrendered to the 37th Division at the end of the war. *37th Veterans Association*

37th Division Band troops the line for final review, October, 1945.
Ohio Historical Society

Frank Mathias and Ed "Pappy" Harrington in downtown Manila,
December, 1945.

Starting that "Sentimental Journey" home! *37th Veterans Association*

Sergeant Mathias aboard the
U.S.S. *Marine Swallow,*
sailing for San Francisco.

Neither of us knew much about the thirty-seven, never having fired one, but we knew it would be a bother, for it would have to be towed behind trucks, jeeps, weapons carriers, or any other vehicle we could hitch-hike. At least we would ride, the small rubber-tired cannon bouncing along behind. Before long we dubbed our strange and troublesome weapon, the "Damn Thing."

Jimmy and I relaxed one evening after setting up our thirty-seven, its muzzle pointing to the dangerous east flank. A Filipino man approached us out of the twilight. He wore the usual white shorts and shirt, greeting us in a "Hello" thick with Spanish accent.

"I want sheet," he announced as he stopped alongside our gun.

"You're out of luck pardner," I responded. "We don't have any sheets; all we carry are blankets."

"I don't want blankets, I want sheet, onnerstand, sheet." He bobbed his head as he carefully pronounced each word.

He must be bullheaded, I thought, so I snapped back: "Damn it all, I said we don't have any sheets, only blankets, and if we did have sheets we don't have any beds to put them on."

"I no want sheet on bed, I want sheet on garden." He shifted his feet, waiting for a reply as a smile creased my face.

"You mean shit—you want shit on your garden."

"Yes sir, sheet, like I say, sheet on my garden." His gold teeth flashed in the setting sun as he smiled, seeing he had finally gotten through to two dumb Yankees.

"You want us to fertilize your crops, is that it?" Mayfield asked.

"Yes, you tell your buddies to be nice and come over and sheet on the garden tonight. Makes it all grow. I sell much stuff soon in Tarlac." He bent over and hoisted a large sack he had brought. "Here, I give you muchos mangoes for you and your buddies. They make you sheet good."

We promised we would do our best. He walked us over to a well kept garden with many rows of small vegetables, happily clapped his hands and left us. We passed the word around as well as the mangoes. Everyone laughed and agreed to get his garden off to a roaring start.

We were soon calling Filipinos "Flips," a natural twist of our untrained tongues. Tagalog was the major language of Luzon, and we soon picked up key phrases, saying *magandang dalaga* (you're pretty) to every giggling girl we met, pretty or not. *Magandang umaga* (good morning), *magandang hapon* (good afternoon), or *saan ka pupunta* (where are you going?) brought wide smiles any time we used them. A sentence that became useful later was *Nasaan ang mga hapon?*—"Where are the Japs?"

Although we lived closely with the people, we were convinced that the American way was best, and anything else was "a couple of bubbles off center." We chortled at the sight of peasant women naked from the waist up as they pounded clothing clean on rocks in streams. Old women smoked cigars two inches in diameter and over a foot long. "They smoke them backwards," I wrote in astonishment, "putting the firey end in over their teeth, then knocking the ashes off inside their mouths!" "Are you seeing things?" my mother asked in a later letter, perhaps worrying that the hot sun had finally done me in. I assured her I was all right, adding that "these Filipinos wash their teeth with sand from the creeks. It gets on your nerves to watch them."

I liked the people, however, noting that "they are very bright and intelligent. They are nice looking, spick and span as their depleted (by the Japs) possessions will allow. They dressed up in their carefully saved 3 yr old Sunday clothes to meet the Americans. The men all wear rakish straw hats, polo shirts, slacks and two tone shoes when dressed up. When working they wear sandals, shorts, straw hats. . . . The people really felt Jap oppression. Some wore burlap sacks and were in a bad way." There was no doubt that I was enjoying the campaign, for I concluded this letter of January 17 by noting that "I am really enjoying myself here in comparison to New Guinea. When I was at Buna we never had anything to see but jungles and Fuzzy Wuzzies." By this time my parents knew I was on Luzon, for they subscribed to the Cincinnati *Times-Star.* Although our censors clipped any reference to our location, the newspapers back home followed the Buckeye Division in detail!

Swarms of new fighter planes we had never seen began supporting us from the huge new air base at Mangaldan. These rakish North American P-51 Mustangs tarnished our long love affair with the Corsairs, the reliable hallmark fighter of the South Pacific. Although the Mustang justly earned its ratings as the best fighter of the Second World War, some of the pilots left much to be desired: "Not long after moving inland we set up house in a small Lingayen town. We were sleeping peacefully when we heard sirens, a roar, and machine guns. One of our own planes got mixed up in the moonlight and buzzed up and down the highway tearing up a convoy of our trucks. I was out of the house in a second and into an armored bulldozer parked in front." The pilot's mistake had tragic consequences and enraged the veterans, who said with seething contempt in their voices: "You'd never have caught a Marine pilot pulling such a damned stupid stunt!" Maybe not, but worse was coming.

A few days later we watched as Mustangs dive-bombed a village tucked into a copse of trees. Debris caromed skyward as 500-pound bombs dug up the terrain in giant blasts. They swooped, dived, and returned like crop dusters, but they were dusting everything with steel and lead instead of paris green. Unknown to the careless pilots, our own soldiers had moved into the village and were being killed and wounded by the attack. Unofficial sentiment now swept the division: "We'll kill the dumb bastards if they do it again." Fortunately they learned from their errors; it did not happen again.

Beautiful days piled on one another as we went our unopposed way. The rice harvest was in, and I described the Central Plains as "closely resembling flat Ohio farmland, if you can imagine a few palm trees and bamboo patches along the roads. It looks like a wheat field after harvest, for the rice is cut and stacked like straw at home. The stubble hides the little dikes running through it. Carabaos, or water buffaloes provide the farmers with draft animals."

"Have you two zeroed that gun in?" a lieutenant asked us late one afternoon.

"No sir," we replied, then wished we had lied.

"Hell fire, men, get that thing lined out and ready to go. What do you think would happen if Jap tanks broke in here this afternoon?"

Jimmy and I hated to think of what would happen, for we barely knew how to load the "Damn Thing." But orders were orders, so we lined up on a nipa hut under a railroad embankment some five hundred yards away, The embankment would stop our shell, and the hut was obviously empty. Besides, its one, small, open window made a black target against the yellow-green of its bamboo and nipa palm sides. We adjusted the thirty-seven as best we knew, then let fly an armor-piercing shell.

There was no doubt that the small shell had slapped through the hut, for a Filipino family began tumbling out like clowns from a small car in a circus tent. We were terrified, running in their direction as they shouted and jabbered. They accepted our profuse apologies, admitting that they had been told to move to safer regions, but had instead decided to sweat it out at home. After returning, I turned to Jimmy: "I never had to zero my saxophone in, so why fool with this thing?" He agreed, but neither of us smiled, frustrated with a situation where such a thing could happen in the first place.

Several evenings later we emplaced our thirty-seven along the same railroad embankment, but several miles further south. Across the embankment, which rose some fifteen feet above the dry rice paddies, a fire fight was under way between the reorganized Philippine army and the *Hukbalahap*. The Huks, as everyone called them, had chatted with us at times. They were fighting to get land away from the rich landlords. According to them, most Filipinos lived in poverty. Dividing up the land would remedy this; besides, they always added, "why should one man own a hundred thousand acres while a hundred thousand of his countrymen owned nothing?" We had no answer for this, most of us concluding that the Huks had a good point. They could sense our approval, and had no quarrel with us.

Carbines, Jap rifles, Enfields, Nambu machine guns and any other weapons the Huks could lay hands on blasted away across the tracks. The army replied in kind. Mayfield and I were unafraid, knowing that both sides wished us well in our battle against the Japs. It was strictly a family fight going on over on the adjacent hundred acres. I jerked my head to the rear as I heard something behind me.

"Pssssssst Joe; hey Joe." The whispered voice was followed by movement behind a clump of bamboo. Jimmy and I both had our carbines on him as he walked slowly and carefully into view, both hands open to prove his peaceful intentions.

"What's up?" Mayfield asked him, slipping quickly around to one side to check out the bamboo thicket.

"You hear battle across track?"

"Sure, how could we miss it?"

"I'm Huk; you know about Huk?"

"Yeah," Jimmy replied, "we know about you Huks. We like you but we like the Flip soldiers too. What are you doing here?"

"We want to borrow your cannon. It would be a big help—mebbe we win with it—can we borrow please the cannon?"

"The cannon!" we both gasped, "you want to borrow the cannon!"

Of course he wanted to borrow the cannon and repeated the request. Jimmy and I started laughing: "We'd like to let you have the son-of-a-bitch—one way to get rid of it—but we'd catch hell if we let it get away from us."

"No no no no," our friend said, "I don't want you in trouble. I bring cannon back early in the morning before you leave; maybe only shoot a little cannister so nobody even miss shells."

As we argued with the Huk we unconsciously moved up the embankment, standing by a large heap of logs on the tracks, probably put there by the Nips. A slapping sound awoke us as a string of bullets went by and into the logs, sending us rolling for cover. I got up scared and mad. "Get out of here before you get us killed and ain't nobody can have that thirty-seven." The Huk understood, cast a longing eye at the little cannon, shrugged, then slipped silently back into the thicket.

Somewhere along its path inland the band picked up a mascot. A small, swaybacked little dog had adopted a tuba player, following him everywhere and attracting attention by his disreputable appearance. Before long he was inducted into the band and named Douglas MacArthur, but called "Dugout Dog," for short. Dugout was too feisty for his own good, becoming a casualty during the Battle of Manila. It was even money whether a Jap bullet had done him in or whether he had been eaten by hungry people in the city. (We mourned his loss, but picked up a monkey, which stayed with us to the end.)

In addition to our new mascot, the band was sporting flashy new watchbands made by ex-jewelers in headquarters company. These bands were made of very special material, as I revealed in a letter home. "I saw my first Jap Zero up close—it was nearly intact and I climbed up in it. It must be more fun to fly than anything I can imagine. What a plane! Impressed! It was soon sliced up for watch bands. I got one made from the piece cut out of the rising sun on its side. It cost more than one from other spots."

Jap field rations, however, were not as impressive as their Zeros. I found some and tried them out. The Jap soldier needed a minimum

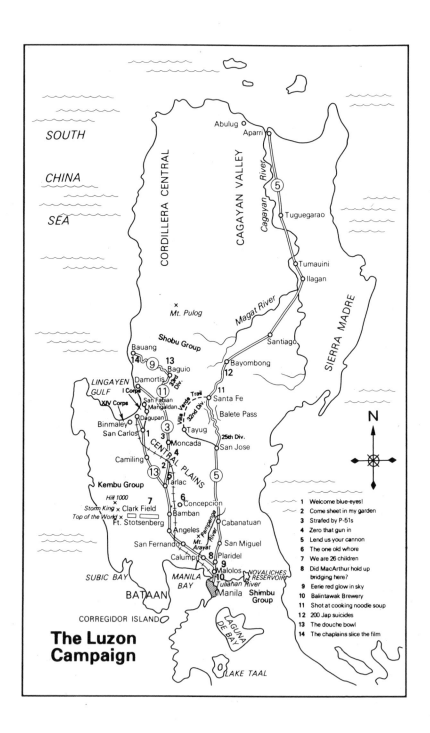

The Luzon Campaign

SOUTH CHINA SEA

CORDILLERA CENTRAL

CAGAYAN VALLEY

SIERRA MADRE

Cagayan River

Abulug ○
Aparri ●

⑤

Tuguegarao ○

Tumauini ○
Ilagan ○

× Mt. Pulog

Magat River

Shobu Group

Santiago ○

Bauang ○
⑭ ⑨ ⑬ Baguio ○
Damortis ○ Bayombong ○
⑫

LINGAYEN GULF
I Corps
⑪ Villa Verde Trail
32nd Div. ⑪ Santa Fe
XIV Corps San Fabian Mangaldan Balete Pass
× Dagupan ③
Binmaley ① Tayug
San Carlos ④
Moncada 25th Div.
Camiling ⑬ San Jose
② ⑤
Tarlac

Kembu Group
Hill 1000
× Storm King × Clark Field ⑦ Concepcion
Top of the World × Bamban
Ft. Stotsenberg ⑥
Angeles Cabanatuan
× Mt. Arayat
San Fernando ○ San Miguel
Calumpit ⑧ Plaridel
⑨
SUBIC BAY Malolos NOVALICHES RESERVOIR
⑩
MANILA *Tuliahan River*
BAY Manila Shimbu Group
BATAAN
CORREGIDOR ISLAND ○
LAGUNA DE BAY

N

LAKE TAAL

1 Welcome blue-eyes!
2 Come sheet in my garden
3 Strafed by P-51s
4 Zero that gun in
5 Lend us your cannon
6 The one old whore
7 We are 26 children
8 Did MacArthur hold up bridging here?
9 Eerie red glow in sky
10 Balintawak Brewery
11 Shot at cooking noodle soup
12 200 Jap suicides
13 The douche bowl
14 The chaplains slice the film

of two and one-half pounds of rice per day, but this did not always come in the familiar white grain for cooking. Field rations were often in the form of puffed rice, pressed tightly into small blocks. These were augmented with cubes of sugar soaked in cod liver oil. They seemed like punk fare to me, but the Nips fought effectively on such rations, picking up poultry and fruit along the way. They were far better than Aussie sheepy shagnasty.

The fun-and-games campaign down the Central Plains continued. The next evening Mayfield and I set up our gun at one of the angles of a street intersection in a pretty little town named Concepcion. We were downtown, amidst a mixture of two-story, concrete and stucco businesses and homes. They were nicely painted in whites and light blues, with typical airy porches overhanging the street and many-paned windows swinging in and out. We decided to sleep in the vacant home next to our position, each of us standing alternate four-hour shifts of guard duty during the night. Nice beds with springy bamboo slats were upstairs, as well as a kitchen with utensils and a charcoal pit. We commented on this, puzzled that anyone with such a nice home would use something as primitive as charcoal. Papers left behind by the owner told us that we were in "the home of a prominent provincial agriculturist—a glorified county agent."

The sun was setting as we finished a meal of mud-baked *camotes* and hot C-rations. We agreed that charcoal was not bad for cooking such as that, then went downstairs to our sand-bagged position. Our attention quickly turned to a line of perhaps twenty GIs across the street.

"Wonder what's up?" Mayfield asked, studying the line.

"Looks like a movie line," I ventured, but soon decided a crap game must be in progress. "They keep filing into the building while others come out."

One of the soldiers stepped out of the open door and walked toward us out of the gathering dusk. We stopped him and asked him the score.

"Aw hell!" We waited for him to say more, studying the look of disgust on his face. "They've got a sore and sleazy old whore back there in a little room and these nuts are waiting to bang her. I couldn't stomach the sight—God, what a mess!" He walked on, shaking his head.

Jimmy and I watched the scene with conflicting emotions of shame, rage, pity, and confusion. Some of the guys were from division headquarters. Nearly all of the ones we could identify were married men. We pondered our band's "philosophers," who held that deprived married men were much more sex-crazy than the often-accused bachelors. We also laughed at the town's name, this in light of what was going on. Later, when I read *All Quiet on the Western Front,* this scene in Concepcion flashed back into my mind, for a very similar scene is described by Erich Remarque. Perhaps the line in Concepcion was but the tail end of a similar line stretching back through every war in history. The real "whore" was war itself, not some poor woman in a steamy brothel.

We lingered several days at Concepcion. Maybe our officers needed time to put together the pieces of this puzzling campaign. In any event, Jimmy and I gladly accepted invitations to eat with local families. "I was out twice to people's houses," I wrote home in late January. "Their names were Senador Wyangco and Tan Ye Sen. They had large families, as all Filipinos do, and treated us like heroes. . . . We passed out those good American cigaretts they go for so much and the family musicians serenaded us. We ate roast pig called letchown [*lechon*] and it was delicious. I don't know where that pig came from!" Pigs had become as scarce during the Jap years on Luzon as they became during Sherman's stay in Georgia!

While walking around Concepcion I admired "the most intricate network of enemy positions I had ever dreamed of. They excavated such positions under the stilted concrete or brick buildings in what we would call 'crawl space'." Although the enemy had left without a fight, his excellent positions made me think. Infantry alone would take huge casualties before such fortifications; thus I was glad our army had superior tanks, artillery, and air power. But once taken, the land still had to be held by men on it—infantry. These nineteen-year-old ruminations came back to me during the Vietnam War, a time when an enemy nearly equaled American firepower, but above all he was able to put a continual stream of men back on the land. There was truth in a statement repeated by many GIs: "If the Japs had our equipment we'd still be fighting back on Guadalcanal!"

By January 23 the 37th had covered seventy easy miles in from the Lingayen Gulf. We were forty miles north of Manila. I Corps to our left had met sharp resistance from the first, thus we had forged ahead to the extent that our left flank was exposed for about fifty-three miles. Patrol reports began indicating that the Japs were in defensive positions at Clark Field, a giant air base just southwest of us. I was of course ignorant of any of this, still "having a ball," I wrote home. The "ball" was near its end, and the Cinderella aspects of our advance would quickly turn into a rotten pumpkin called War.

General Walter Krueger by this time held a powerful deck of Sixth Army cards. He was ready to gamble. He had Griswold's XIV Corps, composed of the 37th and 40th Divisions, wheeling along Route 3 to Clark Field. Since the newly arrived XI Corps was pushing across the Bataan peninsula and tying up Jap forces to his west, and since the 25th Division had left its reserve role to aid the 6th in its fight along Route 8 to the east, why not take Clark Field and at the same time keep elements of the 37th moving south toward Manila? It would keep the enemy off balance. It was worth a try. Besides, reinforcements would arrive at Lingayen on January 27: 1st Cavalry Division, 32nd Division and 112th RCT. He would have them if things did not work out. If the Jap 2nd Armored Division finally showed its hand, Krueger now had the cards to trump it.

Clark Field and Fort Stotsenberg, a nearby army base, were defended by the Kembu Group, its purpose being to deny the air field to Yank planes. Awaiting the 37th and 40th Divisions were eighty-five hundred combat troops and thousands of men in auxiliary units. They were well armed with tanks and artillery, and infantry with automatic weapons was dug into the surrounding heights like beetles under the bark of a tough old tree. The flat terrain of the base itself was covered by murderous fields of fire. Minefields, made by burying aerial bombs nose up, their triggers awaiting unwary heels, wheels or treads, made the entire area treacherous.

General MacArthur, with his usual flair for showmanship, and a continual wild optimism concerning the Luzon campaign, issued a communique on January 27 stating that Clark Field and its surrounding areas had been secured. This was the day the savage five-day battle began, the men hoping to live up to Dugout Doug's communique.

Mayfield and I were off on a far flank of this operation. Some officer must have heard of the incompetents manning the antitank gun, for we were taken off the Damn Thing and put behind a light machine gun. We were told to keep any intruders out of our area of rice paddies, then left alone. Neither of us was sure of where we were, or of the location of division headquarters. Things were moving rapidly. We could hear the distant din of battle as the 129th and the 145th regiments began the attack on Clark Field. The 160th from the 40th division was aiding them. We were confused as to our role, so we decided to improve our position. Rice straw was thrown over a camouflage net, then lifted on a pole above our machine gun. It looked like a straw sack. We were proud of our machine gun nest, but worried a bit as an artillery barrage flashed and bit into the mountain above us.

The enemy had excellent prepared positions in the high ground. They mounted counterbattery fire against the 6th, 135th and 136th Artillery Battalions of the Buckeye Division, knocking out several guns and inflicting casualties. It also stopped our infantry—this after two tanks had been knocked out by mines. The attack continued, however, and by nightfall the division had deeply penetrated the Clark Field-Fort Stotsenberg area. To our right, the 40th Division's 160th regiment had moved along the Bambam River to the base of the mountains. Jimmy and I were not far from this river.

As Mayfield and I warily assessed the events to our front, we noticed life in a nearby nipa hut. Two children ran over and started chatting, as if this were no more than a pleasant afternoon on the farm. "How many are in the hut?" we asked with worried impatience.

"Only fourteen are here now," said the barefoot girl.

"Only fourteen!" we both exclaimed—"You mean there are more?"

"Oh yes, sir; we are twenty-six in all, but the older ones don't live with us now. Mother made them leave."

"You don't mean all of you have the same mother, do you?" Mayfield asked in unbelief.

"Yes sir, all twenty-six." The young boy pointed proudly to a slender woman standing on the bamboo ladder leading into the stilted hut. We looked at her, then at one another, shaking our heads in admiration at such a feat. After we talked with her a while, it was obvious she had no intention of leaving. She would stick it out, no matter what, and her husband agreed. Their decision, added to the similar affair with our cannon shell, made us believe that civilians often die victims of their own ignorance in a battle zone.

The battle in the mountains above us ground on through January 31. Colonel John D. Frederick's 129th RCT finally took a crucial height known as Top of the World, losing four hundred men before it was over. This thousand-foot upthrust commanded the flatlands beyond, and had to fall before planes could use Clark Field. The Japs used scores of automatic weapons, point blank cannon fire, and tanks on the lower levels. Grenades were pitched back and forth like baseballs from ravine to ravine on the high slopes. The doughboys prevailed, however, and on January 31 General Krueger raised the stars and stripes over nearby Fort Stotsenberg, an army base adjacent to Clark Field. As the flag reached the top of the pole, every Jap cannon in range zeroed in on it, splattering the ceremonies with steel and wood splinters. A shell landed in a gun pit of the 6th Field Artillery Battalion, starting a fire that was extinguished even as it burned into ammunition cases. The Japs, of course, were still back on the far ridges. They had lost twenty-five hundred killed, with only ten taken prisoner, a good indication of the tenacity of their defense. Although the Kembu Group was still intact, and a force to reckon with, enough progress had been made to free one division for the drive on Manila. That division was the 37th.

10. The Battle of Manila

We privates knew as well as MacArthur that a speedy capture of Manila would best ensure the survival of thousands of American prisoners interned there. The enemy must be rushed and kept off balance until our people could be rescued. Everyone hoped Manila would escape destruction, for we had heard of the beauty of the Pearl of the Orient. We also relished the thought of city lights after our time in South Pacific jungles.

MacArthur decided to rush the city, even at the risk of going a bit too fast. Our 148th regiment was started south along Highway 3 even as its sister regiments were busy at Clark Field. When the 148th started south on January 27, it was taking the first step of what would culminate in an all-out race between the 37th and 1st Cavalry divisions to enter Manila first—the "Great Manila Derby." The 1st Cavalry had landed at Lingayen on January 28. MacArthur unleashed its tanks in a hell-for-leather drive on Manila on January 31. By this time the entire 37th was on the road to Manila, but he thought this "flying column" could rush the Japs more effectively than infantry, and would be better able to break into prisoner-of-war compounds. On the same day, the 11th Airborne Division dropped south of Manila, but stood little chance of beating the two divisions racing across the northern flatlands. The rank and file did not know it yet, but the great race was on.

The race for Manila developed rapidly during the first four days of February. As the cavalrymen left northern Luzon on their drive south, Buckeye foot soldiers were already closing on Plaridel, a small town sitting near the crucial junction of Highways 3 and 5. These two roads ran parallel down the east and west sides of the Central Plains, meeting at Plaridel to form one highway for the remaining twenty miles into Manila. It was an obvious spot for the Japs to throw up a powerful roadblock, which they did, forcing the 148th to kill 350 of them in a two-day fight before breaking through. This delay, greatly aggravated earlier by the delay of bridging material for crossing the wide Pampanga River at Calumpit, made it possible for a lucky 1st Cavalry Division on Saturday, February 3, to beat the Buckeyes into Manila by several hours.

The 1st Cavalry had unbelievable luck at a bridge over the gorge of the Tuliahan River, just south of Novaliches. The Japs had the bridge mined and the fuse to a powerful charge of dynamite sizzling when a naval officer from a fleet bomb-disposal unit showed up, ran out on the bridge and cut the burning fuse. The same officer then threw the mines over the side and into the river below. Had this not happened, the cavalrymen would have had at least a 24-hour delay, and the 37th would have garnered the big black headlines accorded the winners of the "Manila Derby." As it was, the navy should have been given half the credit!

We simply threw up our hands in the face of such luck. But we chortled in glee the next night when the cavalrymen were not able to defend the Tuliahan bridge, and the Nips blew it, thereby trapping the cavalry's flying column down at Santo Tomás with the 3,768 internees. It fell to the 37th Division to rescue the rescuers, thus bringing a safe end to years of internment for the civilians, and red faces for General William C. Chase's cavalrymen.

The loss of the Manila Derby became a sore spot, nagging the division's pride. It was jokingly held that the cavalrymen faced their only real opposition from the 37th MPs, who tried to misguide them as they closed on the city. I wrote home on March 19 that "the 37th did a lot of fighting recently that other divisions got credit for. The papers played up the sensational advance of the 1st Cavalry. They never said however that the ground they advanced over had already been passed through, captured, or cleared by the 37th. Who couldn't ride over fine highways when the other fellow has done the fighting."

A bitter rumor, widely circulated and fervently believed, was that MacArthur had purposely held up delivery of the missing sections of the Calumpit bridge in order to put the cavalrymen in position to win the race. Why? "He secretly hates Beightler's guts for his having outscored him at the Army War College," I wrote, echoing a widely held canard. Moreover, it was said that "Doug could not stand the thought of having a national guard division beat a regular army outfit at anything, especially a crucial race for glory into his old hometown."

The truth about these charges may never be known. But the actions of MacArthur in other areas and times reveal that he could be petty, and not at all above such manipulations as those he was accused of by the soldiers of the 37th. Whether they were true or not, we believed the accusations, and so did our artillerymen. When they got within range of the Manila Hotel, they may have taken revenge on one of its owners and former lodgers—MacArthur! During the battle within the city I spotted my Carlisle classmate, Soda Shrout, a sergeant with the 140th Field Artillery Battalion. "Every time we traverse by Dugout Doug's hotel," Soda said, "we lay one in for effect!" Soda, of course, may have been joking, but the fact remains that the hotel was riddled with shell holes. Although MacArthur visited it with a patrol from the 37th, he never, so far as I know, accused anyone of treating it any worse than the numerous other shell-riddled buildings.

The approach to Manila was an exciting time for every GI. From the north, Manila started growing along the highway with string towns interspersed with fields, bamboo thickets, and builtup areas, finally displaying solid commercial zones found only in major cities. Highway 3 turned into Rizal Avenue, indicating that we had arrived. We hardly dared believe we were nearing a goal that had seemed impossible just under a month ago when we stepped ashore. The 110 miles had been covered in unbelievable time. The city was a believable goal for us, not just another dank jungle or "vital airstrip," but a great city of nearly a million people. We knew that thousands of our fellow Americans were within the city, hoping and praying with clenched fists that nothing would go wrong during the last few hours before their rescue.

The night before we entered Manila, the bandsmen (we were still part of headquarters defense platoon) spent the night in a small town north of the city. As we marched into the town, taking over vacant homes for sleeping quarters, an eerie red glow became noticeable along the southern horizon. The Japs had started burning supply depots along the Manila docks and storage areas. This was the beginning of the end of central Manila.

Sunday, February 4, found us hiking toward the Manila city limits. Our eagerness to enter the city was sidetracked by shouts of "beer! beer! beer!" The entire column broke, running toward a huge building with a sign on top: Balintawak Brewery. As we neared we saw a scene unique in the annals of the bejungled Pacific War. Soldiers were sloshing helmets full of beer over their heads and any other heads nearby. Others were drinking greedily, as if this mirage might vanish into the tropic air; and some simply sprawled out in the liquid, which was an inch or so deep on the brewery floor. They lay there like cats under a cow's udder, their open mouths the targets for streams of beer spurting through bullet holes in the vats. The first men inside had shot the vats up, not knowing where the spigots were. One of the hallmarks of the coming battle was the presence of this beer. It was in lister bags instead of the lemony "battery acid," carried in most canteens, as often as not in five-gallon water cans, and more than a few water-cooled machine guns had jackets full of Balintawak beer. If the Japs had poisoned it, much of the Buckeye Division would have gone down the drain that Sunday afternoon.

Balintawak beer was fine, though still a bit green. Downtown, however, was the great San Miguel brewery, still untapped. It was rumored to be owned by MacArthur, but this was not held against him. Surely the artillery would spare such a monument of civilization. It did, targeting everything nearby and blowing it out at a record clip. But the brewery came through as unscathed as the capitol back in Columbus.

It was the fourth day of February. Division headquarters troops went south on Rizal Avenue to the Ang Tibay shoe factory, which would serve as Beightler's command center during the coming battle. At the southwest corner of this large, ochre-colored building, Mayfield and I set up our machine gun in an abandoned Japanese blockhouse constructed of sod slabs.

Meanwhile, in downtown Manila, the civilian internees and their cavalry rescuers were trapped when the Nips destroyed the bridge at Novaliches. Beightler sent the 148th into their España Street neighborhood to reestablish supply lines and provide a force adequate to counter a Jap change of mind. This done, elements of the 148th rushed a mile south to Old Bilibid prison, located at Quezon Boulevard and Azcarraga Street. Some fourteen hundred civilian and military prisoners, including some survivors of the infamous Bataan Death March, were inside hoping for rescue. Most were in pitiful condition. They could hear the crackle of small arms fire outside, and smell and see the flames and smoke of burning buildings near the prison. Many of them were puzzled, having been kept ignorant of events. As the first Buckeyes broke into the gloomy prison, some of the prisoners began talking to them in German, confused by the German-style pot helmets, which had been adopted by the United States after their capture. Germans were all right, they thought, for judging from the shooting going on outside the Japs and Nazis were no longer on good terms. Rescue was rescue, no matter the source. But they were overjoyed to learn that their rescuers were from the Buckeye State and not from Berlin.

Great fires were now blazing in buildings around the prison, threatening to engulf it. Snipers had crept in, taking a toll. There was no time to waste. Every available truck from the 37th and 1st Cavalry was commandeered and flung into an all-out effort to save the prisoners.

Many of the trucks from Bilibid unloaded their emaciated prisoner-of-war cargoes near division headquarters, in Manila's Grace Park district. They were in woeful condition, some without arms, others missing legs, all of them suffering from malnutrition. After censorship was lifted, I wrote home that "the people we met from the prisoner of war camps often had beri-beri or some horrible skin disease. I talked to a number of them. Beri-beri is a pretty bad disease to see. Swollen legs that seem ready to burst open; after laying down awhile the watery stuff runs back up into the body from the legs and causes awful aches and pains. Old men as thin as skeletons had legs shaped like Popeye. Pretty bad sight to see." Mental disease was present, for some just sat and stared the time away; others blabbed rather incoherently. Our cooks and medics cared for them until they could be sent to fully equipped hospitals. All of us did the best we could for them, now more certain than ever of the bestial quality of the enemy.

One prisoner was in better shape than the others, telling a story I recorded in a letter home. Early in the war he had been sent to a small work camp in northern Luzon. The prisoners did repair work on roads and bridges—a miniature version of the later tale, *Bridge on the River Kwai,* but with a happier ending. The Jap officer in charge told each prisoner upon arrival: "You do your work, stay out of my hair, and I'll stay out of yours. You can't swim back to America, so make the best of it. Give me any trouble, though, and it will be the last you ever give me." The officer probably hoped to avoid assignment to a battle zone through peaceful and efficient road and bridge work. In any event, the prisoners took him at his word, putting in a day's work and then returning either to their camp or to the homes of Filipino friends in nearby villages. They led a fairly decent life until the Leyte invasion upset the applecart, bringing their internment at Bilibid.

Manila was now surrounded, the 37th holding the northern areas, the 1st Cavalry the east, and the 11th Airborne cutting of Jap retreat to the south. But what was this city we were attacking? Why was it important, and what was its past? I only knew that it was a large place and that Americans had to be rescued. But it was much more than that. It started as an ancient Tagalog village, was taken over by Spain in 1571, and between that date and American entry in 1898, it rose as center of the Spaniards' far eastern empire. Spain ruled from behind the thick walls of Intramuros, a walled city running along the south side of the Pasig River and adjoining Manila Bay. The deep Pasig River split the growing city into northern and southern halves.

Following the Spanish American War, the United States subdued Manila and the Philippines, making these islands part of an American empire. Much new building was done south of the Pasig, as huge government buildings constructed of steel-reinforced concrete arose. (These were going to be easy to defend and costly to take, when the battle reached them.) North of the Pasig River, a great commercial district lay in the west-central area, with movies, restaurants, large retail stores, and many factories. Toward the bay front lay the Tondo District, Manila's most populous, occupied by workers of all sorts and burdened with much substandard housing and narrow streets. As one moved east from the business area, better housing and wealthier areas appeared. And on the north shore of the Pasig, in the center of town, sat the Filipino White House. Malacanan Palace had been the center of government for both Spanish and American governors-general. Finally, off to the west lay vital Manila Bay and the great docking and port areas, with cranes, shipyards, lengthy piers, and other installations. The city ran for some nine miles north and south along the bay, inland perhaps five miles, with a total built-up area of over a hundred square miles. The cityscape was flat, although it did slope perceptibly from the north down toward the river.

The city entered by Sixth Army forces in 1945 probably had some seven hundred thousand inhabitants left, out of a normal population of over a million. Judging from what was to come, those who fled the city before the battle had either great luck or great wisdom going for them. Their beautiful city was to face destruction more dreadful than that of any other city during World War II, except for Warsaw and Stalingrad. And the Japanese sailors who made up the bulk of the seventeen-thousand-man defense force slaughtered an estimated hundred thousand civilians. These deaths, added to those of some eighteen thousand Japanese and Yankee soldiers, make the Battle of Manila by far the deadliest battle of the Pacific war. It was also unique in being the only battle of that war fought in and for a major city.

MacArthur had fully expected the Japs to declare Manila an open city and move out. It was the logical thing to do. It was what General Yamashita wanted to do. He reasoned that it would be impossible to feed a million people in a besieged city, that most of the structures were highly inflammable, and that the city's flat terrain would require tremendous strength to defend it. But neither MacArthur nor Yamashita had counted on the Jap navy and its weird hatred for the Jap army. Rear-Admiral Sanji Iwabuchi was not subject to Yamashita's control since he was a naval commander, and he is the man responsible for Manila's destruction.* Despite Yamashita's pleas, he determined to fight to the last in defense of

*Robert Ross Smith, *Triumph in the Philippines* (Washington, 1963), pp. 243-46.

the city. He ordered aircraft stripped of cannon and machine guns, sunken ships in the harbor of their heavy weapons, and using the already adequate supplies of weapons and ammunition at hand, he built up formidable strong points in each major structure south of the Pasig. Each floor of these reinforced concrete buildings had fire slits and sandbagged guns, each covered from other floors, buildings, and barricades. Tunnels connected many of these positions, and mine fields were laid with cunning and care throughout the southern city. Automatic weapons abounded, backed by huge naval guns and the heaviest mortars yet to appear in the Pacific war. There were practically no tactics. Iwabuchi assigned specific areas of defense to subordinate commanders, and they were to hold strong points and use demolition to wreck buildings and block streets leading to these points. As a final retreat, they had Intramuros, the old Spanish walled city, with its walls sloping up from a base thickness of forty feet. The seventeen thousand defenders intended to die, and they also intended to take as many Yankees and Filipinos as they possibly could to death with them.

Some miles to the north of the Pasig River, in an abandoned Japanese blockhouse, I sat as Iwabuchi set up his defenses and the prisoners at Bilibid scrambled aboard the trucks and out of the growing conflagration downtown. I confess that I had no knowledge of what was going on anywhere except in my blockhouse at the dusty intersection of two small, dirt streets behind the southwest corner of the Ang Tibay Shoe Factory. Mayfield and I had set our light machine gun on a wide board laid in the gun port of the small blockhouse. Something ran out from under the board, down my fatigue pants and on across the floor. "It's a scorpion!" Jimmy cried. I leaped back, quivering with disgust. One had bit a friend of mine in New Guinea, with painful effects. This was a small one, but some of the small ones were worse than the big ones. We gingerly looked the place over, finding that the crumbling old sod blocks and grassy clumps were as thick with scorpions as the back of an old hound with fleas. We cursed our luck but moved across the dirt street and sandbagged our gun under the overhang of a deserted frame building. That night the Japs threw banzai attacks against Highway 3 north of us, but Jimmy and I escaped with nary a shot fired–our ignorance of this was bliss.

By the time we had finished our position and eaten our rations, it was getting dark. Division headquarters was in the shoe factory, so I wandered in, up some stairs, and out onto the roof. I simply followed the crowd, for scores of soldiers were there watching as Manila burned. Fires downtown were now far beyond any control, and Japanese demolitions were adding to them by the minute. Great, leaping gouts of fire erupted steadily from burning oil and gasoline storage tanks, casting flickering light against the smoke filled, copperish clouds above the dying city. We were looking several miles south as if from the rim of a very shallow basin down to its center—the downtown area. Shimmering sheets of flame swirled up from hundreds of small and large buildings throughout the commercial district north of the Pasig. A sullen roar emanated from the hellish scene, reaching our ears along with the stuttering sounds of automatic weapons firing as infantrymen retreated from positions overtaken by the spreading conflagration. Our building trembled as ever larger blasts went off, ignited by the Japs or triggered by great burning sections of the fire which, with seeming lives of their own, careened upward away from the central blaze, only to drop like burning drapes over untouched buildings, igniting them also. Jimmy and I watched throughout the night, taking our usual turns of guard duty on the machine gun.

General Krueger's tactical planning for Manila makes good sense when I read it now in U.S. Army historical accounts. It did not make sense at the time to a nineteen-year-old. Krueger saw the necessity of quickly seizing all dams, lakes, pumping stations, and electrical installations. Without these, sanitation problems would soon get out of hand for the civilian population. But I was puzzled at all the action thrown at such places as Novaliches Dam, the Balara Water Filters (what in the hell are they?), San Juan Reservoir, and the Provisor Island Power Plant in the Pasig River, an installation paid for in blood by our infantry.

The battle's first phase began on February 4 as the 145th and the 148th raced for the Pasig River in an attempt to engage the main enemy force. The 1st Cavalry was attempting the same thing to our left. Sharp, deadly fire fights ripped up and down the narrow streets leading to the Pasig bridges. Civilians stood in streetside doors, heads turning to and fro as if this were a tennis game, watching as one side fired and the other answered. They swarmed around intersections, hindering the advance.

By February 6, the Pasig River line was firmly in American hands. The enemy was now in prepared positions south of the river. During the latter part of the advance, however, Jimmy and I were told to set up our machine gun on a small balcony jutting out from Far Eastern University's big concrete building. We were ordered to fire on any Japs trying to make it to the river. Our gun overlooked the inner court of this U-shaped building, commanding a street intersection beyond. We almost opened fire on one of our own trucks shortly after arriving, and this so unnerved us that we decided we would not fire at all, no matter what came by. Instead, one of us watched the gun while the other rambled the vacant rooms looking for souvenirs.

I went first, and souvenirs were everywhere. We did not know it, but this building had housed the headquarters of the Kempetai, the Nip equivalent of the Nazi Gestapo. There were large stacks of unmailed postcards from prisoners of war back to their families, propaganda literature, records of every kind—material any historian would have guarded with his life! I bypassed most of this in order to carry off such inconsequential things as flags and bamboo fans with the rising sun emblem on them. But I did grab a stack of prisoner postcards, shipping them home to my father, who sent them on to often bereaved families. (Some families replied with curses, thinking he was a con man.)

I returned to the gun, telling Mayfield of my discovery, but he pointed to one of his own. Under the trees of the inner court were stacks of Japanese aerial bombs—long black things with yellow bands around them. As we watched, two civilians began nosing around the stack. They paid no attention to our shouts, so Jimmy fired a burst into the trees above them. They ran around the corner of the building and a minute or so later mortar shells began dropping in the nearby street. Whoever was firing the mortar knew the bombs were there. The "civilians" had probably been disguised Japs, but we did not figure this out until later. Each of us grabbed a piece of the gun and its ammo and raced out of the building, heading north. Although we were told later that bombs were hard to set off this way, at the time we could imagine the whole building rising on a giant blast of fire and smoke, with Mayfield and Mathias topmost.

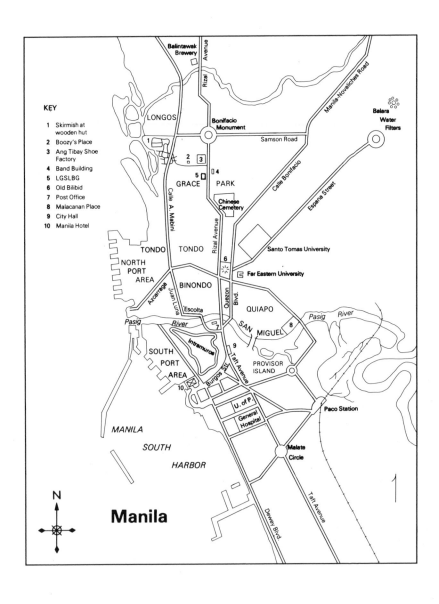

KEY

1 Skirmish at wooden hut
2 Boozy's Place
3 Ang Tibay Shoe Factory
4 Band Building
5 LGSLBG
6 Old Bilibid
7 Post Office
8 Malacanan Place
9 City Hall
10 Manila Hotel

Balintawak Brewery

Rizal Avenue

Manila-Novaliches Road

LONGOS

Bonifacio Monument

Balara Water Filters

Samson Road

Calle Bonifacio

Espana Street

2 3

5 4

GRACE PARK

Calle A. Mabini

Chinese Cemetery

Rizal Avenue

Santo Tomas University

TONDO

TONDO

NORTH PORT AREA

6

Far Eastern University

Azcarraga

Juan Luna

BINONDO

Quezon Blvd.

QUIAPO

Pasig River

Escolta

SAN MIGUEL

8

Pasig River

7

Intramuros

SOUTH PORT AREA

Burgos St.

9

Taft Avenue

PROVISOR ISLAND

10

Paco Station

MANILA

U. of P.

General Hospital

SOUTH

Malate Circle

HARBOR

N

Dewey Blvd.

Taft Avenue

Manila

The battle had hardly begun before tales of Japanese atrocities were exchanged as infantrymen told other infantrymen what they had seen. It was becoming apparent that thousands of Filipino civilians had been killed north of the Pasig River on Friday and Saturday, February 2 and 3, as the American army neared the city. We found hundreds of murdered men, women, and children, their hands bound, and their bodies riddled with bullets. Scores were found, for example, in the Paco Lumber Yard along General Juan de Luna Avenue. Many others were discovered with their bellies slit open by bayonets along the estuaries in the city's western lowlands. My senses still shudder at the memory of a dead Chinese sprawled alongside a small shed just off northern Rizal Avenue. Mayfield and I came upon him just as his friends were preparing to take the body away. His bulging eyes stared unseeingly at the sun from a head hanging askew, the result of a Jap saber slash across his throat. His intensely polite friends said that the Japs had murdered many Chinese this way. We left with curses of anger and frustration--anger at the animal-like ferocity of the Japs, and frustration that the army had not swept in fast enough to have prevented much of this.

Our disgust and fury with the enemy grew as Filipinos related tales concerning "water torture," a technique long used by the Kempetai against political prisoners. A hose was shoved into the prisoner's mouth, bloating his stomach with water. He was then hurled to the floor where soldiers jumped up and down on him, rupturing his inner organs and usually bringing an agonizing death. We found much evidence of this as our infantry entered the deep dungeons under Walled City. What kind of men were these Japs? They of course asked no quarter, but from this time on, no quarter would be given, nor would the nuclear flash at Hiroshima erase these atrocities from our memories. The Japs had done worse at Manila.

After the Japs had settled into prepared positions south of the Pasig, their artillery and mortars fired steadily but erratically into the northern city. Walking the streets was a matter of luck and guess-work, a sort of Russian Roulette. And in this early part of the battle, American artillerymen were furious at MacArthur's order strictly limiting battery fire for fear of killing civilians alleged to be hiding in buildings near those the Japs occupied. (This was not true except in several well known cases.) This order cost extra lives and brought heated arguments between Beightler and MacArthur. Later, when it became clear no civilians were involved, the order was lifted. There can be no thought of either general wanting to harm civilians; it was a case of Beightler being much closer to the reality of the situation than was his commander. It also started another round of damaging gossip about MacArthur: "Old Dugout Doug is afraid we'll damage his property—he loves this friggin city more than the lives of his own men."

If one sound must be taken as the hallmark of the Battle of Manila it would be the sound of automatic weapons. They could be heard at all times of the day and night. The enemy had thousands of them and used them freely. But another sound entered with stunning force one day, soon promising to become typical as well. I was walking a street near Rizal when a shattering blast shook the flimsy buildings. I knew it must be something awful as I cringed in a doorway. It was. The Japs had unleashed huge rockets—one of 200mm and a bigger brother of 447mm. The things could be seen lumbering through the air before hitting with an explosion heard for several miles. Shortly after this, I vaulted into the open top of a half-track as another lit in a Grace Park street. They landed as erratically as the German buzz bombs in London, adding to the unease mounting in all of us as the battle enlarged and ambulances screamed by loaded with casualties. Our artillery knocked the rockets out after a few days.

This did not end my trouble with Jap weaponry. Another brush with it came as the 148th's 3d Battalion made the first crossing of the Pasig River. One of the few good spots to cross this river, which elsewhere had high sea walls, was at Malacanan Palace. General Beightler had his advanced command post there with that of the 148th. Several bandsmen had been detailed to take something or other from the shoe factory headquarters—I forget exactly what—down to the general. We had no idea of what was going on as we pulled in and unloaded various items from our truck. As we were leaving, the Japs across the river began spraying the area with machine gun fire and mortar shells. Our driver, a trombonist called "Slushpump" could either stop and hit the dirt or step on the gas. Slushpump never hesitated, later stating that he knew right away he had to "shit and git!" The truck careened around the corner and into the street, gaining speed as we headed north, with each of us scrooched up in a tight ball in hopes of making as small a target as possible. Once our truck was in behind sheltering buildings, we calmed down as we slowed down. Meanwhile, the second wave of troops back on the Pasig suffered numerous deaths and wounds in this barrage. Nevertheless, the Pasig was crossed, and a bridgehead was established firmly by nightfall of this Wednesday, February 7.

I knew I was lucky not to have been in those boats crossing the river; the Jap fire that had merely slopped over toward our truck had been bad enough. And had I remained in G Company with Clark, I would have been engaged in savage house-to-house fighting in the Tondo District at this time. This large, shacky, swampy residential area of 160,000 people faced the sea, and gave the 145th Regiment many problems before they secured it. I was glad to be in the band.

The second phase of the battle started once American forces had landed and dug in south of the Pasig. As noted earlier, the Japs had used every trick in their book to fortify the excellently constructed buildings in this area. And inside these heavy-walled buildings, the Japs turned each corridor into a fire lane. When infantry attacked, as for example the 129th at the German Club, they faced interlocking streams of machine gun fire, losing nine men in as many seconds. A smoke screen had to be laid by mortars in this instance to get the wounded out. By this time, however, artillery restrictions were lifted by MacArthur, and point-blank fire against Jap positions began pounding buildings to rubble. Trouble was, the Japs climbed out of the rubble, firing as usual.

On February 9, the battle south of the Pasig reached a new fury as the Japs tried to drive the newly arrived infantrymen back north of the river. Three Medals of Honor were won by soldiers of the 37th during the course of this one savage day, these being added to another earned by a lieutenant three days earlier. The stories of their exploits passed by word of mouth throughout the proud division. "The Heavyweight" was giving the enemy all he could ask for, slugging and sending him reeling into the ropes, but the battle was still in its beginnings and destined to grind on for another three weeks.

While the two armies were locked in a death grip along the Pasig River line, by-passed Nips were causing trouble all along the swampy northern reaches of Manila's bay area. Jimmy and I blundered into an understanding of this while the battle was thundering along downtown. Bored with life at the shoe factory, we left our position in charge of some buddies and hiked westward along our dirt road to see some salt water. I think we planned to do some swimming as well as sightseeing.

We took our carbines from force of habit and set out, exhilarated with our freedom. We joked and chatted with Filipinos and other soldiers as we passed nipa huts, several built-up areas, and bamboo groves. An hour or so later our little road curved through a bamboo thicket. We walked around the bend. The ripping sound of a Nambu machine gun stunned us, then sent us scrambling for cover behind the weedy dike of a roadside rice paddy. Automatic weapons answered the Jap gunner as we sized up our situation; we had stumbled into a fire fight. Our jovial mood of a few seconds before was now shattered by fear and by anger at our own stupidity.

As nearly as we could tell, several Japs were cornered in a wooden hut several hundred yards to the right and front of our position. They were covered by GIs from positions we had not yet spotted, though we could hear the return fire. We had been very lucky, for the Japs had not seen us as we rounded the bend, but their guns covered any retreat back around the bend. We had no choice but to join in the battle to eliminate them. Unknown to us, similar small fights were under way up and down this coastal region.

A deadly silence now returned to the steamy surroundings as we lay in the sun, wide eyed and whispering to each other. A clattering sound from the hut brought a new burst of fire from the GI positions, one of which we surmised was not far away to our north. We had our carbines ready for whatever action might come, but silence returned, only to be shattered by explosions in and around the hut and a rush of gunfire from automatic weapons and rifles. Someone had called in mortar fire on the hut, and the job was suddenly over. A dozen or so infantrymen had shot their way into the hut, finding three dead Nips.

We ran over, then found we had been seen as we walked around the bend: "What in th' hell were you two guys doing out on that road?" a corporal grinned, shaking his head. I murmured back, with no grin, "I guess we were just sort of out sightseeing." It was the truth, but it puzzled the corporal and his crew. Jimmy and I decided to leave well enough alone, slung our carbines over our shoulders, and made it back to the shoe factory in half the time it had taken us to get there. "Did you guys make it to the sea?" our buddies asked. "No," Jimmy replied, "we just wandered around for awhile." We told them later; had our officers known of this escapade, we would have been busted to buck privates.

By February 10, the American army was fighting to enclose Manila in a circle of steel. Paratroopers of the 11th Airborne Division had finally run into stiff Jap defenses as they moved into southern Manila. Two days later the 1st Cavalry swung around Manila's south side to join the paratroopers in a successful drive to Manila Bay. This encircled and isolated Iwabuchi's defenders, leaving them with the Pasig to their north, the sea to their west, and a cordon of steel knit solidly across any escape to the east or south. We heard this, realizing that there would now be a fight to the death for sure. And that was what happened.

As the three divisions closed the net tighter on the city, the fighting continued in unabated fury, never to lessen in intensity from beginning to end. Every advance was heralded by smashing barrages from the division's 6th, 135th, 136th, and 140th Field Artillery Battalions. Thus the 145th, supported by all the artillery it could muster, sent a battalion against City Hall, a vast building on Padre Burgos Street. Before this fight was over the 145th's men had been forced to use every weapon in the infantry catalog. The Nips stopped the first assault by touching off mines as the Buckeyes approached. Later it was room by room. Flamethrower nozzles were stuck through holes in the walls and ceilings; oil was poured through cracks in the floor on Japs below, then it was ignited. When 382 dead Nips littered this rubble heap, the building was taken. But many more remained.

The 129th Infantry got itself involved in one of the toughest battles the 37th ever experienced when it attacked the New Manila Police Station. It took a week of horribly savage fighting to take it, and the loss of a hundred men. The enemy chopped holes through second floor ceilings, dropping grenades down on the Yanks below. Hundred of rounds of artillery smashed into this extremely tough edifice before the 129th, finally aided by the 145th, was able to say that yet one other building was secured.

Meanwhile, the 148th was just as heavily involved in assaulting the

University of the Philippines and the Philippine General Hospital. It teamed up with the 5th Cavalry in a week of blasting and hacking paths into and through these large structures. Thousands of Filipinos were rescued from these buildings as the two regiments did their best to limit artillery fire and protect civilian life. With the fall of these bastions to the 148th and 5th, and the earlier Jap defeats at City Hall and the New Police Station, the way was open to attack Intramuros.

As position after position was taken, two thousand of the enemy were forced inside of the old Intramuros District. This would be the scene of their last stand. The old walled city was built by sixteenth-century Spaniards. In area, it covered some forty blocks of stone and brick buildings. It was enclosed by walls forty feet thick at their base and sloping upward twenty-five feet in height. A wide moat, filled in as a public park, covered three sides, and the Pasig River ran along the north wall. The inner bastion, or castle's keep, was Fort Santiago, built in 1590. The Kempetai had tortured scores of political prisoners in its gloomy dungeons. Intramuros lay completely within the zone of the 37th Infantry division, and it fell block by block and gun by gun to the soldiers of that division. No military attack had ever succeeded in capturing Intramuros in the 350 years it had guarded Manila, but it and its Nip defenders were now doomed, as one of the heaviest concentrations of artillery in the Pacific War started round-the-clock shelling of the old walled city.

Mayfield and I of course had no inkling of the plans to shell Walled City. We had returned from our scrape with the Japanese in the wooden hut glad to resume life in our small world surrounding the shoe factory. We lived in a decrepit frame house next to the factory with several other bandsmen, our cots strung with the essential mosquito netting. Most of us spent spare time in a ramshackle small cafe standing by itself along the dirt road to our west. The owner, whom we nicknamed "Boozy," was a jolly practical joker, glad to be back in business so soon after the Yanks arrived. We liked him. He had a large carabao, which grazed nearby but was tethered every night to the cafe wall. These creatures love to be splashed with water, something they have to have to cool down in the tropical heat. We knew this, using it in a plan to repay Boozy for his practical jokes. Someone had discovered many buckets of yellow paint in the shoe factory. That night we went down to the cafe, splashing paint over the approving carabao. When we left, the happy beast was solid yellow except for his face and snout.

The next morning we trotted down to Boozy's cafe, sure we had one on him. The carabao was missing, and we puzzled over this as we walked in and sat down. Boozy walked over to our table with a long, sad face. "Boys," he said, with unaccustomed seriousness, "I had to shoot my poor carabao." We turned stunned looks to each other, thinking we had painted it to death; but Boozy continued: "There wasn't much else I could do, you see, for the son-of-a-bitch turned into a Jap last night!"

Boozy had hidden the yellow beast before we arrived, then repaid us in kind. The carabao was called "jap" from this time on. Jap became a landmark of sorts, turning heads as he pulled loads for his owner up and down Rizal Avenue. Patches of paint stayed on his hair for months, for I saw him as late as December, shortly before I sailed for home.

The afternoon before the shelling of Walled City started, Jimmy and I were told to pack up our machine gun and board a truck. We unloaded after a mile or so and were ordered to guard a battery of 155mm howitzers, probably from our 136th, but my memory remains unclear regarding the unit. We emplaced the machine gun, wondering what was up. The tropic night fell quickly, and with this the artillerymen sprang into action. Their four howitzers joined scores of others in a thunderous barrage against the ancient fortress. We watched in awe as the Intramuros area was outlined by the exploding shells. White phosphorous shell bursts sent fire-tipped fingers arcing lazily upward, as if to claw the black sky. I stood my watch, looking at the fireworks, but my musician's ears resented the impact of the nearby muzzle blasts. Then Jimmy relieved me. Neither of us had brought a blanket, so I lay down on the dusty turf, thinking I would never get to sleep because of the roar of the big guns. But I was soon asleep, and I slept well. When one is nineteen, a little noise seldom disturbs anything so important as sleep.

The next day I decided to go downtown and see what it looked like. I hitched a ride with a southbound truckload of infantry. The truck picked its way slowly through debris-cluttered side streets. At an intersection a screaming Filipina ran toward us. She was carrying a baby, its blanket flapping wildly behind her. Two Japanese soldiers were lunging after her, cursing and swinging sabres. Every gun found its hand as soldiers began tumbling off the truck to kill the bastards. By this time the Filipina was waving her hands wildly at us, screaming "NO-NO-NO-NO!" The Jap soldiers were on their knees, having dropped their swords as if from burning fingers. But our trigger fingers were really stopped by the sight of a large movie camera on a tripod some forty feet away. The movie crew was running and screaming at us in panic. We relaxed. It was a close thing, a drama lasting perhaps three seconds, but not one planned by the producer. He had picked up authentic Jap uniforms and weapons to concoct his scene of Nipponese nastiness, but reality replaced make-believe as he and his actors missed death only by the tiny length of a trigger pull.

I jumped off the truck downtown, gawking at the fire-blackened hulks of shattered buildings. Shells were swishing by above me as the pounding of Walled City continued. A young soldier lay in a gutter, his foam-flecked mouth emitting groans as he stared blankly at the sky. I paused to help him, but I knew it was hopeless. He was one of many who had drunk poison liquor purchased from Filipino moonshiners. I had seen others. Chaplains, I suppose, had erected a large billboard at the Bonafacio Monument, the northern entrance to the city: Deaths From Poison Liquor To Date—Total: 48. Many more died as the ignorant moonshiners blended captured Japanese motor alcohol into their whiskey. Others wound up with jake-leg, a permanent disability of the nervous system resulting in a stumbling walk. A child of the Prohibition Era, I had seen this walk on the streets of Carlisle. My dad had told me why they walked that way, attributing it to lead in the whiskey. In any event, I could do nothing for the soldier in question. I walked on, like the rest, leaving him for the medics to pick up.

By February 23, General Beightler and his staff, after much worried planning, were ready to launch an all-out assault on Walled City. The north and northeast sides of the walls were to be hit simultaneously. This meant that the units attacking the north side would have to cross the Pasig River and land under the great walls on a narrow shelf of land between them and the water. As usual, Mayfield and I were not consulted on any of this, but ordered to pack up our light machine gun and board "that truck." We were driven with other machine gun crews downtown to the Escolta area, a section of large burned out commercial buildings crowding the north bank of the Pasig River. Directly across the river to the south of the building we entered was Walled City. We climbed up burned and blackened concrete stairs until the officer in charge guided us into a room. It was on the sixth or seventh floor, with a window overlooking the river and the great walls some five hundred yards away.

"Set up your gun in that window, and sandbag it and so on," he said, assuming that we were "quality" machine gunners, which we were not. We nodded in agreement to everything he said, wondering what was up.

"Tomorrow morning at 8:30, we will launch assault waves against the walls over there—infantry in boats and so on. You are to fire at anything you think has a Jap behind it—flicker of guns from wall slits, movement of any kind, just anything at all. You've got to cover the landing parties. Any questions?" We of course had none.

By the time the 117th Engineer Battalion had the assault boats filled and ready, some thirty machine guns were sniffing the breezes above the Pasig for Jap movement. Gun crews were on every floor, including the roof.

Mayfield and I were nervous but ready. We jumped as the air filled with a sharp swishing sound heralding the instantaneous arrival of a thunderous artillery barrage. Intramuros was covered with shell bursts. We stared in amazement, feeling the air shudder as the powerful shells ripped into the ancient buildings. There was a lull. Artillery and mortars now shifted to smoke and white phosphorous to blind the Jap defenders. We sensed that the infantry attack would soon come.

Landing craft bearing the 3rd Battalion, 129th Infantry, came into view, heading across the Pasig into who knew what reception. I felt proud of them and sorry for them at the same time; I was glad to be where I was. Jimmy and I began firing at anything suspicious, letting our imaginations guide us. Gunners on other floors joined in, dust flying as streams of .30-calibre bullets bit into the centuries old mortar and brick. We did our best as the troops crossed and climbed out on the south bank. They had encountered little enemy resistance.

The 129th was soon inside the walls, fighting the two thousand Jap fanatics still alive. The 145th had entered through eastern walls broken into rubble by our artillery. As the Japs were compressed back into their redoubt, they released some three thousand prisoners, mostly women, gaining time by dribbling them free little by little. They murdered most of the men, and these were found later by horrified soldiers. Fighting through this shell torn forty-square-block rubble heap finally ended as the last Japs were killed in the old Fort Santiago bastion. Of the two thousand defenders, only twenty or so shell-shocked and dazed men were captured.

I doubt that any army of history fought so consistently to the last man as did the Japanese army and navy of the Second World War. Many armies have said they would do so if required, but only the Japs backed such words with deeds. And that is perhaps the reason they were so hard on military prisoners—they could have no respect for a man who would rather surrender than fight on to the honorable death!

With the fall of Intramuros on February 24, the Battle of Manila entered its last phase. Some thousand Japs, including Admiral Iwabuchi, fought to the death in the giant legislative, finance, and agricultural buildings. These steel and concrete edifices were defended by an enemy who knew there would be no tomorrow. The end came after a savage fight by the 37th and the 1st Cavalry Brigade. The last holdouts were seventy-four Nips in the elevator shaft and roof appendage of the Finance Building. They joined their ancestors on the morning of March 3, courtesy of the 148th Infantry Regiment. These were the last Japs killed in Manila. The 1st Cavalry Division may have entered Manila first, but the last Jap in the city was kicked out by the Buckeye Division. The battle was now over, one month from the time it began, and one month from the time General MacArthur issued his optimistic communique that Manila was secured for all practical purposes!

The Buckeye Division bore the brunt of the Battle of Manila, killing well over half of some sixteen thousand Japs who died there. It also suffered half of the 6,575 casualties inflicted on the Americans by the fanatical defenders. It alone had stormed and taken Intramuros, the centerpiece of Jap defenses, whose great walls had resisted assault for 350 years. The exhausted men looked forward to a period of relaxation in the now conquered city.

11. After the Battle

Although the battle was over, the memory lingered on in all five senses. Thousands of Japs and civilians lay buried in the warm rubble. The rotten-sweet odor of death hung over the city like a fog. Hordes of rats were at work along the estuaries and in the corpse-clotted rubble. Vision was assaulted by the widespread destruction, and sounds from the nearly dead city echoed like a ticking clock in a vacant house. Everything was gritty to touch and taste, as the dust of war had settled over every inch of the city and its suburbs. There was no public transportation, the schools were destroyed, water and sewage services were gone, all major and most minor bridges were wrecked, lower and middle class homes by the thousands were smashed, the four-hundred-year-old Intramuros landmark was razed, and the port areas and docks were reduced to twisted metal and collapsed, tide-washed rubble. The bay was littered with scores of sunken ships leaning at crazy angles and turning rusty around the gaping shell and bomb holes in them. Only God knows what Manila ever did to deserve such a fate, but that was far beyond the thoughts of this soldier boy. I had once again survived, and now I looked forward to some good times.

Things looked bright for the Buckeyes. We were assigned the job of patrolling, protecting, and serving as temporary police in the Manila area. We were placed under direct control of the Sixth Army, leaving XIV Corps for the time being. Spirits were high, and some bandsmen began taking classes at newly reopened Santo Tomás University.

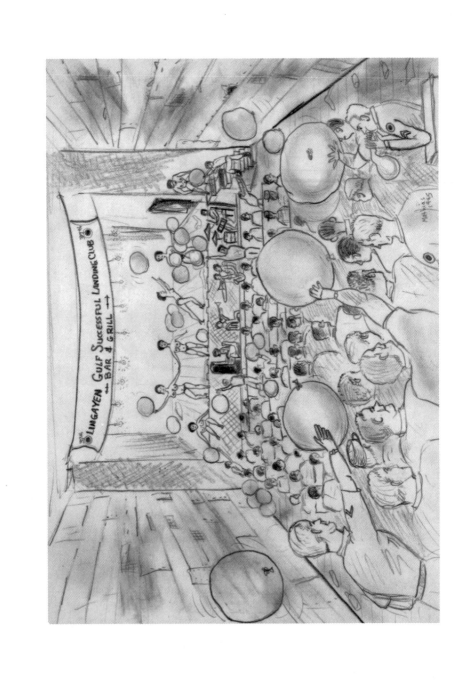

Santo Tomás was not the only thing to reopen. Scores of tawdry little night clubs, bars, whorehouses, dance halls, and honky-tonks flourished all along Rizal Avenue and other areas north of the Pasig. One of the first to open was the Lingayen Gulf Successful Landing Bar and Grill, an imposing name for a club built with scrap timber and rusty tin. Drinks were served here—a risk I did not dare take—and topless women cavorted on the stage in a pathetic imitation of burlesque houses in happier cities. We knew the Filipino musicians playing there, so we often went to the LGSLBG. Boredom with the floor show usually brought our condoms into play. Handfuls of these "rubbers" were forced on us by the medics, and military police could and did ask for them in the same way they might ask for a pass in the States. Their purpose was to prevent veneral disease. We blew ours up into soft, fat balloons, batting them around the GI audience like volleyballs and swatting them up to the girls on the stage, who squealed as they kicked them back to the audience. Scores of these balloons caromed around the club, a forerunner of what is now called "audience participation."

Brothels often operated to the rear of the clubs, not that such places were restricted to the rear of anything, for often they did business in street-side locations. The word for sexual intercourse in these places was "pom-pom." Pimps were everywhere, asking: "Pom-pom, Joe?" But these "pimps" were not of the odious variety one might encounter in a peacetime city; instead they were often young boys trying to attract trade to a sister or even a mother, hoping to earn enough money to buy sufficient food, shelter, and clothing.

I succumbed to the lure of visiting a whorehouse. Five or six of us decided to visit one near the Lingayen Gulf Successful Landing Bar and Grill. It was said to have true professionals who could "put you in high cotton," whatever that was. Six or seven women were lounging around in the gloom of a red-painted room. A candle burned before a small religious shrine in one corner; this seemed sort of out of place to me. Several of the girls approached, volunteering their services. I began to have second thoughts as one neared me. She was well built, the color of creamy coffee, and very probably was a professional who had recently switched smoothly from serving Japs to serving Yanks. She smiled broadly, revealing gold teeth, and then wiggled a red-laquered fingertip inside her ear:

"Only place is virgin, Joe! You like, Joe, you like?"

Suddenly I did not "like" at all. I saw only gold teeth super-imposed on those movies I had seen back at Benning. She was VD personified, as if hordes of syphilis germs were speeding around all over her—a giant chancre I wanted to get rid of pronto! But I stood there a moment, paralyzed with fear at what my buddies would say if I answered my urge to get the hell out of this place. I mumbled something, making an excuse of some sort, all the while backing up. My act was not very convincing, and someone shouted "Mathias is backing out." That was not quite true, for by this time I was running toward the street, as laughter filled the narrow hall behind me. The bright tropical sunlight bathed my senses. I felt as if I had emerged from a tunnel just inches ahead of a thundering train. Jimmy Mayfield stumbled out behind me. We knew we had had a close call, wondering if any germs had settled on us. Maybe we should go to a pro-station, "just in case," but we decided we had probably escaped in good shape.

Jimmy and I did not back out solely because of remembered VD movies. Lurking in our memories also was a weirdly dramatic story then circulating through the ranks of every outfit in Manila. I told the tale to my brother in a letter home. A GI from the 37th decided to go to a brothel. On the way, he saw several large buildings sur-rounded by a high fence. He walked along, pausing to look in through a shattered place in the fence. His gaze met that of a beauti-ful white woman seated enticingly alone in the shade of a poinciana tree. She turned her head as he approached, but he was not to be denied. He argued that death was just around the corner for him, pointing to the smoke rising from the battle in the central city. Would she consent to be the last woman he would ever love? She sighed a strange sigh, saying she would.

He left her, saying farewell forever, then hurried to a prophylactic station down the street. He told the medic of his good luck with the lovely woman back up the street. The medic's response was shatter-ing: "My God, don't you know what that place is? You have been in the Philippine Leper Colony!"

The story was believable. Lepers wandered the city during the battle, one serving as a spy for General Beightler, and the colony walls had been broken down in many places. Certainly I believed the story, telling my brother that they had to wash the poor guy "in every solution known to man. Even with this he will have to remain in the Philippines under observation for three years before returning to the states. It shouldn't be very hard to see the moral to that story."

Once the battle had ended, sailors began getting shore leave. They wandered in knots through the downtown area. Here was an opportunity not to be made light of—a chance to make some money. We heard that a bandsman sold a Jap gas mask flag to a swabby for $5. These small silk flags were enclosed in every Jap gas mask, each with a red rising sun and appropriate slogans written in Japanese characters along the sides. We did not have many of these flags, so we hated to part with a real one when sailors did not know the difference anyway. We scrounged up a white parachute and took it to a tailor shop where it was cut to exact size; each piece was then printed with a red ball in the center. A Japanese interpreter was happy to letter them for us, always with such enlightened messages as these: "Screw Swabbies!" "Piss on the Navy!" "Sailors eat shit!" We then took our wares to the bars and areas the sailors soon monopolized and began thinking of as their own. It helped sales tremendously to put on dirty and torn fatigues, wear a bent helmet, and carry an M-1 or carbine casually slung across the shoulder. After starting a conversation with a likely prospect—all sailors were likely prospects—I would tell a bit of the recent battle, then almost shyly pull the little flag out of my pocket:

"Look here, I picked up a little memento of the battle—you might like to take a look at it."

"Hey, look at this, gang!" came the eager response. "You wouldn't want to sell it would you?" By this time a small crowd would be awaiting my answer.

"Well, I don't know; I do have another one, but it's not as nice as this one. What do you think it's worth?" (It was worth anything I could get over five dollars.) The deal was quickly made, and those flags are hanging today over fine fireplaces somewhere as cherished mementos of "Dad's great days in the Navy."

Following the battle, mopping up operations continued out in Manila Bay. A few Japs had to be shot out of the old hulks sunk all over the harbor. In the process, it occurred to some imaginative

soldier to inquire about the liquid that floated the large compasses on these ships. It was good, drinkable alcohol, and the rush was on. Fears of the contaminated stuff being sold by Filipino moonshiners added to the demand. It was no problem to rent or wheedle a Filipino with a boat to take one out to a ship. There, the alcohol would be drained out of the compass and taken back to shore. For some reason, it was held to be necessary to strain it through bread before drinking it. This belief may have come via sailors, who as "everyone knew" stole alcohol propellant from torpedoes, strained it through bread, and spent many a happy hour drinking torpedo juice. In any event, much was made of this source of alcohol. I did not join in these excursions, but I doubt that as much was gleaned from the compasses as claimed, else half the division would have been drunk all the time!

Another GI pastime I did not join, owing in this case to religious scruples, was stealing food from the Chinese cemetery. A large cemetery of beautiful edifices and decorations lay along upper Rizal Avenue. Chinese worshippers would leave fine dishes of rich foods there for the dead, as their religion held ancestors to be worthy of such attention. Although involved in a fire fight with our infantry during the advance to the Pasig, the cemetery had escaped in better condition than other areas of Manila. (We had learned that the Filipinos did not like the Chinese in their midst, viewing them with that same disdain some Americans hold for Jews. Indeed, the Chinese were called "the Jews of the Orient.") Filipinos said they had sometimes survived by picking up the food left at the cemetery during the latter harsh days of the Jap occupation. In any event, some of the GIs in headquarters company held that the best meals in town were those left behind at the "little houses" clustered throughout this city of the dead.

I lived with my friends in the old shack across from the shoe factory during the first few weeks after the battle. I sat outside one afternoon, drawing a picture (most musicians can also draw) of "The Old Manila Home," which I sent back to "My Old Kentucky Home." I wrote that "the weather stripping is so loose that everytime the artillery went off the sides would flap like a butterfly. . . . We have running water out back in a shower attached to a 50 gal. water drum. The road is dirt and gravel. One thing we don't have is a chimney. You never see chimneys here except for cooking. No heat has been needed here since the world started I guess."

Soon we had good Filipino friends. One of these was named Napoleon Saludar. "Nappy" simply attached himself to the headquarters gang somewhere along the road to Manila and stayed until we went north for another campaign. He was a smart young man of my age, worshipped Yankee soldiers, and all of us liked him. He was an excellent interpreter, speaking Tagalog, Spanish, English, and some Chinese and Japanese. We could depend on him to be on our side in negotiations with businessmen or simply Filipinos we needed in one way or another.

Another valuable adopted member of headquarters company was a Filipino who swore that he had been the head bartender for the swank Manila Hotel. Whether that was true or not, he had bartended somewhere swank, for he was never stumped when it came to mixing drinks. He could stack the different liquors in a "Singapore Sling" into layers, each occupying its own place according to its relative weight. His most valuable qualification was that he knew where to go in Manila to get good, safe liquor. He too had to be left behind when the division moved north.

I was experimenting with foods I had never eaten before. "I like crab meat fine," I wrote. "One fellow's Filipino sweetheart's family does his clothing free and gives him a crab everytime he pays the girl a visit so we buddies eat crab nearly every day." I also noted that I ate a lot of milkfish, papayas, and shrimp, none of which I had ever eaten at home. I could have "milk if I wanted it, but I don't trust it." And I got cheated in trading a pack of cigarettes for "7 cooked comotes (sweet potatoes)." But all of us relished those packages from home. "I got three packages today—potted meats, Hunts candy, 3 books and cough drops! Why the cough drops? It's 90° in the shade here! The candy was mashed but still edible. It had been on the road 5 months." But I concluded this was better than nothing, yet not nearly so fast as letters from home, most of which "reach us in ten days."

I felt that my fellow soldiers missed much through their own prejudices. "Most things over here are interesting, but the G.I.'s are so anxious to get home they never seem to notice them, or shrug them off with, 'Oh well, we've got something better back home.'"

One item, however, was a never-ending mystery to many soldiers, and this was the time differential between the South Pacific and the United States. They never understood the assumptions behind the arbitrary assignment of "international date lines," Greenwich meridians, and the like; thus they lived in a world of mystery they never tired of talking about. "It's 9:00 a.m. here now, Thursday, March 22, so that means it's 8 p.m. Wednesday back home." In a world before John Glenn, moon landings, and TV documentaries, things like this stirred interest hard to imagine by today's person who can think of Earth as a small spaceship hurtling along with our galaxy.

I was saving money regularly from my sales of Jap flags to sailors as well as from my paycheck. "I place my money in 'soldiers' deposit.' After 6 months you get 4% interest. That is 100% better than stateside interest, 2% after a year. When you're discharged you're paid the lump sum." And to this I added the information that "the army has forbidden girls to put lip stick on their V-Mail letters—clogs the cameras!"

As the battle drew to a close, the band was relieved of its duties in the defense platoon and given its instruments. There was a lot of blowing, rebuilding of lips and embouchures, after months away from trumpet or clarinet. We recovered rapidly, and soon had arrangements worked back into passable shape. On the morning of February 24, we were loaded into trucks and taken over to Santo Tomás University. The internees, happy now, gathered around our bandstand as we serenaded them. "The dance band was cheered," I wrote, "as we played many of the old songs as well as the new ones: The Flat Foot Floogie, Dipsy Doodle, The Music Goes Round and Round, Fools Rush In, GI Jive, Moonlight Cocktail, Brazil, and All or Nothing At All." Some danced, some smiled, while others were still sick and dazed by it all. We also had a comedy act featuring Paul Benzaquin, who pretended to be a nightclub waitress selling "cigahs, cigahretts, and ah-ah-monds." As the night wore on, her dignified accent changed radically, and our comedian wound up taking his tray through the audience peddling "nuts 'n butts! nuts 'n butts!" It always got a laugh and it did not fail here at Santo Tomás. We sensed the need to play well here, to provide entertainment after their three harrowing years as prisoners.

Music filled the dusty air of post-battle Manila. Funeral dirges gradually gave way to popular ballads and stirring marches. The band worked day and night as life oozed back into the veins of the stricken city. First came the ceremonial jobs. The British army, represented by a four-star Australian general, awarded Victoria Crosses to two Buckeye generals as the band played "God Save the King." "Newsreel cameramen were there," I wrote home, "so you may see me." They were also present for the first fashion show, held in a Chinese garden. "We played background music, stuff like 'A Pretty Girl is Like a Melody'. . . ." Our dance band played almost non-stop for riotous regimental parties, but we also played a dreary affair for recently arrived "stateside commandoes"--pompous asses shipped in to administer everything." I continued: "It was a very beautiful dance hall. One fellow had recently made colonel and was taken out and pitched into the swimming pool. We played 4 hours and got only 2 cokes for it so you can see what kind of guys some people are. We had to go to the toilet to even get a drink of water. They thought it was Camp Wheeler instead of Manila. We enlisted men were put in our place." Later, however, we played a grand ball at Malacanan Palace. It was a celebration of victory, with Allied officers mingling with Filipinos who had resisted the Jap occupation—men destined to lead the islands into the postwar years. Filipinas in lovely island costume swirled to our music in a columned ballroom ornately paneled in teak and other tropical woods. As I played I remembered my visit to the palace a month earlier, when the 148th was being raked with mortar and machine-gun fire as they crossed the Pasig. "Everybody was here but MacArthur," I wrote proudly. He would hear me play sooner than I expected.

CWO Hower called us together a few days later. He was nervous. "We have a really big job to play," he said. "General MacArthur is arriving on the first train over the rebuilt tracks from Lingayen. Newsreels and everything else will cover the event; everybody of importance in the South Pacific will be there. We've got to get ready to play for it."

Hower had a unique problem to share with us. It concerned "The General's March." Military bands play this march upon the arrival of an officer of general rank. The march is preceded by trumpet flourishes, one flourish for each star the general has on his shoulder.

Our problem was this: MacArthur had recently been promoted to five-star rank, but the rule book listed four flourishes as the absolute limit. MacArthur was one of the first officers ever to receive an additional star. Do we blow the usual four flourishes called for by the rules? MacArthur was held to be a stickler on such things. He might be embarrassed and mad if we gave him too many flourishes in spite of traditional regulations. On the other hand, it was argued that he was a noted egotist, and might get much madder if we denied him what he felt he so richly deserved—five brassy flourishes heralding forth to the world his unique rank and proud position! We finally put our money on his ego. The band's philosophers clinched it by pointing out that Dugout Doug can change rules anytime he wants, but he cannot change his ego. Our trumpeters thereupon practiced flourishes until it sounded as if the Lord himself was stepping down from the skies.

The next day we went to the railroad station. The Philippine Carabao division lined the tracks into the blue distance, awaiting the arrival of their much esteemed hero. Newsreel cameramen checked and rechecked their equipment. Our nervous trumpeters blew often but needlessly to clear dry spit valves, with the rustling sound familiar to all brass men. Everyone was waiting, with mixed emotions.

"There it comes!" The line of high ranking officers strained a bit forward, watching the small, flag-decorated engine pull its cars down the tracks and into the station. As the train eased to a stop along the concrete platform, a roll of movie film escaped a cameraman's grasp, unrolling itself across the platform as the frantic photographer stooped after it. I chuckled to myself, but hardly dared laugh in the presence of such powerful brass.

Suddenly he was arrived, wearing his famous campaign hat and with pipe in hand. Hower lifted his baton and the trumpets performed beautifully: taaa-ta-ta-ta-ta-taaa, five times in a row, followed by "The General's March." MacArthur stood at ramrod attention, the lines of officers equally stiff. He was only five feet from me, and I fancied I could see his ear cock as the fifth flourish rent the air. Numerous Filipino civilians were weeping with joy. Tears also dimmed the eyes of several tight-lipped officers. A microphone was handed to the general. He took it in hand, pausing as he scrutinized the silent scene on all sides of him—silent except for the whirr of cameras. Then he spoke: "Thank Gawd this is con-struction"—again he paused, offering his profile to the cameras—"and not dee-struction!" He turned on his heel with the last word and strode over to a waiting staff car.

The band went from MacArthur's reception to new quarters down the street from the shoe factory. The only things reminding us of our South Pacific environs were the heat and the bathing facilities. Fifty-gallon oil drums hanging above duckboards provided our showers, while similar drums, cut in half, and with a hole torched out of the remaining end, were set over pits for our latrines. Tarpaulin shields were erected only on the side facing the street. An unexpected invasion of our privacy began immediately. Filipinos of all sexes and ages came to watch us using the facilities. They squatted on their haunches, chatting amiably but whispering occasionally in admiration of the physical equipment displayed by a few of the musicians. We at first resented this un-American intrusion, but gradually we accepted the change, the art of conversation taking zest from the arrival of new faces among the daily crowd of observers. No one, of course, commented on the clouds of buzzing flies that swarmed up between our legs whenever we used the latrines. Insects were as much a part of life in the South Pacific as the heat and rain.

The band played on, once again secure in its world of music. We traveled to Rizal Stadium on March 31 to play for a baseball game between our 145th Infantry and the 544th Engineer Boat and Shore Regiment. The stadium was of big league size, but shell holes let light in through the roof and pocked the concrete bleachers. We revived happy memories as we played "Take Me Out To The Ball Game," then cheered the 145th on to victory. A photographer from *Yank* was present. Four months later the story of the game was in *Yank,* with a cover picture of the Buckeye band playing in the grandstand.

Little things came along occasionally to mar our otherwise happy lives as occupation soldiers. During mid-March the matter of poison liquor had flared up again, as I revealed in a letter dated March 20: "I hear nine soldiers died last night after drinking Filipino bootleg. The M.P.'s are out in force all over the city. They were breaking all the bottles they could find yesterday and believe me you can find plenty of them. Every little shop has a sign: '1 jigger—1 peso'."

Another intrusion into our happy lives came one afternoon when the men of division headquarters were assembled for a lecture. Ferdinand the Papal Bull strode up on the lectern, and he was roaring mad. He suddenly spouted a stream of oaths and vulgarities. It sounded awful coming from a chaplain's mouth. "How do you like it!" he shouted in rage. "You ought to; you use it all the time. But that's not why I'm here. I'm here for worse than that. I know what happened last month at Concepcion." There was an uncomfortable stirring in some seats. "I know what you did to that poor woman even while your comrades were dying elsewhere. What do you think the Japs would do with this information. I can hear Tokyo Rose now: 'American GIs lined up for a block in order to creep in and abuse one poor Filipina woman. These are the ones claiming to be your "liberators." Rise and strike them down and join your friends of the Greater East Asia Co-Prosperity Sphere—your Japanese allies!' Is that what you punks want? Is it?"

The padre was not finished nor had his rage subsided. He lambasted several unknown GIs who had walked up and asked him to direct them to a pro-station during the Battle of Manila. At the time he was standing outside a medic tent full of wounded and dying men. His face flushed as he recalled the episode. He was a fine chaplain, and his speech was needed, but some of us felt he had showered the entire company with verbal shrapnel instead of zeroing in on the guilty ones. Nevertheless, I reported home that "if his speech doesn't help things nothing will. He appears to be a regular 'Father Duffy'." This was an esteemed World War I chaplain I had seen portrayed in a popular movie—*The Fighting Sixty-Ninth.*

Beggars continually wandered into the band building, attracted by the music as well as hopes for a soft touch. We gave what we could spare, but we sometimes turned the tables. "The other day," I wrote, "a 7 year old Filipino boy kept pestering us for cigarettes. Somebody finally said, 'Hey, if this kid's old enough to smoke, he's old enough to shave.' We grabbed him, lathered him up, and shaved him with a stick. Filipinos standing around joined in the fun. But he has quit pestering us for cigarettes."

I never played in a finer dance band than the Manila version of the Buckeye Danceband before, during, or after the war. A dance orchestra, like any other team, reaches a peak of perfection. Our band reached this peak during a dance for the 140th Field Artillery Battalion. It was held in a large ballroom somewhere north of the Pasig, built in the style of the great dance halls of the swing era. We had five saxes, four trumpets, four trombones, four rhythm, and a vocalist. The band had great power, yet it could play with a whisper. Every section carried its weight, with talented soloists fitting tasteful rides into the superb arrangements. It played with a sound much like that obtained by the Glenn Miller band in "The Moon Is a Silver Dollar," an upbeat number never recorded by Miller but picked up from a radio tape and issued later as a record. Perhaps only a musician will understand me when I write that if I could go back to one night in my life it would be to this job in a dance hall of forgotten name, but whose bandstand, dancers, and even walls remain emblazoned on my memory.

Replacements flowed in after the battle to bring the 37th back up to strength, for XIV Corps credited the 37th with 3,732 battle casualties. Two of these, John Graham from Merced, California, and Ed "Pappy" Harrington from Syracuse, New York, joined me to form a trio of best buddies. Johnny was an easygoing lad of eighteen whose parents had migrated to California from Kentucky during the 1930s. His ambition was to follow in his father's footsteps as manager of a J. J. Newberry five-and-dime store. We called Ed "Pappy" because he was six years older and because he had a wife and children back in New York. We shared details, patrols, and much else together for the remainder of the war.

"Well, I've been in this game 18 months and one day," I wrote home on March 16. "We heard Roosevelt promise us that every man with 18 months in over here would be home by Christmas. Most of us laugh. According to him not one of us was ever going to set foot on foreign soil. I hope he is right this time." What Roosevelt knew that we did not know, was that an atomic bomb was going to be used sometime before next Christmas!

As on Bougainville, the 37th band began broadcasting over the armed services network out of Manila. "We sing ads we've heard on the radio. At present we have Little Orphan Annie and Jack Armstrong theme songs sung by our trio. We also do Rinso White, Bromo Quinine, Carter's Little Liver Pills, and others." These ditties were very popular, and show again the hold advertising has on Americans—a love-hate relationship, but a sure sign of home to boys away from home.

Meanwhile, my younger brother was casting about for advice on which branch of the service to join when he came of age. I advised him to join the Navy, since he could not get into a band. "The Navy has always got good beds, good food, shorter tours of overseas duty, more rapid advancement based on competitive exams, no mud, marches, and not much work. . . . Anyone who has been in the infantry wouldn't hesitate to tell you to join the Navy. If you want to be interned in the Frankfort Insane Asylum write and tell me you've joined the marines."

The Philippine economy was flattened by the war. Millions of small, worthless, paper Japanese bills blew through the streets after American peso notes replaced them. These notes were presumably some of the ones I had guarded as the invasion currency was unloaded from the *Monterey* at Hollandia the previous autumn. The peso was valued at two for the dollar, or 50¢ each. Any kind of merchandise, however, was preferable to money in Manila's starved and ragged economy. Much price gouging took place: one mango sold for $1.25, silk stockings for $5, and three photos cost up to a dollar each, depending on the cameraman. I learned to dicker almost endlessly over prices. When my patience wore out, or I could plainly see I was being cheated, I used a line that never failed to work: "If the Japs were still here they'd simply take these bananas [or whatever] and shove your stand down your throat." They had to admit this or make a liar out of themselves and every other Flip in sight.

The black market blossomed during the battle and grew rapidly thereafter. I entered it by chance one afternoon while reading in a newsstand along Rizal Avenue. These stands bought magazines from soldiers and hung them on long tiers of nail-studded boards, renting each one for a nickel. Customers were provided with benches. While reading, "Pappy" walked up, asking if I wanted to get in on a good deal. "Sure," I said, asking what the deal was. He reported that instruments captured from a Jap army band had just been unloaded at our band building. Someone from one of the regiments had sent them over, not knowing anything else to do with them. We ran back, hoping to clear them out before too many bandsmen became involved in the deal, especially the powerful noncoms.

We arrived to find only five or six lowly enlisted men anxious to move them out. They would sell at high prices on the black market, for Filipino musicians had constantly begged us to sell them our army instruments. We could not do this, but we had given them pads and reeds for their woodwinds, valve oil, drumheads, and other supplies. They played amazingly well with the worn junk they had, and one band, called "The Glenn Miller of the Philippines," was good enough to play in any American city. Their livelihood depended on good instruments, and as we tried them out we realized that the Japs had made good ones. I received an excellent tenor sax and a box full of supplies as my share, leaving immediately for a downtown club. I walked in with utter confidence, showing a musician friend what I had. He was delighted that I had remembered him, paying $120 in cash for the tenor and supplies. I could have charged much more, for the Jap tenor was an exact imitation of the one I was using, a costly American Conn instrument.

I left a happy musician behind me as I walked out into the sunlight, fingering my wad of crisp bills. A sherbet vendor stood by his push cart on the corner, hawking his paper tubes full of flavored ice as traffic roared within inches of him. I bought a tube for 50 centavos, sticking my new wealth in a hip pocket. A truck with division marking came by so I flagged it, jumping aboard as he slowed down. We had traveled no more than a block when I decided to transfer my money to my shirt pocket, where I usually carried anything of value. I slapped both pockets excitedly; it was gone! I flew off the truck like a loose hubcap, lifting the strap of my .45 automatic sidearm as I ran cursing back to the corner. I meant business if I could catch the pickpocket. He was gone, of course, but I stood watching everything for the next fifteen minutes. I finally had to swallow the fact that a 50-centavo sherbet had cost me $120!

During a musical show several nights later I made a new Filipino friend. His father had been a high police official in prewar Manila, and the family still lived in a nice home near the downtown area. I liked him, writing home that "I ate Sunday dinner at Tony Reyes. Really was fine. I tried on his sport coat and felt like I was home again. He is 20 years old in April, and I will be the same in May." Reyes told me of the sudden onslaught of infantry and armor as the 37th raced into downtown Manila. Jap officers, who had commandeered quarters in his house, looked out the window to see what the approaching clatter was all about. They were shocked, leaping to their feet as a tank bearing a big white star roared by in a cloud of dust. They rushed out the back door, leaving Samurai sabres, hara-kiri knives, and other equipment Tony showed me.

The Jap officers were probably killed in the ensuing battle, but initially they were victims of their own overblown propaganda, believing until the proof roared by outside their window that the Yanks had been stopped north of the city. Tony gave me an English language newspaper the Japanese distributed throughout the islands. I saved it. It reported that in the five weeks after October 12, 1944, the Japanese forces had sunk 24 American carriers, 4 battleships, 16 cruisers, 10 destroyers, 18 troop transports, and damaged others for a grand total of 375 ships. Similar claims were made for the ground forces. Little wonder that the average Japanese soldier and officer gradually became unable to sort out fact from fiction. In any event, "the Filipinos say they all laughed at such figures. They hid in cellars to hear the news from San Francisco."

It worried me that everyone did not get along well with the Filipinos. "Some of the men look down on the Filipinos because they don't understand them. A Filipino believes in courtesy above all. He is always ready to give a helping hand. If you ask him how far it is to your destination he will say only a few miles even if it is twenty. He never wants to hurt anyone and likes to take it easy. . . . Many of us are browner than the Phil. people. Negroes call the Filipinos "Paleface" in fun. There is no race prejudice here except between whites and negroes."

The army remained strictly segregated throughout World War II, modern television shows notwithstanding. In Manila, black troops were assigned to docks, loading and unloading the ships and driving the trucks of the "Yellow Ball Express," which took supplies and other materials all over the area. At a dance I talked to one of these drivers. He was drinking, and bragging about his role in the black market, claiming he had laid away over $50,000. Later revelations regarding the extent of nefarious sales from these supply trucks forced me to believe that my informant may have been drinking, but he probably was not lying.

Sometime during this campaign—and I think I remember it correctly—the first word about a wonder drug called penicillin was bruited about. It was held that it could cure syphilis and gonorrhea overnight. This was scoffed at by the old hands who had been through the scraping and other agonizing treatments for these venereal diseases prior to the war. But this "miracle drug" lived up to its name. The medics noted a sharp increase in soldiers admitted for the social diseases, and nearly all of them knew about penicillin, asking for it as if they were asking for an aspirin after a night of boozing!

About this time I lost patience with a question my father posed in one of his infrequent letters: "Would you rather fight Japs or Krauts?" I tried to talk this over with some of my buddies, then wrote back that "We all would rather fight Japs. What formerly made it so bad were the jungles. If the Japs had Messerschmidts [sic], tiger tanks, and 88's we'd rather fight Germans, I guess. If you all would not let your imaginations run clear away with you you would see that there is nothing to worry about. I'm right here and not worrying except for how to chisel seconds at meals." I was unable fully to understand the worries of parents, and since I was so obviously healthy and in good shape in my own mirror, I could not visualize the blank mirror they faced in my bedroom back in that tiny Kentucky town.

I was still an avid fan of radio news broadcasts and propaganda from Japan and Japanese-controlled stations elsewhere. Near our band building was a short air strip used by observation planes. An excellent radio was housed in the flight shed, and several of us made numerous trips to listen over this fine receiver.

We can get nearly anyplace in the world, and we hear Berlin and Tokyo very easy. Tokyo's quit telling . . . a lot of stuff about invincibility and lost island bases being "unimportant." The people no matter how stupid know something's wrong when a bomb lands in Uncle Fujie's back yard. The announcers say that just like Britain, an island, they can't be taken either. If the Germans couldn't take Britain, they think the Americans can't take Japan. Of course they don't tell the people that Japan, unlike Britain, has no navy to keep supply lines open, Japan has no country like the U.S. to supply her and that Japan on an island of comparable size to the British Isles has twice as many people to feed. I remember Daddy used to say that if the Germans couldn't take Britain then we would have an awful time with Japan. Well, the Germans never tried to take Britain. If they had been ready, as we are, they would've taken Britain, in my opinion now.

It was near the end of the division's stay in Manila that I began questioning the ceaseless remarks directed against General MacArthur by the rank and file. It hardly seemed logical that a leader so often disparaged could win the undying admiration of Filipinos, win brilliant campaigns, strike fear in the heart of Jap commanders, and otherwise do such an excellent job of soldiering. I concluded, first, that what little any of us knew about him had come from the usual latrine rumors. With this in mind, I asked critical friends a simple question: "Who would you want to replace him?" The answers were revealing, in a word: "Nobody." A typical answer, however, went like this: "Hell, I wouldn't want nobody to replace Dugout Doug, but I'd still like to kick his butt, or scrape that egg salad off his hat." In short, his being a showboat was almost as bad as if he had been a losing general—but not quite!

He was recognized by every soldier as a great leader. We knew he valued our lives and that he won. He may have been an egotistical old showoff, but the casualty lists told another story entirely. We did not consider the Aussies and Marines so smart for losing a lot of men MacArthur would have saved through patience and planning. The men I talked to admitted that he could be trusted to pull them through alive if there was any possible way to do so. This, and not MacArthur's self-preening, nor his infuriating tendency to play up to the press by announcing campaigns over before they started, lay at the root of his great success as a leader. When the chips were down for keeps in the Southwest Pacific (as his command was officially designated), Dugout Doug never lacked for followers. The whole gang trooped along in his footsteps, grumbling and cursing his egg salad hat every inch of the way!

12. Baguio and Balete Pass

Unexpected news, all bad, came to the Buckeye Division on March 25. We were to move to a new battlefield high in Luzon's great mountains against a place called Baguio, the cool summer capital of the Philippines. The 37th was transferred to the Sixth Army's I Corps, commanded by Lt. Gen. Innis P. Swift. Since I had no code for such a place as Baguio, the folks at home assumed I was still in Manila. They learned better shortly, for their *Cincinnati Times-Star* soon carried news of the division fighting in three places at once.

General Walter Krueger called the 37th his "trouble shooters." In late March he ordered the Buckeyes to split their talents three ways. He ordered the 129th Infantry into the battle for the mountainous city of Baguio. They began moving east along corkscrew Highway 9 at mile-high altitudes. The 33rd Division was slugging toward the same goal from the south and southwest. We were now in the northern Luzon bastion defended by Yamashita's Shobu Group, a force of 152,000 men divided among five divisions and supporting units. The band had moved with division headquarters into a new command post in the foothills not far from the Lingayen Gulf.

Meanwhile, Krueger sent our 145th Infantry to campaign with the 6th and 38th divisions east of Manila in the Wawa and Mount Pacawagan areas. A terrible and costly campaign developed in this mountainous and well fortified stronghold of the eighty-thousand-man Shimbu Group. Walter Clark later told me that G Company took greater losses here than it had in Manila. They were trapped one

night by point-blank artillery fire. He laughed when I credited my
saxophone with pulling me out of that company back on Bougainville.

As if to make sure nobody escaped, Krueger assigned the 148th
Infantry to the Baguio sector, later releasing them for duty with the
25th Division in a terrific fight for Balete Pass. This pass was the key
to the great Cagayan Valley of northern Luzon, and its precipitous
terrain was called worse than that of the Burma Road by a man who
knew—General "Vinegar Joe" Stilwell. In short, there were few parts
of the Luzon campaign that did not have units of the Buckeye Division involved someplace. It can be argued that this division's action
on Luzon is more representative of this campaign than that of any
other unit.

Division headquarters was established in the Bauang area, not far
from the Lingayen Gulf nor from the mountains. I wrote on April
20 that "I've been swimming in the ocean every day for about a
week now and really have a tan. We are living in the midst of thousands of palm trees. The weather is still dry as a bone as the Island's
rainy season hasn't started yet."

Our infantry was making good time in the mountains above us.
The enemy fell back steadily toward prepared positions, then began
contesting every hairpin turn as Route 9 zigged and zagged higher
and higher into the formidable mountain spine. These mountains
looked somewhat like the American Smokies, but shaded them by
nearly three thousand feet, their cloudy ridges rising to more than
ninety-six hundred feet at Mount Pulog northeast of Baguio. Although the Buckeyes had fought across some high ground on
Bougainville, it was nothing like this cool, cloud-wrapped terrain. It
was a new experience for men who had fought on city streets,
sandy beaches, and in the swampy morass of steaming jungles.

There was nothing new about the heavy casualties involved in
mountain fighting. The 129th was to list 317 men killed or wounded
along this spiraling highway, and the 6th Field Artillery Battalion
lost its commander during an artillery duel. Meanwhile, the 148th
Infantry had been packed up and shipped out of Manila to "pass
through" the 129th along Highway 9 and spearhead a drive on into
Baguio. The 148th continued the same pounding that had been administered to the Japanese by the 129th- a slashing attack always

preceded by heavy concentrations of artillery and air strikes. General Yamashita, in an interrogation after the war, believed that the 33rd Division had undergone a complete change of tactics around April 10, when the 129th first hit him. He never thought of the 37th since his intelligence sources held that this division had joined the attack on Okinawa. This was his first direct experience with the "heavyweight."

The 148th Infantry ran into six days of real trouble at Irisan Gorge. The highway dipped into this vast crevice, crossing a bridge at the bottom before winding up the other side. Some fifteen hundred Nips were dug into the surrounding ridges, like ants licking the rim of a deep bowl. They had all of the usual weapons as well as tanks. Fighting man to man, the infantrymen clawed their way from ridge to ridge, pausing only when screaming aircraft engines heralded the arrival of an air strike. Irisan Gorge fell on April 21, but the 148th had lost two hundred men in taking it. The Nips retreated toward Baguio, dying in their tracks as they contested every twist of the road. Meanwhile, the 129th passed through the 148th, digging in throughout a cemetery along the city's outskirts. That night hordes of screaming Japs attacked with tanks, hoping to fling them out in one last battle. They failed, and the 37th entered Baguio first, sharing the occupation of this small city with the 33rd Division. It was April 24, 1945.

When the line regiments moved into Baguio. division headquarters packed and headed up Highway 9. As our truck climbed the fifty miles of twisting road to Baguio, we were presented with a magnificent view. Below us, to the west, we could see the entire Lingayen Gulf, its shimmering silver surface reflecting the morning sunlight and ending only at the distant blue mountains guarding its western flank. "Gee!" Chick sighed, "the Japs could see every move we made down there last January!" There were the invasion beaches off to the south, and we tried to imagine how our invasion fleet had looked to the Japanese watching from this lofty position.

Our truck pulled into a roadside turnout to cool its engine, giving us a better view. We jumped off only to duck warily as Gil Silvius began shouting; our bass man was leaping and laughing wildly: "It's cool! It's cool! The weather is cool!" Everyone joined Gil in his discovery, shaking shirts to let the cool air in and breathing deeply. "I haven't been cool since leaving Mount Morris, Illinois in 1940!"

Gil gurgled happily, but added: "God but I would like to see some snow." Then we noticed the pine trees, hundreds of them on all sides. The sunny air was heavy with their fragrance. These and the cool dry air were exciting reminders of our temperate homeland. We had been in the humid tropical heat so long we had forgotten the way things used to be.

As our truck twisted on into the mountains, the difficulties faced earlier by the line regiments became obvious to us. Caves had been dug into every curve, sunk back into the clay and rock, and defended fanatically with automatic weapons. Many of the defenders had been buried alive when tanks blew the caves in on them. Seeing these caves verified our belief in a story circulating through the division. One of the guys in a line outfit was said to have entered one of these caverns, a vacant one. He was on the point of a patrol, quite a piece out in front. He came running out, shouting and pointing back to the cave he had entered. His patrol ran up and into the cave. It was full of bags and boxes of prewar silver Philippine pesos. The Japs had trucked it out of Manila to Yamashita's mountain stronghold. An air strike had destroyed the truck and the survivors had cached the money in the cave. It remained to be discovered by the first Yank in. The Buckeye dogface had stumbled onto a fortune but he had given his secret away to his patrol. The patrol leader thought only of asking an officer. The officer immediately summoned a truck, thanking the soldiers and giving them another assignment. The officer and the truck disappeared down the highway with the horde of silver safely aboard. No one knew the officer involved nor his outfit. The silver never turned up back at division headquarters, with the Philippine authorities, or anyplace else.

The story was widely believed, and always brought this response: "Told about it, did he? th' dumb shit."

"Yeah, he shouldn't of done that. I wouldn't, I'll tell you that."

"What would you have done?"

"Hell, I'da done what anybody with a mind woulda done—I'da taken a grenade and blown that old cave right in on the silver; I'da said I found a Jap inside and nobody woulda known the difference!"

"That's all right, but how you gonna get the silver with all that dirt on it; besides, all these caves look alike and a lot of them have been blown in."

"Look, dummy, I would'a marked the spot some way in my

mind. After this old war was over, Id'a rented a little truck and eased back up here to do a little diggin'. Boy! what a life with $100,000 to ease the pain!''

Who knows the truth, if any, in the above story? Wartime movements of vast sums of money are not unusual. Philippine authorities sank much of the public treasury in Manila Bay shortly before the Japs entered the city. Again, there were few survivors to account for the vast sums in gold and silver the Japs brought into the Philippines or confiscated while there. It may well be that one day after the war the neighbors in some small Ohio town enviously noted that "the boy next door has come into an awful lot of money!" It was an inheritance, they said, agreeing that he deserved it. "After all, he was a lieutenant with our own Buckeye Division in all that hard fighting on Luzon."

A somewhat similar story of finders-keepers circulated during the Battle of Manila, but the finder in this case was not an innocent by-stander. A safe-cracker from one of Ohio's big cities finally found opportunity to practice his specialty once the division got back into civilized surroundings. He blew safe after safe as the division moved through abandoned towns and cities of the Central Plains. Vaults in Manila's crumpled banks and business houses only added to his fortune in jewels, bullion, and valuable certificates. An especially attractive safe caught his eye in a small bank south of the Pasig River. He tinkered with it, but was blown through the wall with the combination knob still clutched in his hand, like Casey Jones's throttle. The Japs had booby-trapped it! At this point a knowing glint darted from the story-teller's eyes as his voice dropped to a confidential tone: "Nobody has ever come up with all the loot this guy hid away before getting killed."

Baguio was a beautifully situated resort city, with a gracefully sloping central plaza, an excellent golf course, and cool pine forests shading streets and homes. The band moved into several vacant homes bordering the golf course. These were lovely stuccoed dwellings built in Spanish style, obviously the homes of wealthy people who had fled the recent fighting. As we moved in we agreed that the house was better than any we had lived in in the States. We were told that a "White Russian" owned the house we were in, and this started an argument:

"A 'White Russian?' What in th' hell is that?" Pappy asked. "I thought all Russians were white; don't tell me they have black Russians too."

"Naw," Silvius replied, "it has something to do with being a Red Communist Russian and the other kind the Reds kicked out when they took over. The captain said the guy who built this place ran from the Reds and wound up here in the Philippines. Russia and Japan aren't at war, so he lived high until we got here."

We pondered this colorful question as we inspected the large, well furnished home. When we entered the beautifully appointed bathroom another argument started:

"Ain't that the queerest little john you ever saw?" Johnny Graham asked, a puzzled expression clouding his face. We agreed as we gathered around it. Whatever it was, it sat by itself in porcelained splendor, but next to a regular commode and water closet. It was low, wide and flat, being perhaps a foot above the tiled floor.

"What in the world is that spindly little spigot in the center of it?" Chick asked.

"Yeah," I put in, "and it has two faucet handles on the end; I don't see how it can be flushed or crapped in either."

We debated the matter for some time, but we were stumped. Fortunately, the warrant officer came by later, and we showed it to him. We grimaced as he laughed, telling us it was a douche bowl; we marveled as he explained its uses. We had easily coped with the outdoor privies used by most Filipinos, for we had grown up with them. Rudy suggested that we call it a "slit trench," so we did, delighted to think there was something in the world as weird as this gadget in the White Russian's bathroom.

While in Baguio, we ripped the division shoulder patches off our sleeves. They were prohibited in a combat zone lest the enemy gain information regarding the unit facing him. I had never seen the shoulder patch until after the Battle of Manila, when most of us had seamstresses sew up several for our sleeves. The patch was a simple red disk circled with a white border. The design came from the letter "O" on the Ohio state pennant. It looked like a sunny-side-up egg, so we were sometimes called "the fried egg division." Every man in the division, however, referred to the patch as "the flaming asshole."

We were soon moved out of our cool mountain sanctuary. The 148th Infantry was ordered east to join the 25th Division in its efforts to break out of Balete Pass. There was great urgency in the order, for the oncoming rainy season would soon make any action impossible in the Pass. The 148th went into action on May 5, and three days later the 37th entered a fifth Congressional Medal in its Luzon ledger. Pfc Anthony L. Krotiak and his squad were subjected to intense small-arms fire and grenades, driving them into an abandoned Jap trench. A grenade landed in their midst. Krotiak jammed it into the soft earth with his rifle butt, then fell over it, successfully shielding his men from the explosion. He died a few minutes later. His self-sacrifice won him his nation's highest honor.

While the 148th was at Balete Pass, and "one-four-five" still hammering away over at Mt. Pacawagan, the rest of the division meandered down to the hot lowlands near San Jose, an inland area in north central Luzon closer to our two embattled regiments. We spent most of May here. The band was near a village named San Isidro, living in a tent city along with division headquarters.

News came upon our arrival of the end of the war in Europe. I wrote home on Jap stationery I had picked up while searching out a cave system: "We heard the war was over (VE) on May 5th but there was no shouting. Just a few sighs of relief and speculation on how long it will take to get the power from Europe over here. Three men go on rotation this next quota & one on furlough. It has been just one a month so the new quota naturally caused excitement."

While here we heard of the new point system, by which men received points for each month in service, each month overseas, for each child, and later for certain medals won. Cynics said there must be a catch in this system somewhere. Many GIs who had been over from the beginning doubted they would ever see home again. I had some forty points, compared to veteran bandsmen with a hundred or more.

Bad news now arrived for all of us. The death of Franklin Delano Roosevelt struck everyone like a thunderclap, for with him a source of friendship and security departed. His presidency filled the memories of most of us as completely as if he had been our father. We knew, with the sure sense of childhood, that things had gotten better in our homes after FDR had come to office. It seemed impossible to envision anyone in the White House but him. I felt a keen loss, as if a dear and well loved uncle had died.

News of Roosevelt's death was followed by a worse blow— Andrew Metcalfe, my Carlisle neighbor, had been killed in action in Italy. I suddenly felt very old, as if this war had lasted forever and would go on through eternity. It seemed to have swallowed my life, destroying things as they used to be before 1943. It was making me old before my time. I dreaded the thought of what must be going on back in my Main Street neighborhood. It was useless to write Uncle Ed and Aunt Elsie, Andy's parents—what could I say? Instead, I raged to myself in frustration. I now knew enough to pass judgment on his death, for we had heard of the stupid leadership in Italy, the cavalier wastage of men hurled against worthless objectives. That this was still being done through the last few days of the war made me reel in disgust. I felt that Andrew's death was needless, that if a MacArthur or Beightler had been there he would have lived through to the end.

Life was easy at San Isidro, and it was meant to be. Various units of the division, including the 129th Infantry, were recuperating after the battle for Baguio. One night, after the feature movie, the projectionist announced that a short would follow, but those wanting to leave should now do so. With this, the open-air screen filled with one of the most pornographic movies of the era. The Japs had captured the film from the Yanks when they had taken Manila, and we had captured it back. It is worth noting that neither army had destroyed or harmed it. I sat there in stunned silence, as did everyone else, for I had never seen anything like it. The silence lasted only a minute, then whistles and catcalls began, followed by a rustling of seats as embarrassed soldiers started showing their Filipino friends to the exits. I sat there gawking as it played out.

The next day, a great furor broke out over at a tent in division headquarters. The chaplains had heard of the movie and they were looking for the film. We were hoping against hope that they would not find it, but of course they did. One of the chaplains had brought a pair of scissors, and he cut the entire film lengthwise down the middle. From our way of thinking, this was one of the worst atrocities committed during the entire war in the South Pacific!

The band provided a combo each night for "The Mosquito Bar," a large tent serving drinks to the soldiers of the 129th Infantry. One night, while playing, I began drinking, and drinking and drinking. I did not know how to drink, and I passed out. I have no memory of being dumped into the back of a truck and unloaded into my cot back at the band tent.

My memories begin when I opened my eyes the next morning. I was beyond just being sick, for I could not raise myself off the cot. My entire body seemed filled with spidery stands of spaghetti, each with its own violently complaining nerve ending. I retched and rolled into the dirt by my cot, landing with a painful thump. "Leave me alone," I gasped to my buddies, then dragged myself through the dirt to a nearby urinal. I grasped two large bamboo tubes stuck into this gravel pit, hanging between them as I vomited until I had the dry heaves. Somehow it felt good to be so sick I could not be any sicker—it was beyond worrying about. I could not walk, so I crawled back to the tent, where Johnny and Chick lifted me into my cot. I began walking the next day, still sick and still unable to eat. The hangover cleared up the third day, but I felt bad all week. The savage hangover had been caused in great part by the fusel oils and other impurities in the Filipino whiskey. It had been tested for lead and other poisons, but it still had ample qualifications as rot-gut booze.

Several days later Gil Silvius handed out photos taken that night. One of them showed me late in the job, leaning on my saxophone with drooping eyelids and slack mouth. I was even drunker than I looked. When I sent the photos home, I censored this one by slicing my face out of it, writing: "I spilled a lot of ink on one. When I tried to erase it the laquer rubbed off and ruined half of the picture."

By the end of May division headquarters moved into Balete Pass. Most of us were following on the heels of our infantry. When censorship was lifted, I wrote that "it made us wonder how the 25th Division ever got the Japs out of this natural defensive terrain. We reached the top point at three thousand feet, then began the long trail down. At every curve the Japs had dug through rock and clay to make very sturdy pillboxes. Our planes dropped jellied gasoline bombs on them and you can still notice the black sides of mountains burnt off. Only the black stubs of trees are left." It had indeed been a bloody fight for the "Tropic Lightning" division, costing them 650 men killed and 1,920 wounded. Our 148th Infantry had taken 165 casualties during its brief time with the 25th. In spite of the cost, the crucial junction point of Highway 5 at Santa Fe had fallen. Joining also in this fight for the junction, but coming toward it along the Villa Verde Trail, was the veteran 32nd Division, the old "Red Arrow" outfit of New Guinea fame. They had engaged the Jap 2nd Tank Division in a grinding battle, losing 835 men killed and 2,190 wounded. The Buckeye Division now relieved the 25th and 32nd divisions. Our job was to bull through the downhill side of Balete Pass with a goal of breaking clear before the rains came. If this could be done, the wide, flat Cagayan Valley would lie open to attack, thus splitting Yamashita's Shobu Group. Thousands of Japs did not believe it could be done, so breaking clear of Balete Pass was going to take some doing.

Division headquarters dug in on the meager flatlands centering a deep mountain-shrouded valley. To our right, Highway 5 clung precariously to the flanks of the eastern ridge, meandering around ravines and gorges until it disappeared over the valley's misty northern rim. The Japs were using mountain caves in the western flank as artillery positions, poking the guns out to fire point blank across the valley at opportune targets on Highway 5, then pulling them back like turtles into their shells. These guns were hard to knock out, but Mitchell B-25 bombers got more than their share of them. Each B-25 had a 75mm cannon in a nose mount. The navigator loaded the fifteen-pound shells, firing them at a rate of fifteen or twenty per minute. They swooped over our position with motors cut back, gliding toward enemy caves with the seventy-five thumping above the sound of their machine guns. The planes were shooting directly into the caves, their exploding shells entombing the defenders deep inside the mountains.

As daylight faded I prepared to eat, pulling out a package of dried noodle soup shipped from home. I used it often, for it never spoiled in the tropic climate. Since I had no primus stove to heat it, I built a tiny fire on the lip of our deep trench. I knew better, but I built it anyway; I was hungry. The fire flickered up, beginning to heat my canteen cup full of watery soup. Sergeant Rogers ran over in a rage: "Put that damned fire out, you nut—you'll get us all killed!" I felt insulted as I obeyed. It was almost ready, I thought, just a few more min—Z-z-z-z-z-z-t-t-t-! Puffs of stinging dirt rippled along the trench top as bullets from an automatic weapon came looking for the nut building the fire.

While I was apologizing to everyone for the fire, and cursing Mrs. McGrath's damned patented noodle soup, General Beightler and I Corps brass were pondering a rapidly changing situation. Jap defenses had practically collapsed following the capture of Santa Fe, leaving the Americans with no immediate plan. Yamashita had counted confidently on the rainy season, but we had beaten it to the pass. Beightler realized that the Japs must not be allowed time to erect a new defensive line, suggesting that the 37th launch a running attack while the enemy was still off balance. His plan was approved, and on May 31 the 129th Infantry spearheaded a drive north on Highway 5. The objective was to break out of the pass and push rapidly on through the Cagayan Valley to the sea, some 260 miles away. What was shaping up was a twenty-six-day campaign involving constant rotation of leading companies, battalions and regiments in lightning-like thrusts of tanks and motorized infantry. The division flowed by strongpoints, always hitting the enemy before he had time to erect effective defenses. This was to be the only instance of lightning-war, or blitzkrieg, in the Pacific theatre.

13. Cagayan Valley Blitzkrieg

All of us sensed that the campaign just opened was different from any of the others. We moved constantly, usually by truck, digging in at a more advanced locale each night. Information regarding this strange new campaign passed by word of mouth. The name Cagayan Valley was on our lips by the time we moving through its hilly southern reaches. The valley ran north and south for some 260 miles, was up to 30 miles wide, and bore the name of its major river. It was hemmed in by mountains on three sides, but opened on the South China Sea to the north. The valley floor was as flat as an open book except for a brief but rough folding of terrain at Orioung Pass, a defile all of us erroneously called "Oran Pass." Balete Pass was the southern gateway to this lush region, but its fall had quickly shifted the advantages of terrain from the enemy to the armored columns of the mobile Americans.

The Cagayan Valley was the last stronghold of imperial Japan in the Philippines. It had become a catchall for Jap troops driven from other parts of the islands. Yamashita was up ahead somewhere in person, laying plans to blunt and perhaps halt the oncoming Yanks. He still had plenty of power. His 101st Division lurked in the flanking mountains while the 2nd Armored Division dug its fuel short tanks into the soft earth as deadly pillboxes at most road crossings. From Aparri, on the northern coast, Yamashita's 103rd Division was moving south. Many other Jap units wandered through the valley, an ever present danger. (Division headquarters learned this to its sorrow one horrible night in mid-June.)

As the 37th uncorked its unique blitzkrieg, I watched in awe the firepower now at the beck and call of our regiments. War's end in Europe was beginning to bring military abundance to the Pacific. Swarms of Mustang fighters swept over, strafing and bombing the enemy. Tanks and tank destroyers rolled on heavy tracks as 240 mm artillery and self-propelled howitzers softened enemy positions before them. I liked the Long Toms, watching their great barrels slowly turn to sniff out new targets, then roaring their shells off at an enemy twenty miles away and out of sight through the valley mists. I did not feel sorry for the Japs receiving this onslaught, but I respected them for standing up to it.

The Mustang pilots loved their planes. I knew this as I watched them. They often played follow-the-leader after finishing a mission. Three or four of these sleek fighters would dart in and out of steep valleys, sailing like leaves driven by a windstorm up and over the mountain crests. One afternoon I lay flat on my back in a tiny mountain stream, letting the gurgling water cool me. Three Mustangs whirred up my valley, so low their propellor blasts blew sticks and water out of the stream. I jumped up, standing naked in utter envy of such a life as that.

We were one week into the Cagayan campaign on Thursday, June 7, the day the 129th crossed the Magat River and entered the town of Bayombong. The division headquarters gang arrived a few hours later. I saw a sight I shall never forget, a vision of horror beyond the powers of Edgar Allan Poe, and proof that in the Japanese of the Samurai Code we faced soldiers we probably could never understand. As I wrote home later: "We came across a hospital in Bayombong where about 200 Japanese sick and wounded had been killed by their own hand or by their officers before we arrived. It was a horrible and stinking sight. Bodies were everywhere and were bloated and torn. Some sprawled with bayonets in their bellies, others minus bellies because of grenades, and thousands of blue flies buzzing everywhere."

No charnel house of old Europe could have matched this, nor could the reasoning behind this mass suicide-murder pact have been duplicated in most other eras or regions of our planet. We walked in silent amazement through the twisted heaps of dead flesh and tattered clothing, hearing only the squeaking of the scabby wooden floors in what had been a low-flung Filipino school building. I wandered through, inhaling the gases and odors now rising and mixing in the heat of this tropical day. A small bridge crossed the creek in front, and near this our mess hall was going into operation. Flies from the hospital mingled and consorted with flies buzzing around the food. I was thinking of protesting this blatant lapse of sanitation, when a burst of rifle fire came from the hospital. It was over even as we ducked and grabbed for our guns. A live Nip had been lying with the dead, planning on taking some hated Yanks into death with him. He moved slightly as he prepared a grenade. A wary soldier whirled and shot him to death. Later, a small bulldozer scraped out a long pit. The bodies were unceremoniously dragged out and sent flopping one after another into the pit. They were soon covered by the dozer. Meanwhile, across the creek, mess was served as usual.

We left Bayombong and the dead Japs behind us, but soon encountered worse trouble from live ones up on Orioung Pass. Yamashita was defending it with everything he had, including banzai attacks. It took our 145th Infantry three days of bloody fighting to cut its way into the flatlands again on June 12. Some of the enemy now doubled back into positions above the pass, "setting up an ambush . . . and knocking out two tanks and five trucks, killing 30. At the time I was just down the road. One of the trucks was loaded with 81mm mortar [shells], so for a few minutes our area was peppered with these 10 lb. shells."

That night on guard duty I picked up a nickname. I thought I heard Japs sneaking through the darkness in front of me. I needed a grenade, but I had none; instead, the muzzle blast of my machine gun revealed my position. A Nip grenade was sure to come—I leaped clear of the machine gun, awaiting results ten yards to the left with my carbine. Every bandsman had rushed to his gun, sure an attack was coming in. We perked our ears into the darkness, but identified only the chirping of crickets and the rustling sounds of some small animal in the tall grass. "Go back to bed, Gunner," someone said disgustedly. I was Gunner Mathias from that time on. Other nervous trigger fingers used this knowledge to satisfy doubts in the gloom of a rainy night, knowing that Gunner would be blamed as usual for disturbing the peace.

After the shootout at Orioung Pass, the Cagayan Valley campaign developed true blitzkrieg proportions. At times over fifty miles separated the 37th's leading elements from the rear guard. Division headquarters was as likely to be up with the fast-moving armor and infantry as anyplace else. We were astonished when hundreds of prisoners were taken—what was the world coming to when you could not count on a Jap to commit hara-kiri! But these were not Nips, even though they dressed like them; they were Korean labor troops glad to be rid of their oppressive masters.

Division officers welcomed the unusual inflow of prisoners, pumping lifesaving information from this talkative crowd concerning Jap positions and plans of ambush ahead of us. During these interrogations, I was walking along a small ridge above General Beightler's tent. My friend Meatnose Findor walked behind me, his rifle slung through his arm. He was tall and I was short, and I had a very close haircut. We were silhouetted against the sunset when Beightler saw us: "Bring that Jap down here," the general shouted. Meatnose and I were puzzled, looking around to see where the Jap was. Then we laughed and trotted down to the tent, for I was the "Jap." When we arrived, Uncle Bob laughed as he looked me over: "Son," he grinned, "you'd better get yourself a better haircut next time and grow up some—I thought for sure your buddy was bringing in another prisoner!"

We became filthy as the campaign wore on. Our fatigues reeked of sweat-caked dust and our bodies stank. Pasquale "Patsy" Marchette, the band's friendly barber, spied a tiny stream meandering through a thicket of bamboo and tall reeds. He guided Johnny and me to it and we stripped and rolled eagerly into the water. But this stream "had some very unfriendly inhabitants. Before we knew it we found ourselves covered with big 3 inch leeches. It didn't take us long to vacate that place. They just seemed to swarm up off the bottom."

Other loathsome inhabitants of this valley were vicious ants. They had powerful jaws on one end and a hot stinger in the other. One of the officers was a pompous perfectionist, needling his dog-robber (orderly) continually. Everyone felt sorry for him. One night the dog-robber set up his boss's tent over an ant hill, not noticing the slight rise of the mound. Before going to bed, the officer laid a cake of sweet-smelling soap on top of the mosquito bar covering his cot. The ants came after the soap, forming lines up and down the sides of the netting. Early in the morning the officer had to use the urinal. He lifted the netting, but as he rose it bushed down his bare back, transferring the lines of ants to his skin. They bit and stung as they hit, sending him flailing and shouting into the dark. The next day the greeting around division headquarters was: "Say something good for ants!"

The blitzkrieg up the Cagayan Valley was nerve wracking, for the unexpected often hit with stunning force. Take, for instance, a peaceful looking little town named Ilagan, near the Cagayan River. Things had gone well that day as our infantry approached. Streams of bullets and shells suddenly came from nowhere, inflicting deaths and wounds as the seeming peace of a sunny day was abruptly shot to shreds. Nine or ten Jap tanks had been dug in as pill boxes and cleverly camouflaged. They were backed by hidden infantrymen. Casualties mounted alarmingly before they were knocked out. The division had to dispose of over seventy such tanks during this campaign.

The band continually provided men for patrols to investigate areas and positions by-passed by our fast-moving armor. Was the enemy still there? No one knew; it was up to the patrols to find out the hard way. We moved down small ravines, checking cave systems as we went. The Nips favored meandering creek beds, digging deadly fire pits into the weed-hidden banks. We gingerly searched these places, hoping no one was at home. We noticed the heavy, jagged pieces of bombs scattered about, glad that the Mustangs had been here before us. It was sobering to think of these huge shards of shrapnel splitting the air, each capable of shearing a man in half. We kicked open the flimsy doors of nipa huts, braced against the unexpected. The grassy hills of northern Luzon offered no cover for patrols. I felt eyes watching me. Somewhere out there a Jap was waiting for me to get too close. Complex caverns dug under some of these hills were worse. The Japs stored supplies in them. We eased tensely into the gloomy interiors. Often we found stacks of valuable things inside. One cavern was full of communications equipment, with stacks of short wave radios modeled after the fine American "Hallicrafters" of that era. Another had scores of tool kits and chests, all of enviable quality. I took two tool kits, writing later that "the Japs made junk toys, but their ability to make quality army goods is as great as anybody's." After the war this ability was turned to civilian production with spectacular results. I found many things on the patrols, but the Nips had gone—which was just as well.

Letters from my girl friends back home had dwindled alarmingly. The war seemed of eternal length, and absence did not make the heart grow fonder. "Thanks for the sprig of bluegrass you sent me," I replied to Frances Henry, "I'm sending back a piece of banana leaf." This was hardly the kind of banter we had exchanged two years ago, but the world had changed for both of us. The romance of war had faded like a dying ember in the loneliness and mounting casualty lists. War had become a crashing bore and worse for the girls at home. Dread had replaced the excitement of 1943 when our class had rolled away on the bus for Fort Thomas.

The war had stretched me thin in ways I did not understand nor would understand until I had returned to the secure tranquility of my Kentucky home. One night I tied one end of my jungle hammock to a large banana plant, mistaking it for a palm tree. It sagged and collapsed on me after I had gone to sleep. I thrashed wildly before fighting free of the "Jap" who had attacked me. We laughed, but all of us were keyed more tightly than we knew.

I had given up hope of getting home soon, writing in mid-June, 1945, that "this war might drag on for another two years." I knew I had no chance of rotation, in which a soldier with enough points was sent to the States for a three-week furlough. Many veterans had three times the points I had, but they carried a very special fear with them when out on patrol. "Suppose a 100 pointer got caught in a stupid Jap raid and got killed," I wrote my brother, "about like those guys killed on November 10, 1918, or like Andy [Metcalfe] just before VE day. Wouldn't that be a shame?" Noncoms and officers were conscious of this, assigning hundred-pointers less dangerous duty whenever possible.

Censorship was a nuisance for most soldiers and civilians. It was overdone. I had a letter returned "as having too much prohibited information in it. . . . We must stick to the facts I guess and not add our opinions to it." Two weeks later a letter dated June 30 made it through the censor, but was cut typically: "A.P.O. 43 means [censored] . J.E. is in that [censored] in the [censored] regiment. There are [censored] regiments in a division." I was trying to reply to a question from my parents concerning the whereabouts of my Carlisle classmate, J.E. Soper, as follows: "A.P.O. 43 means 43rd Division. J.E. is in that division in the 169th regiment. There are three regiments in a division." Yamashita couldn't have cared less about the whereabouts of Private John Estill Soper, and he already knew enough about the redoubtable 43rd Division to last him a lifetime!

One afternoon Joe E. Brown walked into division headquarters. We were pleased, for he was a noted movie comedian of gentle but sharp wit. He opened his famous gaping mouth wide, then snapped it shut with a tiny little "hello." Joe was a native of Ohio, and he lived with us for several days. We heard he had killed several Japs while on a patrol. This was verified later in the *Navy News,* January 2, 1946: "Maj. Gen. Robert S. Beightler revealed that Joe E. Brown was credited with killing two Japs on Luzon."

Brown probably got his Japs somewhere along Highway 5. They were constantly being flushed from cover under culverts and roadside huts. Their bodies sprawled here and there along the road. We became used to seeing them. I sat alongside the road one day eating K-rations. Five or six bloated bodies were in a ditch below me. I absent-mindedly watched bubbles of gas and liquid moving around under their tightly stretched skins as I munched my crackers. The June sunlight was bright and hot. They were in their world and I was in mine. I had to eat, didn't I?

Live officers worried me more than dead Japs. Division headquarters was full of them. "They pile unnecessary stuff on us. I'm petered out." Their "whims" were especially irksome, I wrote. "The general had one tent with enlisted men move because it blocked his view (of more tents!). Another tent had to roll their rear flap down presumably because the general just couldn't stand to have to look in on enlisted men. Of course this doesn't apply to all officers but it is the few that make it hard." I failed to reveal whether the erring general was Beightler, Kreber, or Craig.

Sometimes it was possible to help materially some of the Filipinos so hard hit by the war:

We were tented by a little Filipino house several days ago and inside we found not only Britanica [sic] but the Harvard

Classics, not to mention all the books on general subjects like physics, math, English. I took a world atlas, turned to page 36 and pointed out Carlisle to every one, not that anyone was interested in it in the least.

The Filipino was a school teacher and agriculturist and had only recently been killed in an air raid so we learned from his wife and daughter. The Japs had torn their house to pieces by kicking much of the sides out and all the windows, so just this woman and her daughter were in bad shape. We helped them all we could with [food, clothes, repairs, and money]. We've met many people in like condition or worse however.

Everything was going extremely well as the division rushed northward toward the sea. We crossed the swollen Cagayan River on a pontoon bridge, walking our trucks gingerly across flooded segments. We paused for a break, and I washed my socks in a small stream, "looking down in amazement to see a crab carrying one of them away. I didn't get it back but I know the ocean must not be far away." It was much farther away than I thought, for crabs lived deep into the tidal waters of this flat valley. We also used socks to hardboil eggs. The cook was given an egg to let us hang a sockfull in the boiling coffee water. The coffee always tasted the same no matter what went in it.

During the early evening of Saturday, June 23, we called a halt north of Tumauini, and set up the division command post. It was flat country, not far from hills nor far from the Cagayan River. The band set up its tents alongside an airstrip. I dug a shallow hole, flopped down my machine gun so it covered the airstrip, then went to eat. I returned, tied my messkit to the tent flap, then joined my buddies in talking about the war and wondering when we would arrive at Tuguegarao, the next town of any size to the north. The campaign was seemingly over, and most of the men in division headquarters did not dig holes. A beautiful moon arose over the scene by the time we hit our bunks. We soon were asleep.

A splintering, shattering roar lifted me from my cot. I hit the ground scrambling for my foxhole, terrified, knowing my survival was at stake. Confused shouting was on all sides, immediately smothered by the smashing roar and hot blasts of big shells landing in our midst. I made it to the shallow hole, cursing myself for not digging deeper. My steel helmet was in the tent. I covered my head with the machine gun. Suddenly the entire area lit up; they had hit the airstrip's gasoline dump. It erupted in a large fireball, burning furiously and providing a perfect marker for the Jap artillerymen. They poured it on. I could hear the crump of their cannons, followed almost immediately by the uneven rustling of the shells coming in. They had caught us in point-blank fire. A shell hit several feet away, the shrapnel's fluttering whine turning to a rattle as it punched holes in the dangling messkits. I was getting wet! A shell had exploded by a water truck parked in front of the next tent, tearing a wheel off, but saving the men huddled in the tent. Jets of water spurted from the ruptured tank, much of it running into my hole. I prayed with my face in the mud: "God don't let them have timers—don't let them have aerial bursts." They were using daisy cutters, shells that burst on impact, showering the area with man-killing shrapnel. Shells timed to burst in the air above us would kill or wound everyone in division headquarters.

I lay there as they pounded us, no longer terrified but numbly resigned to whatever fate held for me. The shallow hole vibrated as duds thudded into the nearby ground, tumbling and caroming about the area, impersonally smashing their dead weight through tents and against trucks. There was a lull of a few seconds: "Infantry attack—watch out for infantry attack!" My heart leaped at this warning. I pulled my machine gun into position, squinting into the flickering light across the flaming airstrip. I was almost relieved as the shells started smacking in again; nothing was going to walk across that airstrip. I pulled my gun back over my head. I hung on, grim and numb, becoming puzzled by a new sound above me. The shells seemed to be going two ways at once, none of them dropping on us. A murmur, then a chorus of shouts greeted the new sound. Our 140th Field Artillery Battalion had moved up, mounting counter-battery fire against the Japs. Shells were going both ways as the Nips lifted their fire, trying to reach our gunners. I knew Soda Shrout was back there with the 140th's big guns, trying to target the Japs. "Give 'em hell, Soda!" I mumbled through clenched teeth. We milled around above ground, listening to the artillery duel and checking for wounded. We should have used the time to dig deeper.

The 140th did its best, but they were unable to pinpoint the Jap guns. When the Nips found this out, they turned their guns back on us. The familiar sound of incoming mail scrambled us for cover. I plunged into my muddy hole, wondering what had gone wrong. Showers of dirt and debris dropped on my back as the Jap gunners pumped several hundred more shells into us. An observation plane laid our artillery on the Jap guns by dawn's early light, knocking them out.

No one was laughing as we surveyed the damage. The division had by-passed three well hidden batteries of Jap 105mm cannon—twelve guns. They had hit us with hundreds of shells between midnight and dawn. The first shell in—the one lifting me from my cot—had struck a nearby tent killing men I had been with throughout the campaign. A heavy hot piece of shrapnel had dropped on Chick's back just before dawn, causing him to shriek that he was wounded. He was not, but his cry wrenched my emotions at the time. Five were killed and many were wounded, however, and division headquarters was a shambles. The tents were in shreds, much equipment shattered, and our vehicles punched full of holes with flat tires everywhere. Dud shells, shiny from having slid and bounded through the area, lay in silent menace around the torn tents. We were offered all the fresh eggs we could eat for breakfast, a treat long planned by the cooks. Few of us could eat. It was a severely shaken gang from headquarters that stumbled around that Sunday picking up the pieces.

The command post trucks, each suffering from a bad case of shrapnelitis, finally limped into Tuguegarao on Tuesday, June 26. The 129th Infantry had moved through this small city the day before, and was now covering the forty-five miles between it and the coastal city of Aparri. The Luzon campaign was nearing an end. The next day, as our infantry moved forward, elements of the 511th Parachute Infantry of the 11th Airborne Division dropped on Aparri. Shortly after noon the Buckeyes and paratroopers met with cheers, hugs, and a shaking of hands. The Luzon campaign, biggest operation of the Pacific war, had ended for all practical purposes. The official end was designated at midnight, June 30, five months and three weeks after the landings on the Lingayen beaches.

Most of us in the 37th were never able to understand why a thousand paratroopers were dropped on Aparri. At first we were angry about missing the big black headlines again, as at Manila. Then we heard correctly that Filipino guerrillas had taken the town earlier, that General Krueger knew this, but that in an empty gesture he still ordered the drop. The troopers themselves admitted they had been greeted by the guerrillas upon landing. They had suffered numerous casualties during the windblown drop; I saw one of their wrecked gliders sprawled in the grass a few days later. It seemed senseless, for Aparri was in friendly hands and the 129th would have been there in a matter of hours.

A seldom told story of the campaign in northern Luzon is that of the Filipino guerrillas. They, as well as units from the Philippines Armed Forces, were attached to the 37th as we swept the Cagayan Valley. They liberated many small towns, patrolled mountain passes, and often prevented the enemy from leaving one area to reinforce another. They outfought the Nips man to man anytime the odds were even. The story of these guerrillas is also that of Col. Russell W. Volckmann, an army man who took to the hills in 1942 after the island fell to the invaders.

When the Yanks returned in 1945, Col. Volckmann offered his force of several thousand guerrillas to the Sixth Army, but at first he was taken lightly. His force soon grew to an enthusiastic eighteen thousand men, after which it was well equipped and sent to disrupt all but the most powerful enemy formations in northern Luzon. They went from one success to another, capturing Jap artillery and blocking such crucial roads as the one between Baguio and Tuguegarao. Volckmann's men knew the terrain and they were fighting for their homeland. Yamashita's plans were given severe setbacks by Volckmann's guerrillas on more than one occasion.

The campaign was over but the mopping up was not. Thousands of enemy soldiers were still scattered through the region, some in pockets containing as many as twelve thousand men. Their situation was ultimately hopeless and many were starving, but it was extremely dangerous to go after them. Patrols continually went forth to check on them. Lives dribbled away daily in savage little fire fights between these patrols and Jap stragglers.

Not long after the band settled into tents at Tuguegarao, three bandsmen were trucked as guards to an advanced supply outpost until headquarters could be moved up. My buddies Gil Silvius, "Patsy" Marchette, and Walter "Bus" Groves were "volunteered" for the duty. They tried to recruit me, making "at least enough guys for cards," but I shrugged off the invitation for some forgotten reason. This was to be one of the luckiest decisions of my life.

The three had not been at the outpost long before hearing sounds of movement in the shrubby surroundings. Several men were spotted moving around a distant hillside. Silvius radioed back to the colonel in charge of headquarters defense, asking that a squad and machine gun be sent up. He was turned down. "What are you trying to do Gil, get a poker game going?" A deadlier game was already under way, with the stakes set at life or death. Silvius later revealed what had happened:

> We settled down for the night in a tent on the ends of the outpost, setting up a guard rotation of two hour shifts. Mattresses "borrowed" from bedrolls in the supplies made the hard ground a bit more comfortable. Bus was on guard when, after midnight, the Japs hit us with at least half-a dozen grenades. They immediately withdrew, evidently thinking the storage tents represented a 20 or 30 man force.
>
> Lucky for us the Japs did not follow up their advantage, for Bus's face was a mess, all bloody, and he lost an eye and couldn't see. Patsy had been hit in the belly and was doubled up in pain, cursing in Italian. The borrowed mattress saved my life. It was ripped to shreds and my back and legs had more than 500 grenade fragments in them. Our rifles had been blown apart. We were completely out of action. I led Bus with one hand and Patsy with the other as we started back toward the lines. After a mile or two, we found a guy with a jeep to take us to the nearest hospital.

I visited the trio in the hospital, shuddering to think how close I had come to going with them. They were in good spirits, especially Gil, who chuckled as he recalled awakening in the hospital "to find the 129th's chaplain sitting by my bed with a bottle in his hand. 'Gil,' he said, 'I thought we should have communion together. I hope this wine won't leak through all those holes in you. Somebody might misunderstand!'"

The band was nervous; first the shelling at Tumauini, and now the grenade attack. The Luzon campaign had "officially" ended, but not for the Nips! Trigger fingers were itching as the band moved its tents outside Tuguegarao's city limits. We faced a wooded ravine and a low ridge to the east. The ravine was wired with flares and white phosphorous grenades to warn us against enemy intrusion. I lay awake in bed late that night. Someone in the distance was shouting: "ben-gay, ben-gay." The voice came again: "ben-gay, ben-gay." I wondered who would be shouting the name of a patent medicine this late at night. Then a chilling thought came to me and others hearing the voice—BANZAI! My God, I thought, maybe a banzai attack is shaping up out there!

My thoughts were confirmed when a flare arched into the black sky, its flickering light wavering over the area. Then another one was tripped off. I rushed to the foxhole, cocking my machine gun. I raised up a bit to see the ridge. There they came, a single line of Japs along the grassy ridge. A musician in a half track turned twin .50-calibre machine guns on them, firing withering amounts of lead from the drums. Others joined in, but I could not; my damn gun was sighted below the ridge line. Silence. No more flares went off. Where had the Japs gone? We waited anxiously, enduring the hordes of blood-sucking mosquitoes. We had nothing on but our shorts. It was soon light enough to see the ridge. There they lay, grotesquely twisted and shot to pieces by the big fifties—a row of fence posts! The uncertain light of the flares had made these vine-covered posts look like camouflaged Japs coming over the ridge. A Jap straggler had been out there, for we had heard him, but he had been shouting something other than "banzai." My title of "Gunner" was now passed to the post-busting bandsman who, we laughed, "played the 'Woodpecker Song' in five flats on his twin fifties!"

14. Atomic Malaria

Early in July the Buckeye Division was transferred back to XIV Corps control, but under the Eighth Army command of Lt. Gen. Robert L. Eichelberger. Though few of us knew it, I Corps and Sixth Army were being readied for the coming invasion of Japan. This left the 6th, 32nd, 37th, and 38th divisions still on the line in Luzon. Forces still available to Yamashita were underestimated by the staff, for he came out of the mountains with fifty thousand soldiers at war's end! I wrote home that "I just saw General Eichelberger . . . His jeep had three stars on it. I've seen all the big shots now from MacArthur on down. Joe E. Brown dropped by not long ago, and I saw Henry Luce, the editor of Time & Life. The 37th is well known."

I wrote a letter home analyzing my ten months overseas. No one had heard of the atomic bomb at this time, and my views were typical of most soldiers my age:

Time seems to fly. June 28 already. July 20 I'll have 10 months overseas. Remember last year from New Guinea when I said a bunch of us predicted the war (VJ) would be over December 10, '45. Be nice if that proved to be true. Lets see, that's around 6 months off. A lot could happen by then. I do think it will end around fall or late summer '46. It has taken around nine months to take the Philippines. Even if they landed on Japan today it would be at least until March '46 before they could have things pretty well in hand. Just to remind you how well the Japs fight look at these figures. In just 2¾ months on Okinawa they killed 13,000 Americans. During the whole Italian campaign the Germans managed to kill 21,000. We killed 100,000 Japs on Okinawa but the Japs say they are willing to lose 5,000,000 men in their war with us. On the same scale as the Okinawa campaign that would take us 650,000 men to kill 5,000,000. 650,000 dead men I mean. I sure hope the Japs get discouraged and give up. That's probably the same thing the Japs would wish if they had fought their way to a beachhead on California. I wonder if we would give up though? Course we don't think like Japs so maybe they will give up. However, they may think themselves into national suicide and give us the problem of killing all 70,000,000 of them. Some situation isn't it? I like to write about it so I'll have my opinions of June 28, '45 on paper. Then if I'm around on June 28, '50, I'll know what I thought about then. I'll also see whether I was near right or not. We have a lot of sayings over here. Home alive in '45—Out of the sticks in '46—Hell to Heaven in '47—Golden Gate in '48. Be real nice to get outa th' sticks in '46.

Victory in Europe seemed to help the Pacific food supply. My opinion of our headquarters cooks, now at Tuguegarao, rose rapidly. "We get fresh eggs now.... I ate 5 hardboiled eggs and 4 pork chops before bed last night. I was on guard from 12 to 1, but I sneaked 2 more chops from the mess hall supper, stuck them on a fork and tied it to a string to the tent to keep the bugs off. . . . As you can see now that the war is over in Europe they really are feeding us. We have good cooks too. They have to cook for 400 men per meal. They have four stoves only. How would you like to cook 2000 eggs for breakfast . . . and hundreds of gallons of coffee, open hundreds of cans and move the whole damn kitchen maybe 20 or 30 miles between breakfast and dinner and have dinner ready usually about 1:00 PM. They're the unpublicized heros."

The great day finally came—the day of my promotion from Pfc. to corporal. On July 15 I wrote my parents that "I made two-striper today, about one year after making Pfc back at Camp Wheeler." I rushed out to find a Filipina seamstress to sew the stripes on my fatigues and suntan shirt. It seemed the folks on the Tuguegarao streets treated me with more respect as I walked by with my corporal stripes. I felt good about this every time I looked at my shirt sleeve—and I looked often.

Novelists and romantics who sing praises of the South Pacific often ignore the blazing tropical heat. We suffered from it in our Tuguegarao tent city. The July sun rose over the Cagayan Valley like a boil in the pallid sky, covering everything with liquid heat. We could smell the waterproofing of our tents under this solar blast. The weblike canvas of our cots held puddles of sweat any time we managed to get in an afternoon nap. Our blood was so thin it seemed to gurgle in our veins. And no cool wave like those of temperate regions was going to descend to make tomorrow any different from today.

It was a challenge to pass time now that the campaign was winding down. We managed to get an occasional pass to Manila. Mostly, we made our entertainment where we were. "We eat, sleep, swim, play, cuss, fuss day in and day out," I told my brother. "One bandsman has 8 chickens and two ducks. The rooster keeps us awake all night but the eggs are good. He had a game cock so we had a cock fight with a Filipino. Cock fighting is a big thing here. We all bet on our cock. But he fed it so much that it couldn't leave the ground so the other cock killed it. The guy with the gamecock is crazy anyway. A Jap grenade hit him on Bougainville. Several days ago he tied a freon mosquito spray can to his belt, turned it on and ran around shouting, 'Look, I'm a rocket ship!' He also chases the Filipinos with a huge samurai saber he found."

The band had some superb artists; one, Rob Romanowitz, painted rotten spots on a collection of fruit an oboist had purchased from a peddler in town. The oboist was amazed at how quickly his fruit had spoiled, and rushed back to the peddler, where the trick was discovered. The reedman slipped back to the tent, finding Romanowitz sound asleep, wearing his thick glasses as usual. He picked up a watercolor brush and painted his glasses black, then shook him awake. The artist paused, thinking he had slept through sundown, then panicked at the thought of sudden blindness as he flailed about the tent before ripping his glasses off. The oboist handed him a "rotten" mango: "They're good for what ails you, Robby!"

We now journeyed north for a two-week stand at the 129th Infantry's famous "Mosquito Bar," reopened along the beaches near Aparri. These lonely, lovely strands faced the Babuyan Channel of the South China Sea, with the sleepy tropical villages of Ballesteros and Abulug nearby. The area was enchanting in its beauty, of which I wrote, mentioning also the contrastingly sharp spine "of Komigin [Camiguin] Volcano rising abruptly out of the ocean . . . 15 miles off the coast." Had I left this northernmost coast of Luzon by boat, I would have landed on Formosa (Taiwan), three hundred miles to the north. Veering to the northwest for five hundred miles would have brought me to harbor at Hong Kong. It was almost that far by winding road south to Manila from this lovely and isolated part of the world.

Our tents were behind the windblown sand dunes, free of mosquitoes as well as memories of the past campaign. We played the friendly and roisterous "Mosquito Bar" at night, and a few parades by day, but tanned ourselves in the roaring surf the rest of the time. Our idyllic life ended in late July when we returned to the command post at Tuguegarao, arriving in time to see Christianity take a minor setback. "We almost had a big bamboo chapel. The frame work was the size of a burley tobacco barn. Well, yesterday, about 50 Filipinos were getting ready to put the thatch roof on when the damn roof folded up like an accordian. Flips were jumping everywhere. I'll bet even the chaplain was cussing." This was seen as an exciting intrusion into the boring routine of garrison duty, stimulating arguments over engineering and architectural problems for many days.

I was more interested in the new chaplain's assistant than I was in the collapsed chapel. Jack Ehlinger had been transferred from the 148th to his new assignment at headquarters. We had gone overseas together from Fort Ord aboard the *Monterey,* shared the training at Oro Bay, then lost touch with each other on Bougainville. "He is a swell guy my own age," I wrote home. "Many of the old guys from New Guinea are under crosses now. . . . Jack told me of one guy we had buddied with that was killed several months ago in the 148th AT Co. I had known him ever since Fort Ord and we were together in the convoy coming to Luzon. He was a fellow of French descent named Marcel." Jack and I talked of Marcel, recalling the time he and I had taken our socks full of "gold" to the chaplain at Oro bay. Now he was gone. I later visited his grave in the cross-spangled cemetery in Manila.

So far, the South Pacific's plagues had passed me by. Not that they were not there, for a steady stream of soldiers passed in and out of the medic's tent, even for such minor things as the great Friday wart-burn. Every Friday the medics burned warts off G.I. hands with electric pencils, the sizzling odor drifting through tents all down the row. One of the chaplains joked about Catholics doing this on Friday.

The more serious ailments were no lauging matter. "The Cagayan Valley," I confided to a friend, "is very disease ridden although I haven't heard any mosquitoes buzzing me yet. We had ½ c.c. of cholera serum shot into us today. If the needle had been much bigger we'd of all had the purple heart." A night or so later the joke was on me.

I answered some mail on the evening of August 2, then went to my cot, utterly exhausted. I awakened around midnight, knowing instantly that something was terribly wrong. I tried counting the holes in my mosquito bar to keep from losing my mind. Nothing worked. I was feverish, and staggered from the tent hoarsely crying for the medics. A voice from the dark shouted: "Go back to your tent and sober up—you'll wake us all up!" I remember being mad at this, but another voice directed me to the medics' tent. I tripped over guy ropes along the way, but finally saw the lantern in the tent. The soldier on duty sized me up quickly: "You've got malaria. We'll send you to the hospital in the morning, but right now I'm going to give you a morphine syrett."

As he prepared the syrett, I thought of the word "morphine," worrying as much about it as the malarial diagnosis. "Will it turn me into a dope-fiend?" I asked, getting no answer. I recalled Carlisle's town dope-fiend, shooting himself in the horseweeds alongside the ball park as hidden kids watched. He had often tried unsuccessfully to get the doctor's son to bring him drugs from his dad's office. The medic administered the shot. I was surprised I did not have the dreams Coleridge mentioned in my high school English books. I felt no better nor worse, but went back to my tent. An hour later I staggered back, feeling worse than ever. This time I received a shot that knocked me out for the rest of the night.

The next morning I joined a truck load of patients for the two-mile ride into Tuguegarao and the 43rd Field Evacuation Hospital. Half of the patients were in a school building, the other half in rows of long tents, some twenty men in each one. I was assigned a tent where a doctor told me I had malaria and also jaundice.

Malaria is a mystifying disease, the attacks coming only at night and ending at dawn, as if in fear of the daylight. Malarial parasites destroy red blood cells, sometimes backing them up to cause deadly blackwater fever. I was found to have a middle-of-the-road variety that usually attacked every other night, leaving ample time for my body to rebuild blood. Another variation, which comes nightly, kills quickly. After an attack my body screamed for food. Some of us occasionally collapsed in the hospital chow line in our eagerness to eat. Breakfast was not served in bed in a field hospital!

Jaundice, another blood disease, complicated my case in that I was taken off greasy foods. I was put on a liquid diet for this, and stuffed full of atabrine for the malaria. The atabrine caused a ringing in my ears that has been with me ever since. Earaches and the like are endemic in the South Pacific, caused first by quinine and later by the synthetic atabrine that replaced it. The jaundice and atabrine together turned my skin a ghastly yellow, with blue lines marking my veins like highways on a road map. I was a feature attraction in the shower stalls. The whites of my eyes were yellow with blue dots in the center, my urine the color of Coca-Cola. I was sick as hell, but still optimistic.

An anopheles mosquito had nailed me somewhere two weeks back, and I soon figured back to the night. It had to be the night all of us lay nearly naked in our foxholes while the machine gunner blasted the fenceposts. We had been swarmed by the little vampires that night. The timing was perfect, according to our doctor, for the disease to get seated and strike me down.

I wrote a cheery letter home: "I knew I would get it sooner or later, as it comes to soldiers here like whooping cough at home. . . . It's just like being sick in the summertime at home as the heat is terrific. You would think that all the Hospitals would be in cool Baguio, but the army doesn't see things that way." I vividly remember the sweltering tent, sitting there day after day in the solar blast, any breeze blocked by neighboring tents. We accepted it, for even in the States air conditioning was unknown anywhere but in movie houses.

My tentmates and I developed an unusual game to while away the hours. The tent had a powdery dirt floor, pitted with ant lion dens. Each one lay covered at the bottom of its funnel-shaped pit, waiting to grab unwary insects that tumbled in. Each patient had a favorite ant lion, one he felt was faster on the draw than any other. We pulled wings off the always abundant flies, dropping them into the pits and betting on the results. This gambling enterprise may well be unique to the 43rd Field Hospital. No one amassed any winnings except the ant lions, which uncomplainingly took anything that came their way.

When the ant lions bored me I looked to the fellow in the next cot. He was an old man of thirty-five, but I admired him and got to know him. Bill had been a tattoo artist in civilian life. His body advertised his craft, covered as it was with tattoos from his collar down to his ankles and wrists. There was the NRA Blue Eagle, grasping a cog wheel, various bewreathed mottoes professing eternal love or simply stating "Born to Lose." Patriotism was promoted by a Statue of Liberty or by the Liberty Bell, which swung to and fro when he flexed his biceps. There were fighting ships and planes. Hula girls danced on his flexing muscles. Bill liked his craft, and told us stories of some of his proudest moments. He spoke knowingly of a woman he had decorated, placing a bluebird on each breast, forever flying toward one another. His proudest feat, he laughed, was having the courage to tattoo a fly on a man's organ. With this he always slapped his pajamas in the crotch, indicating that the fly was still there. We followed him to the shower, finding he had not lied.

A hospital tent was an ideal place to talk out real or imagined problems. The love-hate relationship with MacArthur coursed our veins as surely as the malarial parasites. In fact, Dugout Doug was the greatest one conversation piece in the South Pacific. My letter from the hospital shows that the "hate side" had emerged again, and also reveals the argument against the general in almost pure form: "He's just a publicity hound taking credit for the moves plotted by [Adm. Chester W.] Nimitiz, [Adm. William F.] Halsey and others. He should of gone to Hollywood where he could of shown off all the time. As an example look at his cap. Scrambled eggs all over it and always in style. He even had his wife and kid sent to Manila with him. No other big wigs did. So you can see how things go over here. The good job that has been done has been done by others—not MacArthur. I understand he's considered a 'God' in the states. That will burst like a bubble when these old outfits get home and start talking."

A few days later I wrote home asking the folks to send me canned sardines and candy. In closing, I made my usual reference to the war's end: "I give up trying to guess the war's end. It will come when it comes and that's all I care." This letter was mailed on August 4, 1945. Even as I wrote, a B-29 bomber named Enola Gay was preparing for its bombing run over Hiroshima.

Sunday, August 5, was the usual boring day in the hospital. That afternoon excited jabbering started in the tent next to mine. I heard the words "big bomb" in the rustling of conversation. A pajama-clad patient popped into our tent. "Did you hear what's happened?" he asked breathlessly. "A great secret bomb made of atoms has torn up Japan!" We considered this, knowing how quickly latrine rumors blossomed and vanished. There must be something to it, we decided, for by now the doctors and other officers were as excited as the enlisted men. Word was said to have come over Armed Forces Radio from San Francisco (it was August 6 there) and been picked up at division headquarters. Within ten minutes the report was widely believed; then came doubts, followed by great joy as confirmation started pouring in. With this malingerers underwent miraculous cures, signing out in "tolerable" or "reasonably" good shape. No one wanted to miss the victory celebrations already cranking up in Tuguegarao. The malaria tents could have no thought of this, but visions of a quick return to the joys of Carlisle and Maysville improved my mental and physical condition tremendously. Once again, my world had turned from lead to gold in the space of a few minutes.

I wrote home on August 8 that "all we have been hearing is 'atomic bomb.' It sure means that Japan will be knocked out, but quick. Maybe my guess [that the war would end] Dec. 20th wasn't far off. Heard that anyone entering the area for years after the explosion will be killed by the energy generated in the air. . . . I'm still in the hospital, maybe for 2 or 3 more weeks."

"Well the war is over I think," said my letter of August 11. "That is if we accept their proposition on the Emperor. Boy you never saw so many guys get cured all at once as when the news came over the hospital loudspeaker last nite at 10 till 9 PM. It was Friday, August 10th here. Everyone was shouting, shaking their splints, casts, and hobbling all over the place."

We huddled around the hospital radios. After listening to Radio Tokyo on August 12, I wrote Dad that"the Japanese are denouncing America something awful for using the atomic bomb. Say its destructive power is much worse than poisonous gas and that it would be outlawed from use if we were a civilized nation. Of course they don't say what they would of done if they had invented it. The way they howl it must of really tore hell out of things. As yet they haven't even mentioned Japan surrendering although we heard last night that the allies will spare the emperor on certain conditions. We are sweating out the Japanese answer to our terms."

As usual, a rumor of instant wealth was circulating on the heels of the great event. I believed it and wrote home that "a major at Clark Field will win $175,000 if Japan accepts. He covered every bet on the field three weeks ago that the war would end in 48 days. He probably knew of the atomic bomb some way or other at the time. He gambled and won, I guess."

I do not remember one complaint from anyone, whether American or Filipino, concerning the atomic bombing of the two Japanese cities. The Japanese were thoroughly hated. They had tortured and killed over a hundred thousand people in Manila back in February. This was worse than Hiroshima. War sentiment appeared, for example, in *Yank* magazine of February 18, 1944, before anyone other than insiders knew of atomic research. *Yank* observed that recent revelation of "wholesale torturing, starving, and killing of American and Filipino prisoners of war captured by the Japs at Bataan . . . came as a terrible shock to the people back home. . . . [The Jap] doesn't want to live in the same world with our kind of civilization. The only way to beat an enemy like this is to fight him the same way, [not] . . . settling for anything less than complete victory."

Most soldiers of the time felt this way, including myself. The Japs had asked for it at Pearl Harbor, now they had gotten it. Besides, the 37th Division was slotted to spearhead a ten-division landing just south of Tokyo Bay the next spring. Better the Japs of those two cities perish, than the hundreds of thousands of American casualties an invasion of Japan would bring. Nevertheless, there was a small niggling in my mind at the time that perhaps it would have served as well if the bomb had been dropped out in Tokyo Bay to show what it could do. That would have ended the war and saved the civilians also. Perhaps. Unfortunately, "perhaps" is never good enough to guarantee survival in a global war—or a line infantry company either, for that matter.

On August 15, at eight in the morning, the official unconditional surrender of Japan came through. "I'm happier to write this letter than any other I've ever written because the war is over. I remember back in '42 I was hoping the war would continue in a way as I thought what great fun it must be. Guess I had to learn the hard way with millions more. I heard at dinner (we had chicken) that the Japs are pouring out of the mountains and surrendering. Whether this is true or not I don't know for sure, but it probably is." The next day I took pen in hand again and summed up the feeling prevalent everywhere: "It sure wound up all of a sudden didn't it? One day it seemed it would last for 14 or 15 more months for certain and then the next day we had the atomic bomb, Russia, and the surrender within a week."

Thoughts of getting out of the army began surfacing: "I have 23 months and 12 days in the army now," I wrote home. "Hope I don't have many more months; I'm sure I won't. It's a matter of months now instead of years thanks to the atomic bomb." Still there were signs that we might be overseas longer than we wished, for "rumor is that the entire 37th is to fly up to Japan for occupation duty." Nevertheless, I did not expect to get out of the army as quickly as I did. I wrote home that the division newspaper of August 16 noted "that 5,000,000 men will be discharged within a year to 18 months. This time next year I should be home or almost there." Actually, I arrived back in the States the following February.

I answered a letter from my parents asking whether "soldiers wanted to be buried overseas or brought home?" The Metcalfes had asked them to write me about this following the death of their son in Europe. I asked a number of soldiers and summed up their answer: "Most say they don't care after they're dead, but on consideration would rather remain where they fell with their buddies than be dug up and reinterred 10,000 miles away. The money it would cost (millions) should be given to the widows and orphans."

My financial status at the end of World War II was not bad for a corporal. If I had been discharged August 19, I concluded that I would have "$477.50 in Soldier's Deposit, $255 from insurance, mustering out pay of $300—a total of $1032.50. This is enough to buy a new car if there are any."

I was discharged from the hospital and sent back to duty on August 20. The malarial attacks had been checked, but I was far from being cured; the parasites would course my blood stream for the rest of my life, nor was there any known cure for the hissing and ringing sounds in my years. The doctor's instructions were specific, and I was determined to follow them: never donate blood under any circumstances lest I pass on either malaria or jaundice, abstain from alcohol for several years, and continue taking atabrine until I returned to the States. (I later tested out the alcohol restriction, paying for it each time with a partial relapse.) The guys in the band welcomed me back, joking about my yellow complexion and assigning me to the "mosquito band," a group of our musicians similarly afflicted. I was happy to be back, and felt well enough to return to duty. The war was over, so to hell with the malaria!

The sight of Japanese soldiers strolling into division headquarters flushed our emotions of any lingering doubts regarding the arrival of peace. "The war is really over now," I wrote on August 27, revealing that "yesterday two Jap officers came into Division Hq. and asked for terms of surrender of 8500 men in the hills. . . . It won't be long until the place is crawling with P.O.W.'s." Several hundred former enemy soldiers were soon living in a compound not far from the band tents. They bowed and smiled broad smiles anytime an American approached, accepting crackers, cigarettes or nothing with equal equanimity. We amused ourselves by bowing back, repeating this until we were bowed out or laughing at the scene. The prisoners were often in poor physical condition, ripped with dysentery and near starvation. Some, however, were healthy specimens; in the back of our minds was the thought that without the atomic bomb these guys would still be out there gunning for us. One of our truck convoys, in fact, had suffered casualties three or four days after the official surrender during an attack by a Jap unit ignorant of the fact. Planes were still busy dumping clouds of leaflets printed with the surrender news throughout the mountains.

Now that the shooting war was over, the problem became one of administering Luzon while accepting Japanese surrender. The surrender had to go according to certain niceties that would save face for the Nips, yet move the matter along as rapidly as possible. The task of administering Luzon was decided early; on August 20 Major General Robert Beightler assumed control of the newly formed Luzon Area Command. This meant Uncle Bob took over tactical control of Luzon in relief of XIV Corps, which was scheduled to leave shortly for occupation duties in Japan. Brigadier General Leo M. Kreber now became Acting Commander of the 37th.

Meanwhile the process of saving face was proceeding admirably. General Yamashita signed a surrender document on September 2 for all Japanese forces in the Philippines. Since Yamashita was the big domino, all of the little ones could now fall gracefully. Unit commanders from the Japanese Fourteenth Area Army immediately began negotiating a surrender with the division staff. The band was ordered to play for the formal ceremonies of September 5. General Beightler had returned to Tuguegarao for this from his new post. I described the affair in a letter home, soon published in the *Carlisle Mercury*:

We had a little shindig here this morning. The Jap General Yaguchi [Iguchi] and Colonel Matsui signed the Unconditional Surrender of their troops at a formal ceremony on our theatre stage this morning. They sat at a long table on the stage. Generals Craig, Kreber, and Beightler sat opposite them and read the terms off over a microphone to the G.I. audience and the Japs. The Jap staff officers stood at the left and our staff (numerous colonels, majors, etc.) stood in the rear with the American flag, the Divisional and General's flag. The band stood in front and played the "generals march" as Beightler entered. At the close of the proceedings Yaguchi rose and presented his beautiful Samuri [Samurai] Saber to Beightler. At this the band broke into the Star Spangled Banner. We played it the best we ever had. Many of us cried as we played. It was quite impressive to hear the anthem and see the line of sad little brown Japs on the stage. It was a very appropriate ending that seemed to sound the note of doom on Japan for good. With this the Japs strode off the stage to be taken to the Prisoner of War camps. Probably to New Bilibid about 20 miles south of Manila. We played a concert there for liberated Allied prisoners in February. Now Yamashita, "The Tiger of Malaya," and his coharts are sweating it out in the same cells their once conquered enemies had occupied.

Many of us were thoughtful as we returned to our tents after the ceremony. The Thing—the war—was finally over. Its sudden end had caught us unprepared. We had courted the whore of war so long that the virginal qualities of peace seemed strangely out of place. The powerful war machine on all sides now lay silent, utterly useless for the job ahead. The Jap prisoners did not resemble the beady-eyed fanatics of our imaginations, but rather were mostly farm boys eager to get back to the rice paddies of Kyushu. They had acted like fanatics, to our way of thinking, but individually they seemed to be good men. Even the division, in which we had shared so much, would soon be breaking up.

We were proud of our division as we looked back, for it had entwined our lives together as comrades in blood, disease. and hard times, but above all in friendship. None, of course, wanted to relive any of the division's 592 days in combat, but those days had forged an indefinable unity for the survivors. We had been marked lucky. Over 10,000 comrades had not shared this luck, falling dead or wounded before enemy fire. Why them and not us? A question with no answer, yet in its asking an implied unity of life and death, of past and future. War is always unacceptable as a political solution, unimaginable in its reality, and unforgettable for the survivors.

Some forty thousand men had served with the Buckeye Division by war's end; though it had begun as an Ohio outfit, every state in the union was represented. The men of the 37th sent some thirty-five thousand enemy soldiers to early graves, avenging the Rape of Nanking in doing so. Seven Medals of Honor glittered from its guidons as well as thousands of lesser decorations. There were numerous unit citations, and commendations from Allied nations.

Tomoyuki Yamashita spoke soldier to soldier after the war, saving his best praise for the 37th: "The tremendous power of your attack . . . won my admiration." He was speaking of "The Heavyweight," the one best name pinned on the 37th during the war. Rodger Young would have been proud!

15. Sentimental Journey

On September 18 the division was ordered to its final assembly area, Camp LaCroix, sixty miles north of Manila at Cabanatuan. It was a memorable 330-mile odyssey over war-torn roads. I was driving a weapons carrier that drowned out in the swollen Santiago River. Several others were swept away by the current. Our carrier was pulled into the next town where we pitched jungle hammocks and waited for morning. "We were awakened by Filipinos pumping on the community pump built by the government. The whole town depended on it for water. We cooked our rations, drained the water out of the engine, pitched candy to the usual gang of children, and started off."

That afternoon "we burst out of the hills into what we had been waiting for. The Lingayen Valley stretched out wide and broad before us. . . . Growing rice paddies were as green as an emerald for as far as the eye could see. On the far horizon Mt. Arayat raised its solitary peak above the plain and we knew that sixty miles south of it lay Manila. . . . We passed little roadside stands selling everything from 6-foot poles of sweet sugar cane to bosse or homemade liquor. Finally, we reached the town of Cabanatuan, turned left for 5 km. and came upon our camp. It is the best we've had since Manila. The 43rd division had just moved out so the area was set up and graveled."

I was sorry at having just missed the 43rd, for I was hoping to see J.E. Soper, a Carlisle classmate, and Jim Brannon, a buddy from

Paris, Kentucky. I had earlier just missed seeing Larry Brannon, Jim's brother with the 6th Division. Now I had missed all three, one of the few times during my overseas service that I had failed to find or run into friends from home. By October 1 the 37th had straggled into Cabanatuan. We were wasting away as high-point men steadily shipped out for the States. No more than sixty percent of the men who had landed at Lingayen remained. Righteous wrath was raised when it was learned that the 38th Division, our sister division from Camp Shelby days, but with comparatively meager combat time or overseas service, was pulling out en masse for home. It would be December 1 before the 37th would be on the high seas for home. Forty-five points were needed to return with the division. If I had gotten nicked with shrapnel I would have earned five points worth of Purple Heart, giving me enough points to sail off with the division. I was disgruntled at not getting points for malaria, for few wounds can equal it for lasting damage.

Our combo began playing jobs in the ramshackle clubs and bars in Cabanatuan, a town that at one time had housed prisoners of the infamous Bataan Death March. We used an accordian, guitar, trumpet, trombone, bass, and my tenor and clarinet. The Filipino owners were delighted to have us and the pay was good. Soldiers crowded these clubs, having little to do other than await shipment home. I called up "Clarinet Polka" one afternoon, a rollicking number I had memorized back at Benning, but I was unprepared for the reception it received in this smoky bar and dance hall. GIs started dancing, others shouted and clapped, but a growing number simply stood in front of the bandstand with tears streaming down their faces! We were astonished. They were literally crying—shouting and demanding more polkas. The tumult continued as we gave them what they wanted: "Beer Barrel," "Too Fat," "Liechtensteiner," "Friendly Tavern," "Chihuahua," and many others. Pandemonium swept the throng when Chubby Malewski laid his instrument down, grabbed the mike, and sang, "I don't want her, you can have her, she's too fat for me. . . ." We gradually understood that our music was blowing the dust of war out of their souls. Most of the audience was of Polish descent, lads suddenly realizing they had survived to make it back to the polka bands and dances of Dayton and Akron.

Our combo can perhaps claim a first in this—a thong of infantrymen bawling loudly in front of a polka band!

A brisk black market developed as the men leaving discarded gear or gave it to us "lowpointers." "I have been . . . selling G.I. equipment. It was either sell it or throw it away. The officers never kicked so we sold. I sold three blankets for $50, one mosquito bar for $5, a suit of sun tans for $10, several shorts and shirts for $10; a poncho for $5, and God knows what else. Anyway, I have 300 pesos or $150 in my billfold now."

Many of us worried about our future after the 37th faded away. I noted that "Harvey Berry is flying into Manila from the cub strip . . . to get the low pointers into one of the AGF bands stationed there." Berry returned with good news, for he found that these bands were looking for new members as eagerly as we were looking to join them.

I took a three-day pass to Manila to see the city and to get into another band. I was thrilled with what had happened to the city since I last saw it: "Manila is fixed up now," I wrote, "with running water, electricity, 3 clubs run by the Red Cross, Catholics, and YMCA. The streets are cleaner, there is a good leave center for soldiers to stay, plenty of picturesque little clubs, hole-in-the-wall merchants, etc. Later I went down to the harbor and walked out Pier 13. Manila Bay is packed with boats for as far as the eye can see. I counted 200 in the 90° angle I could span—carriers, cruisers, battleships, transports unloading, big cranes going, troops boarding and troops debarking." Some of the debarking troops disgusted me: "The 86th and 95th divisions are considered stinkers over here. I guess you heard about them begging congress to not send them over here from Europe as they had 28 days of combat." These divisions had painfully come twelve thousand miles at war's end. Small wonder they were griping about it, but they received little sympathy from the South Pacific veterans.

One of the last jobs the band played involved "a long, dirty 450 mile round trip to Tuguegarao to play for the dedication of a monument raised in honor of the division." A fine monument set within a triangular framework of concrete and grass was dedicated on October 17. I enjoyed the three-day trip in spite of myself, shuddering as I passed shell pocked Tumauini, remembered the two hundred Nip soldiers in their pit at Bayombong, and laughed as we drove by the spot in Balete Pass where I had spilled my soup. War fashions memories quickly, so "old veterans" needed no more than my twenty years!

Division personnel was now transferring low-pointers out of the division and bringing in thousands of high-pointers from other divisions for shipment home. Changes caused by this rapid flux of men in and out of the division caused trouble. Camp LaCroix was surrounded by a heavy wire fence; its entrance gate was near my tent. Johnny Graham and I were seated on our cots one afternoon when we saw a soldier and a Chinese stealing from a vacant tent several rows away. Johnny went for the soldier and I headed for the gate, picking up a sub-machine gun as I left. Johnny grabbed the soldier but the soldier grabbed him back, shouting, "Thief! thief!" Meanwhile, the Chinese ambled toward the gate, a stuffed barracks bag bouncing on his shoulder. I was enraged.

"What do you have in the bag?" I asked as he approached.

"Just laundry," he replied in a thick Chinese accent, mincing his steps.

"Drop it!" I jabbed the tommy gun hard into his ribs. "Now, dump it out." Boots, shoes, canned goods, cameras, and souvenirs poured out over the dusty ground. "You call that 'laundee,' you son-of-a-bitch!" I was getting madder by the second, remembering the pickpocket on the Manila street. I had finally gotten the draw on one of these vermin.

Johnny had now wrestled the soldier out into the open. I signaled them to the gate, using the machine gun as a baton. Several men joined them as they walked up. "Let's beat their asses off," one of them growled. This sounded like a good idea, but military police ran through the gate, either called by someone or just lucking into the action. We told our story and signed a form. The thieves later got six months at hard labor in the tropical sun. There was the painful realization that the old division was no more, for theft was almost unheard of before the new men started pouring in.

In mid-October the division passed in full review, the first time since 1942, while still at Indiantown Gap. It was, I think, the last review the Buckeye Division would ever have. The band pulled out a sheaf of marches, taking its position to "troop the line" opposite a stand crammed with Filipino officials and our generals. We played "Stars and Stripes Forever" as the regiments swung through the dusty air of the huge parade ground, approaching the end of a trail started in 1940. Rows of helmeted heads snapped toward Uncle Bob as they streamed by. Pennants, guidons, and colorful citation flags announced the arrival of each battalion and regiment. Sousa marches tumbled through our sore lips one after another—"The Thunderer," "Semper Fidelis," Washington Post." We played "Colonel Bogey," the real name of the march whistled in the movie "Bridge on the River Kwai." Still they came. Our eyes grew moist in realization of the finality of this parade, like the last curtain call for a stage production.

Good news awaited Johnny, Pappy, and me after the parade. Orders had been cut for our assignment to the 237th AGF band in Kyoto, Japan. We had earlier passed auditions held by this unit in Manila. We were to report to the Base X tent area along the Manila docks. From there we would travel as prisoner-of-war guards on a ship taking Japanese soldiers back to their homeland. "How I hanker for some cold weather," I wrote in anticipation of the new assignment.

The three of us reported to Manila's 5th Casual Camp, then to Base X, where three other musicians from the 37th joined us. A rumor started that we would not ship for six months. So, without telling us, two of the married men signed on with the warrant officer of Manila's 234th band; they did not want to miss their mail that long. A few days later the warrant officer walked into our tent, telling us to get moving; he had taken all of us for his band. "We were happy," I wrote, "until this S.O.B. came down and said we were going to his band. Well, we just missed a nice trip to Japan and a lot of new sights. We are helpless to do anything but take it. Now you have a pretty good idea of the way this army is run and why we want to get out so damned bad. From now on address my mail to Hq. Co., AFWESPAC [Army Forces Western Pacific], 234th Band, APO 707." As for the warrant officer, I wrote that "I hope I meet him someday in civilian life." This was a cherished hope of every downtrodden enlisted man at one time or another.

We had hardly settled into our new surroundings when the hated warrant officer left for home. We liked his replacement, and I optimistically reported home that "this isn't a bad set up here at all. It's a big headquarters outfit for all the western Pacific, and the 65 piece band is a cracker jack, full of excellent musicians. We are in downtown Manila close to Far Eastern University." I was assigned to play in one of the two dance bands, with "a steady job at the AFWESPAC officers club, playing six nights a week at $5 per man per night. I'll be making a little over $190.00 per month counting my army pay." A theme of my army life never failed to surface when I was thinking in this vein: "Looks like those sax lessons I used to worry you with are paying off. Also the trips I took to Maysville to get dance band experience not to mention the fact that I owe my life to the saxophone. Remember? A lot of the men from G Company are killed in action or badly wounded. Where would I be if I hadn't gotten into the 37th band?"

Another theme of my army life—chance meetings with friends from home—continued. This time it was with a friend who had played tenor sax with me in the Kavaliers. "I saw Brooks Mattingly Thanksgiving Day and we talked 'turkey.' His outfit is 40 miles south of Manila. He expects to go home soon and said he would drop by and see you all." Shortly after this I barely missed seeing Wilbur Buntin, a Carlisle classmate everyone called "Junior." He was now a lieutenant, but when I dropped by to see him he had "been sent out of town for a week or so."

The theme of violence also continued, though not on wartime levels. Racial problems between whites and blacks erupted. I was as surprised as most white GIs at this, seeing no cause for such "un-reasonable" events. But I wrote home about it. "Jan. 9 we had a race riot out in Quezon City, a nearby suberb. A white guard shot a colored boy trying to steal some supplies from a [supply] dump. As soon as a colored outfit heard about it they broke into a supply room and took automatic rifles, carbines, and ammo. Then the shooting began. 80 of them started running up and down the streets shooting for all they were worth. We could hear them down here but at the time we didn't know what was going on. In reading the *Manila Chronicle* I found out that all 80 are in jail now."

The violence of banditry also found a rebirth in post-battle Manila. We had heard and rather admired the lurid tales of a peg-legged Filipino bank robber. The band's tents occupied part of a square in downtown Manila, protected from the sidewalks and streets by a stone and brick wall. We were playing cards when we heard the crackle of pistol and rifle fire. We hit the dirt. There was the roar of onrushing motors, the squeal of tires around our corner, and the sounds of a running gun battle as Old Peg-Leg and the Filipino police raced out España Street past Santo Thomás University. We heard he later managed to change cars and make his get away. We were rooting for Old Peg-Leg.

Nothing interrupted my attempts at philosophizing, another theme of my homeward bound mail. On December 4 I offered youthful predictions concerning the changes coming in warfare. "The way war is changing I don't see how they can expect to benefit by training teen-agers. More benefit could come of sending them to college in order to produce scientists, what with jet & atomic power. The biggest advantage we have over Russia is our education so why interrupt a lot of guys' education by the damned silly drills, parades and learning to make beds that go with basic training. It's really a big waste of money and time. We should train a large air force however. Volunteers could easily be had if given a square deal." I already viewed Russia as the probable next enemy of the United States. This feeling—for that is all it was or could be—was shared widely among the soldiers, appearing with the news that Russia had attacked Japan after the atomic bombing of Hiroshima. We suddenly felt cheated. Russia was after the fruits of a victory won by us through all of those years from Pearl Harbor to the bitter end. Her handling of the Nazis was an admirable thing, but the Pacific was ours, and she had overstepped her bounds.

If a theme song had been written for soldiers in the Manila of late 1945, its title would have been "Getting a Boat Home." By November, tension was building, and the number of points one had was the key to taking that "Sentimental Journey" home. Our dance band played this piece by request five or six times at some dances. Each letter home was stamped with a very direct political message:

Get Us Home

"NO $\frac{\text{boats}}{\text{votes}}$! "

The overriding theme of the life of every soldier in Manila was the point system. I now had forty-five points, studied all reports on this matter and continually reported home: "All 70 pointers have now [Nov. 29] left the Philippines. They expect to get the 55 pointers out of the way by Jan. 1. Possibly they will get the 45 pointers by Feb. 1st, and maybe I'll be home by middle March. Who knows?" I was not alone in believing the army was screwing up as usual and not processing us as fast as it could. "We read in the *Pacifican* that Marine Pfc Jack Mac Nider, 18, 'son of Brig. Gen. Hanford MacNider, former national commander of the American Legion, was . . . discharged with 38 points'." To us this meant that the Marines were getting their men out faster than the army, for we heard that their discharge requirements for enlisted men was fifty points. But I had hopes things would improve, for "this is headquarters here and the pts. are decided on just two blocks from here." In retrospect, it was impossible to satisfy soldiers so tantalizingly near taking that sentimental journey.

Most mornings the 234th marched down to Far Eastern University "to play four or five numbers for the office boys" stationed there. I regarded this as "chicken shit," remembering my machine gun position there earlier in the year. It was here that I learned that the 234th had its version of the Major Chancroid who had plagued the 184th back at Benning: "The other morning while we were playing over at Far Eastern U. the bass drummer put his drum on the ground to beat it as it was heavy. Here came a full colonel storming across the campus to tell him to get the drum off the ground. The band had been playing in the same spot for 4 months with the drum on the ground. After we had finished he called the warrant officer over and threatened to bust everybody. That shows you the narrow mindedness power produces and just how little the old bastard had to occupy his time."

The 234th's bandsmen played the parades, concerts, and radio shows usual for a military band. The dance band played each night at the Wack Wack Country Club. The Wack Wack lay just outside Manila, boasting a beautiful prewar club house and a fine golf course. AFWESPAC officers used it for their club. The band knew most of them by sight, admiring some, rejecting others. We chuckled nightly at their recognition of advertising before talent. We had a superb clarinetist from the famous civilian band of Charlie Spivak. He soloed brilliantly and should have attracted favorable comment and attention for himself alone; instead, he was seldom noticed unless the leader announced him as "Charlie Spivak's great reedman!" With this, "they all would flock up and say how great he was!" "Many officers," I complained, "never recognize anything unless it is pinned on their shoulders."

The army's class and caste system irked us greatly now that the war was over: "The worst yet are some of these women officers (whores) that dance out at the Wack Wack with the officers. They laugh at us like we were monkeys on a string." I concluded, however, that some of us were worthy of a laugh, for "every band I've ever been in has had at least two booze hounds or lushes. The other night one of ours got drunk, puked all over his music, and fell off of the stand into the floor."

Of more concern than officers was my future after I got home: "I will be home by this time 1946 and I will be in college. . . . Maybe I should just take a general course the first year so I can get back in shape. If I fail I can't continue under the G.I. Bill of Rights, so . . . I would lose out on nearly four years of free education." We respected the wisdom which produced this magnificent piece of legislation. I knew where I wanted to go—the University of Kentucky.

We low-pointers from the old 37th received a letter indicating that the postwar world was already under way back home. "We got a letter from Gil Silvius, one of our 'alumnus' who has arrived home. It took him 24 days to get to Portland, Ore. where his ship landed due to Frisco congestion. He had 95 points. He was one of the 12 that left us in his bunch. Two of them are married already, after being engaged for four years overseas. I was really surprised to hear of 30 applying for divorce in Carlisle. When I do get married I'm going to have to have a case history of the girl."

We killed time on hot afternoons in the band tents watching our mascots perform. Herkimer, a pet monkey, hurtled through the flowering trees in our compound, searching for the large spiders he relished. He was generous, often running up to a horrified bandsman's cot with his little fist full of wriggling spiders, a gift for a friend. We bought him a mate, naming her Her. Her and Herkimer had light lines dangling from their collars. Herkimer could seldom catch Her in a free romp through the trees, but he learned to grab her line, reeling her in when he wanted her. They sat picking at each other's fur, as irresponsible as the musicians idly watching.

Pappy Harrington replaced the monkeys as a diversion one steamy afternoon. "He left the showers to get a letter he had long awaited. He whooped when he read it, dropped his towel and ran from tent to tent naked as he passed out cigars. Pappy was the pop of a baby girl. He joined us last June while we were in the 37th so the 12 points [he receives for a child] will be good to him."

The one most enjoyable day I spent during my two and one-half years of service came as a result of our job at the Wack Wack. A young warrant officer began "sitting in" on tenor sax. He played well, winning our respect to the point that we nicknamed him "Flip Phillips," after Woody Herman's great tenor man. We thought Flip worked with other AFWESPAC "office boys," but we were wrong. One night after a job Flip invited the band for a Sunday cruise on his army crash boat. We were elated to find that our tenor man had charge of a PT Boat without torpedo tubes, an eighty-five-foot craft capable of speeds up to forty knots. During the war these boats were used to pick up downed pilots, but now Flip was telling us to pick up dates for a day of fun in Manila Bay and the sea beyond.

I had been dating Nita Aldape, a lovely brunette whose Spanish family lived in a comfortable home along the fringes of the downtown area. It took much wheedling to get her aboard without a chaperone, but we showed up with the others that Sunday morning. Flip eased the sleek craft into the bay, then shoved the throttle forward. "This thing goes so fast," he said, "that it goes into a 'step' like a seaplane!" We believed him implicitly, enjoying the blast of air blowing over the open decks as we raced by the sunken ships in the bay. None of us had seen Manila from the bay, but there she was in all her wrecked and charred yet somehow majestic self. The city got smaller as we approached Corregidor and Fort Drum. These two bastions held great significance for us, yet we had only seen them lying along the bay's blue horizon.

We picked up the long swells of the open sea west of Corregidor, cruised in and out of coves along the coast, then headed back to the Bay for a picnic. Flip eased over toward Cavite, cutting the engines. We ate and drank beer while the boat drifted in the bright sunlight. Instruments appeared and we serenaded our dates and the startled sea birds hovering around the craft. Our dates donned swimming suits below decks, joining us for a swim in the limpid waters. Evening was heralded by a bright December moon rising in the clear sky over distant Manila. Nita and I decided that we were in love as the craft cruised gently back to harbor. She let me kiss her when I took her home. The day had started and ended perfectly. Almost as an afterthought, Nita invited me to the wedding of her sister Adela the next week.

Nothing in my past as a small town American Catholic could have prepared me for Adela's wedding. The nuptial mass was celebrated in the traditional style of Old Spain, a liturgy that enveloped all five senses in the era before Pope John's ecumenical movement. The incense, the chants, the gorgeous vestments, and the music required one to smell, hear, and see his prayerful way through the ceremony. The beflowered altar of the ancient downtown church was crowded with priests and altar boys. Sprinkles of unleavened bread and flower petals were dropped now and then by an acolyte high in the ornate dome—manna from heaven, as it were. The family was dressed impeccably, entering to music superbly played on the great organ by one of our musicians. Photographers used gunpowder mixtures ignited by flint and steel atop short-handled platters. These flared blindingly for a full second, leaving a smoky blue haze drifting in the afterglow, yet chasing for a moment the perpetual inner gloom of the huge old edifice. The marriage ceremony and the mass that followed lasted two hours.

Numerous people walked in from the streets to share the happiness of the moment. Their smiling faces were mostly Malaysian or Chinese, yet they were at a Roman mass for Spanish people. This meld of cultures, societies, races, and ways of doing things made Manila one of the world's great cities. Perhaps that is why MacArthur loved the place so much.

What a difference a year can make, especially if that year was 1945 and one lived in Manila. On Christmas Eve I wrote of the changes I had discovered since the battle. The shops have "become well stocked up on American goods. . . . You can buy anything from a box of Ritz crackers to a brand new bath tub downtown now." I liked the lighted Christmas trees in the homes and stores, but was more thrilled by the streets full of "Dodge pickup trucks of '46 vintage." I thought of imitating a "G.I. who got his discharge and is now operating a fleet of 40 trucks. . . . If I could get a musical instrument agency for Conn or King I could sell $40,000 worth of instruments the first week if I could guarantee delivery."

There was no doubting the economic opportunities in this great city, for it was in the throes of a massive rebuilding program. "The P.I. are getting $450,000,000 to rebuild with so it has to go somewhere. Guys that pass civil service exams are staying to make around $400 a month often doing no more than ordinary typing and a little bookkeeping. Construction men are getting their discharges and buying what they need of this Army engineering equipment so they will be set when the gigantic reconstruction job gets in high gear."

I was sorely tempted, having had the value of money beaten into my bones by the Depression. Had I proposed marriage to Nita, and assuming her acceptance, my opportunities would have been great in a city that now boasts a population in the millions. I did not have the strength of my economic convictions. Perhaps I did not love Nita enough; instead I compromised myself, promising to come back and settle here. First I must go home. Once there, my plans faded quickly.

My final promotion in rank came on Christmas Day. "From now on you may bow your heads and call me 'old sarge!' I am a Technician Fourth Grade, or sergeant. My arm is beginning to look like a zebra with all the stripes, but I'm not kicking as the pay is $93 a month."

I had put off for too long a visit to the soldiers' cemetery out in Grace Park. I went on January 9, the anniversary of the Lingayen landing. "The white crosses stretched out like a cloud over the burnt ground they are stuck in. Hundreds of 37th men are buried there, including some former buddies of mine." I visited Marcel's grave, remembering our days together aboard the *Monterey* and on New Guinea. My friends from headquarters killed at Tumauini were in nearby graves. Memory returned me to the roaring fires of Manila, the rattle of automatic weapons, the exploding shells and ambulance sirens. A year ago none of that had happened. For many men under the ground on which I stood, those were the last sounds and sights of their lives. I thanked God for His guidance, crossed myself, and left.

In late January the band's forty-five-pointers were trucked south to a processing center along the shores of Lake Taal. These were the first miles of my nine-thousand-mile journey home. We arrived late, finding no mosquito bars in the tents. I crawled inside a mattress cover, sweating and cursing this typical army snafu, trying to sleep as whining mosquitoes probed my refuge. I hated these little blood suckers worse than any of God's creation, but the knowledge that a ship home awaited me made any discomfort bearable. The next day we cleared up our army records with the clerks. I had a good conduct medal, the Asiatic Pacific Ribbon with battle stars for Bougainville and Luzon, a bronze arrowhead for the assault wave landing at Lingayen, an American Defense Ribbon, a Victory Ribbon, and a Philippines Liberation Ribbon with one battle star. I wrote home that day that I was proud of these ribbons, for they are "one thing money can't buy."

My happy group was returned to the Manila harbor, where we boarded the S.S. *Marine Swallow* on January 28, 1946. She was clean and new, a lovely ship. I left a year of my life behind on Luzon, as if cut by a surgical knife, when the ship slowly turned into the bay. I felt a loss at leaving many friends, and above all Nita, but I had to go. We sailed for many hours through the sun-spangled islands of the archipelago, emerging into the open Pacific through the narrow strait separating Luzon and Samar. I watched from the deck with mixed feelings as the blue horizon claimed the islands now behind me.

Ten days later I regained the day of my life I lost coming over, this time having two Thursdays as we crossed the International Date Line. We were at 30° north latitude and excitement mounted as cool breezes began sweeping the decks. By this time I had discovered that a bunk mate was from Millersburg, Kentucky, a village only seven miles from Carlisle. Ross Fleming was the last of the unusual number of men from my home area I met in the army.

Soldiers lined the rails as dawn broke on February 15, watching the California coast come nearer and nearer. The sun broke through the fog over rows of houses on the slopes south of San Francisco. We cheered. The Golden Gate Bridge of our South Pacific dreams loomed before us. This time I was sailing under it in the right direction, no longer the tension-ridden, constipated, frightened kid aboard the *Monterey* so long ago.

I debarked at the San Francisco Port of Embarkation, destined for Camp Stoneman up the bay, then a train ride before discharge at Camp Atterbury, Indiana, followed by a short bus trip to the home folks awaiting me in Carlisle.

We boarded a ferry for the ride to Camp Stoneman. A small combo was playing "Sentimental Journey," the lyrics sung by a WAC. Several more WACs sat nearby. The ferry moved slowly out into the bay. I got a cup of coffee and sat at a table with a WAC, listening all the while to the combo. As I lifted my cup one of the hovering sea birds relieved itself of a brown lump. It flew unerringly, plopping with a splash into my coffee. "Welcome home, soldier boy," the WAC said with a giggle. I stared into my cup for several seconds; somehow, the discolored coffee reminded me of the past two and one-half years, now gone forever. I looked up, feeling good about everything.

"Yeah," I replied, laughing as I tossed the cup, coffee and all, over the rail and into the bay, "Welcome home!"

Index

Aberdeen, Ohio, 24
Adair, Claire, 24, 36
Admiralty Islands, 48, 104
advertising, 115, 162
AFWESPAC (Army Forces Western Pacific), 210, 211, 213. *See also* 234th Band.
aircraft (Japanese): *Jill*, 107; *Zero*, 108, 121
aircraft (US): B-29s (Superfortresses), 26; P-61s (Black Widows), 26; P-63s (enlarged P-39s), 26; P-38s (Lightnings), 26, 106, 112; F4Us (Corsairs), 118; P-47s (Thunderbolts), 106; P-51s (Mustangs), 118, 119, 180; B-25s (Mitchells), 177
Akron, Ohio, 207
Aldape, Adela, 216
Aldape, Juanita "Nita," 215-16, 218
Alliance, Ohio, 116
Americal Division, 88
American Legion, 29, 32, 213
Ang Tibay Shoe Factory, 131.
Aparri (Luzon), 179, 188, 189, 195
ASTP (Army Specialized Training Program): 1, 8, 10; paradox of, 16; disbanding of, 47-48. *See also* Mathias, Frank F; 184th AGF Band
Atlanta, Ga., 36
atomic bomb, 199-201

Australia, 63, 69

Baguio Campaign, 168-70
Baguio City (Luzon), 172
Balete Pass (Luzon), 169, 176-78
Balintawak Brewery, 131
"Ballad of Rodger Young, The," 87
banzai attack, 191
Barkley, Alben, 26
basic training, 10-15
Bauer, Rev. Earl E, 15
Bayombong (Luzon), 180-81, 208-9
Beightler, Maj. Gen. Robert S.: praised by *Yank*, 86; qualifications of, 92-93; cheered by troops, 115; and Manila command center, 131; and dispute with MacArthur over artillery usage, 140; plans Cagayan Valley blitzkrieg, 178; assumes control of Luzon Area Command, 203; accepts surrender of elements of Japanese Army, 203-4; reviews Buckeye Division for last time, 209-10
Benzaquin, Paul, 92, 157
Berry, Harvey Hubbard, 208
Binford, Matthew, 29
Binmaley (Luzon), 114
black market, 163, 165, 208
Blamey, Gen. Sir Thomas, 99
Block, Jack, 37-38